Toward a Theory
of Immigration

Toward a Theory of Immigration

Peter C. Meilaender

palgrave

TOWARD A THEORY OF IMMIGRATION

First published 2001 by
PALGRAVE
175 Fifth Avenue, New York, N.Y.10010 and
Houndmills, Basingstoke, Hampshire RG21 6XS.
Companies and representatives throughout the world

PALGRAVE™ is the new global publishing imprint of St. Martin 's Press LLC
Scholarly and Reference Division and Palgrave Publishers Ltd (formerly
Macmillan Press Ltd).

ISBN 0-312-24034-1 hardback

Library of Congress Cataloging-in-Publication Data
Meilaender, Peter C., 1971-
    Toward a theory of immigration / by Peter C. Meilaender.
        p. cm.
    Includes bibliographical references and index.
    ISBN 0-312-24034-1
    1. Emigration and immigration—Government policy. 2. Emigration and
immigration—Government policy—Moral and ethical aspects. I. Title.
JV6271 .M45 2001
325'.1'01—dc21   2001032760

A catalogue record for this book is available from the British Library.

Design by Westchester Book Composition, Danbury, CT USA 06810

First edition: December 2001
10 9 8 7 6 5 4 3 2 1

Printed in the United States of America.

To Eva,
without whom this book would surely
never have been written.

Teacher, tender comrade, wife,
A fellow-farer true through life,
Heart-whole and soul-free
The august father
Gave to me.

—*"My Wife,"*
Robert Louis Stevenson

Contents

Acknowledgments

Thanks to *International Migration Review* for permission to reprint in slightly altered form, as part of chapter two, my article, "Liberalism and Open Borders: The Argument of Joseph Carens" (*IMR* 33.4 [Winter 1999], pp. 1062–81).

Thanks also to my editor at Palgrave, Toby Wahl, for guiding a novice author through the publication process, for his patience at my delays, and for making it all pretty painless. I am also grateful for the comments from Palgrave's reviewers, particularly Joseph Carens and Dan Tichenor, who were kind enough to identify themselves.

Special thanks to a number of my former professors at Notre Dame who helped guide this work to completion in its initial incarnation as a doctoral dissertation: Edward A. Goerner, who served as my advisor; Fred Dallmayr, Walter Nicgorski, and John Roos, who comprised the rest of my committee and provided valuable comments on various portions of the manuscript; and Donald Kommers, Catherine Zuckert, and Michael Zuckert, who were helpful in a variety of ways during the process.

Thanks also to the Gerst Program in Political, Economic, and Humanistic Studies and especially its director, Michael Gillespie, as well as the Political Science Department at Duke University for providing the time, funding, and congenial environment that allowed me to transform my original dissertation into this book.

My father, Gilbert Meilaender, also commented, with typical insight, on parts of the manuscript. More importantly—as he would surely point out—he provided me with a stellar example of the scholarly life. My mother, I believe, did not comment on the manuscript at all, but she is greatly to be praised for having put up with that stellar example for so many years.

My father-in-law, Erhard Mackenberg, helped me obtain numerous materials relating to German immigration law and policy, for which I am grateful.

Finally, I should note that this project originated in my own fortuitous—or rather providential—personal experience. The debt incurred here cannot be repaid; the dedication offers an all-too-meager recognition of its significance.

Introduction

This book seeks to defend a view that most people probably still take for granted: that states are entitled, within certain wide limits, to craft immigration policies as they see fit, based upon their particular histories, cultures, interests, and desires. In the not-too-distant past, such a defense would not have been necessary. The right to control immigration has long been considered a sovereign right of states in the modern world. It is part and parcel of the state's power over its territory, recognized as a fundamental principle of international law. Needless to say, that power has never been exercised absolutely; people have always crossed boundaries, licitly and illicitly. But that states are entitled to exercise such control has not been in question, nor have states indicated a desire to abandon their right to this authority.

Today, however, the state's control over its borders is being compromised in a host of familiar ways.[1] Illegal immigration to the United States and Western Europe has increased enormously and attracted significant attention. Such migration is fueled not only by the strong economies in those destinations, but also by rapid population growth elsewhere, growth that is not expected to abate until well in the future. Advances in transportation and communications put long journeys to new places within reach of enormous numbers of people. The growth of multinational corporations creates large and powerful bodies that operate across boundaries, possessing both the incentive and the power to influence states in decisive ways. As barriers to free trade fall in many areas of the world, goods and people flow back and forth across state borders in greater numbers, a process with its own internal momentum. The United States saw impressive evidence of this recently when Mexico's new president made a splash by traveling throughout North America calling for the eventual opening of borders across the continent.

Political changes reinforce these economic and demographic ones. Not only corporations cut across national boundaries; so too do a host of extra-territorial interest groups, the familiar NGO's of international relations literature. The growth of international institutions, both political and legal, chips away at traditional state sovereignty in a variety of ways, as does the proliferation of treaties governing subjects such as trade, the environment, and human rights. Numerous domestic factors within Western polities—affirmative action, bilingual education, public support for multiculturalism, the opening of borders within the European Union—combine with economic growth, aging populations, and a demand for labor to make those countries even more attractive destinations. And, of course, as migrants settle in and join democratic polities, they acquire political influence and can oppose efforts to restrict further migration by their former compatriots. Similarly, migrants' countries of origin more frequently attempt to retain close ties to their emigrants; again, Mexico's outreach efforts towards its citizens residing in the United States provide an instructive example.

These transformations in global migration and political reactions to it have sparked relatively little normative reflection among political theorists. Or, to be more precise, they have sparked little reflection on migration specifically. Normative theorizing about various closely related subjects, such as citizenship, globalization, and nationalism, has exploded, so much so that it is difficult to keep up with the endless stream of articles on these subjects. Presumably, (im)migration will begin to attract similar attention—indeed, there are indications (this book among them) that this is happening. Thus far, though, it has remained relatively unexamined. To be sure, the literature on immigration in other fields—history, sociology, economics, as well as other branches of political science—is immense. But this work is often of little help to those interested in the practical moral question of what we ought to do in the face of increasing migratory pressures. What is the range of acceptable responses open to us? What types of responses must we reject as immoral? What sorts of claims do would-be migrants make upon us, and what sorts of claims may we make against them? These are the sorts of questions I wish to explore here.

To the extent that political theorists have addressed such questions, their response has, as it were, supported and reinforced the contemporary forces that are challenging the traditional prerogatives of state sovereignty. Almost invariably—Michael Walzer is the notable exception—they contend that the kinds of immigration restrictions that most contemporary states still seek to enforce are unjust. They do not all go so far as to endorse Joseph Carens's argument for open borders. But there is surprising unanimity around the view that, whatever policies states currently pursue, justice requires a world of far more open borders than now exists.[2] I call this unanimity surprising not because it differs from broader currents in contemporary political theory. On the contrary, any number of signs—the influence of Kantianism following Rawls's *A Theory of Justice,* increasing interest in cosmopolitanism, liberal theorists' response to the wave of nationalism unleashed after the Cold War, the growing appeal and influence of theories of human rights, multiculturalism's status as a doctrine practically beyond question—indicate that skepticism towards the state's traditional right to control immigration is perfectly in keeping with other developments within the discipline. It is surprising because it differs so widely from the ordinary, everyday assumptions about immigration that most people probably hold without even thinking about them. The confluence of and mutual reinforcement between intellectual trends and global economic, demographic, and legal developments has now made it necessary to offer a fuller and more reflective defense of those ordinary, everyday assumptions.

Not only immigration policies are at stake, however. Raising as it does questions about the constitution of a polity and its preservation over time, immigration is also a useful lens for focusing our attention on deep and abiding dilemmas of political theory, dilemmas about the nature of political community, the sorts of bonds that do or do not (and should or should not) connect citizens with other citizens and human beings with other human beings, the relationship between politics and culture. I shall argue that at its core, immigration is one manifestation of a fundamental ethical problem: May (or perhaps must) we prefer "our own"—our families, friends, neighbors, and compatriots, the shared way of life we develop together, even the familiar vistas of our native land—to other people, in different places, with different ways of life? And if so, in what ways and to what degree, and within what limitations? Specifically—since immigration restrictions, if they are to be meaningful, must be enforced—may we prefer our own *politically,* supporting our preference with the coercive force of the state?

Questions such as these have always been at the heart of political theory. We cannot even discuss the attempt to preserve "our own" without some idea of what that means—of who "we" are, of the characteristics we share and that are distinctive of us, of the sorts of bonds that hold us together, ultimately of what sort of thing political community is and of our own particular political community as a member of that larger set. The classics of political thought necessarily address this question, in a variety of ways.

Plato famously spoke of the need to tell citizens the "noble lie" of autochthony, to persuade them that they are all related to each other, sharing the deep and intimate bonds of an extended family and enjoying a special, familial relationship with a particular territory. Aristotle made the concept of civic friendship an important element in his understanding of politics. St. Augustine defined a people as "a multitude of rational beings united by a common agreement on the objects of their love" and, through his description of the Two Cities and their mutual desire for earthly peace, outlined the rough limits on what kinds of loves they could and could not expect to agree upon.[3]

Debate over the nature of political community is central to the rise of modern liberal thought as well. As a theory of political legitimacy, liberalism insists that legitimate government can arise only by consent. But this naturally raises questions about other bonds that join people together and how they affect the granting of consent. Does liberalism's focus on individual consent undermine other kinds of social bonds? Does it simply relegate them to a non-political sphere of civil society about which it remains agnostic? Does it superimpose the additional bond of political consent upon other, pre-existing group ties in a way that might actually reinforce them? Such questions are posed by the development of liberal theory and its attempts to grapple with problems of community, culture, and politics. Hobbes focuses exclusively on individual consent in establishing his "Artificiall Man," the Leviathan, and the centrality of self-interest in his logical grammar of human motivation and behavior can make any broader concern for the larger community appear mere ignorance or sentimentality, as when he describes exile (to pick a relevant example) as not a punishment at all: "the mere change of air is no punishment." Locke also emphasizes individual consent as the sole source of legitimate political obligation; but his account of how "the natural *Fathers of Families,* by an insensible change, became the *politick Monarchs* of them too" suggests that he views identifiable pre-political groups as the natural locus for such a consensual politics, just as his explicit legitimation of tacit consent allows political community to map onto any already existing territorial community. Rousseau famously tied himself into theoretical knots, which political theorists have never fully succeeded in disentangling, when he sought, through "the total alienation by each associate of himself and all his rights to the whole community," to create a social bond so tight that "the sovereign . . . has not, nor could it have, any interest contrary to" that of its members, but in which "each individual, while uniting himself with all the others, obeys no one but himself, and remains as free as before."[4]

Similar disputes have been at the very heart of some of the most important arguments in contemporary political theory. Thus John Rawls, in his restatement of social contract theory in *A Theory of Justice,* held that principles of justice are those that would emerge from "a fair agreement or bargain" among "free and rational persons concerned to further their own interests" in an original situation of equality and in which "no one knows his place in society, his class position or social status, nor does any one know his fortune in the distribution of natural assets and abilities, his intelligence, strength, and the like." His attempt to derive principles of justice from this original position with its veil of ignorance gave rise to the great liberal-communitarian controversy, which dominated Anglo-American political theory for approximately two decades and from which the dust has not yet settled. Central to that controversy is, of course, the question of what constitutes a political community, what kinds of bonds join citizens together, how far they extend, what their consequences are—precisely the questions which immigration forces us to confront.[5]

In the discussion that follows, I shall not often refer the reader to Plato or Aristotle, Locke or Rousseau, but it is worth emphasizing here at the outset that the questions under discussion have this long and rich theoretical background. Because I do not explicitly discuss these canonical thinkers, because my response to the problems posed by immigration seeks to leave as much room as possible for countries to approach these fundamental dilemmas of political theory in different ways, and finally because I shall argue that different positions on immigration are closely related to different underlying views of political community, it seems only fair to give the reader some indication of my own theoretical starting point for addressing such matters. I regard the argument that follows as essentially a liberal argument, though perhaps not of the sort found today in most conventional presentations of liberalism. When forced to give my approach a label, I generally refer to it as "Augustinian liberalism," but since that particular tag may be of little help to many readers, I will describe what I mean ever so briefly here.

I begin with the assumption that humans naturally live in communities with each other, that these communities are of different sorts, that we can characterize and describe them in meaningful and recognizable ways, and that people ordinarily wish to see their particular community and its way of life survive and flourish. Liberal democracy is one way in which such communities order their political lives. What is distinctive about liberal democracy is not merely, as is sometimes suggested, a devotion to individual rights, or even to the ideals of equality and freedom, important though these are. Liberal democracy is committed to pursuing and defending a complex variety of goals, which it does by means of familiar institutional devices (separation of powers, checks and balances) and legal protections (*habeas corpus,* trial by jury, prohibitions on *ex post facto* laws) that emerged through a long process of historical development. Because these goals can be in tension with one another, they may be weighed and balanced by a particular community as it sees best in light of its traditions, culture, and circumstances. Together these goals are necessary to prevent tyranny and preserve independent self-government. They include not only freedom, equality, and individual rights, but also stability, security, and limited government, as well as "majority rule and property rights, personal liberty and domestic tranquillity, popular government and the rule of law."[6] Combining the adjective "liberal" with the noun "democracy" helps to emphasize—as does the inclusion of goals such as majority rule and popular government in the above list—the valuable point (relevant to my discussion of immigration) that, though it is not the aim of liberal democracy as such to give voice to or embody the common life and culture of a people, liberal democracy has no special stake in thwarting such expressions of the broader culture or in preventing its shaping and being reflected in law.[7]

Because liberal democracy so understood pursues a variety of conflicting goals, it contains room for extensive variation. Liberal democracy, in other words, can take a host of different forms; it leaves much to be settled through the contestation and give-and-take of politics. This points toward another insight: that liberalism's list of goals, though complex and broader than usually acknowledged, is not exhaustive, that some communities of people may prefer to pursue a different mix of human goods and may assess some of the goods on the liberal list differently, that they may pursue their ends through very different institutional means than those typical of liberalism, and, finally, that they are presumptively entitled to do so. If there is a case to be made for the superiority of liberalism to other ways of ordering political life (as I think there is), it rests on liberalism's historically demonstrated ability to achieve a variety of very important human goals more effectively than other alternatives. But that is at most a contingent case—in any given place and at any given time, people may wish to pursue different goals in different ways. If the system of their choice allows them to lead decent lives without causing serious injustice, liberalism, in my view, has no ultimate quarrel with them. That "if" is important, of course, because it does indicate the existence of some minimal standards that must be met— a government that slaughters its own citizens does not make the grade. But these standards are minimal, and they are to be balanced against the reality of different communities with different ways of life and different goals. As long as people can maintain a basic level of peace and civil concord, there is no reason for insisting that they pursue our mixture of goals in the ways we think best. Liberalism is one way of ordering political life, perhaps the best way, but not the only or only legitimate way.[8]

This, of course, is only a brief description of my version of liberal democracy, not a defense of it. The latter is a task for another day.[9] The reader familiar with contemporary discussions of liberalism will recognize that, just as my argument about immigration is at odds with broad political and intellectual trends, so too is the underlying account of politics upon which it draws. This dual dissent will be controversial, of course, as almost all important questions are. But it reflects my belief that using the concrete issue of immigration as a lens through which to focus on certain theoretical problems can contribute to our understanding at both levels. And if this attempt at a "theory of immigration" encourages the reader to consider in new or unfamiliar ways questions of political community and the relation between culture and politics, then I will be quite pleased.

The structure of the book is as follows. Before moving into my more theoretical discussion of immigration, it is worth reminding ourselves of just what it is we are thinking about, and in particular of the diverse variety of events included under the general label "immigration." A business CEO relocating to a foreign country in order to head up an international branch is an immigrant, but so is a poverty-stricken refugee fleeing ethnic cleansing. And countries may receive immigrants gladly or with hostility. In the first chapter, I explore this broad range of different kinds of immigration, seeking to give real examples of a variety of reasons why people migrate, as well as why countries do or do not wish to receive them. The implicit purpose of this catalog is to raise doubts about suggestions that any single policy—and here I have arguments for open borders especially in mind—would be appropriate for handling this vast spectrum of very different situations.

Chapter two reviews the existing normative literature on immigration. Because there are few scholarly arguments defending the state's right to restrict immigration, I begin by examining three recent works of intellectual journalism that call for restrictions on American immigration. These, I suggest, have not fully explored their own intellectual premises. I then turn to the scholarly literature, focusing primarily on Joseph Carens's case for open borders. This more sophisticated argument is, of course, aware of its own premises, but it has not, I argue, defended them in a way that is really able to engage those who do not already agree with them. My third chapter seeks to address this standoff by presenting what I hope is a more sophisticated defense of the premises necessary to support the state's right to restrict immigration. Chapter two ends with a consideration of what a postmodern approach to immigration might look like.

Chapter three's argument for broad state discretion in regulating immigration is the theoretical heart of the book. Here I argue that immigration policies are closely linked to particular understandings of political community and national identity; that a broad range of such understandings is legitimate; and that, both because we lack an argument that would persuade all peoples to adopt the same identities and visions of political community, and also because there appear to be quite plausible arguments in favor of a people's right to enact policies designed to preserve its particular way of life, countries are presumptively entitled to craft immigration policies that reflect their own particular national identities and conceptions of politics.

Chapters four and five both attempt, in different ways, to illustrate one of the key premises from chapter three's argument, the claim that immigration policies are closely tied to particular understandings of political community. Chapter four seeks to illustrate this at the level of political practice, through an examination of immigration law and policy in two countries that have recently engaged in fierce arguments over immigration, the United States and Germany. In both cases, I explore how these countries' national identities have shaped immigration policy and the debates surrounding it. Chapter five seeks to illustrate the same point at the level of political theory. Here I reflect upon the arguments of Will Kymlicka and Michael Walzer, both of whom write powerfully about the relationship between politics and culture. Again, I wish to show how their arguments' implications for immigration are closely connected to fundamental ideas within their broader theories about the nature of political community.

Chapter six, finally, is in a sense the counterpoint to chapter three. Having spent most of the book defending broad state discretion over admissions, I conclude by asking what the limits of that discretion might be. This is in part to forestall concerns that my argument is intended as a defense of complete state authority, or that it is simply a relativist position. But it is also an attempt to flesh out my earlier arguments. I criticize the open borders view for conceding legitimacy to an overly narrow range of regimes, and I hope that my own argument is open to a much broader array of different visions of political community. But every argument is based on some premises, and no position can avoid excluding at least some alternative possibilities; and in my final chapter, I ask what possibilities my own views exclude. I thus close by arguing that if borders need not be completely open, neither should they be completely closed.

Chapter 1

MIGRATION'S MANY FACES:
THE COMPLEXITY OF THE PROBLEM

People move for many reasons. A poverty-stricken family fleeing starvation; an international sports star relocating to a country with lower taxes; a man moving to another country to join his foreign wife; hordes of people trying to escape an invading army—all are migrants, but in very different circumstances and with very different motives for their journeys. And the countries that accept them are similarly diverse, with correspondingly different reasons for wanting to accept or reject various would-be immigrants.

In this book I hope to reflect upon cases such as these and offer some modest suggestions for how we ought to think about and deal with immigration. First, though, I simply want to explore the vast range of situations that fall under the general heading "immigration." There is, after all, no obvious reason why examples as diverse as those mentioned above should be dealt with in the same way. It is therefore worthwhile, I think, to begin by simply elaborating as many reasons as we can think of why people migrate, as well as reasons why countries do or, more interestingly, do not want to admit them. This need not be an extremely lengthy, detailed affair (though it could easily become one). Nor will it be exhaustive—further thought would doubtless continue to reveal motives, or combinations of motives, not mentioned here. The purpose of this brief catalogue is simply to open our minds, to make us sensitive to the broad spectrum of cases of which a theory of immigration needs to take account. And if the reader begins to doubt that any single immigration policy could appropriately cover so many diverse situations, then the groundwork for the argument of the following chapters will have been well-laid.

Motives of Migrants

Why, then, do people migrate? Why do they uproot themselves, leave their homes, and seek to settle somewhere else? We can begin, perhaps, by making a general distinction between two broad types of immigration: voluntary and involuntary. In a sense, of course, all immigration is voluntary: one could always simply refuse to leave, preferring to die where one is. Nevertheless, it seems reasonable to call people driven into flight by the ravaging soldiers of an invading army involuntary migrants.[1] On the other hand, it is surely possible to stretch the category of "involuntary" so far that it is no longer helpful. Consider, for example, contemporary debates over so-called "economic refugees," people who, though certainly poor, may not be facing real destitution or the possibility of death. Are such people voluntary or involuntary migrants? In cases like these the distinction between voluntary and involuntary begins to blur. By employing the distinction, then, I by no means intend to propose any rigorous theoretical model for analyzing immigration; I use it merely as a handy way of providing some structure to the discussion. By using the term in a narrow, restricted sense, we can delineate a category of people whom we can meaningfully, and I think uncontroversially, refer to as involuntary migrants.

Even within this limited class of involuntary migrants we can imagine a number of different motives for leaving. I have already suggested the example of people fleeing a hostile army. Thomas Sowell points out that "[t]he havoc and chaos of war raging through ancient China sent refugees fleeing to adjoining lands, where they spread the Chinese culture."[2] More recently, the population movements caused by ethnic conflict in the former Yugoslavia, for example, or between Hutus and Tutsis in Rwanda and the Congo (formerly Zaire) seem similarly involuntary. The westward movement of American Indians in the face of advancing European settlement is a slightly different example of the same phenomenon.

Civil war and political anarchy often create involuntary refugees. Civil war in Liberia during the 1980s and '90s created 1,260,000 refugees, "more than one half of the population of Liberia." They fled to Ghana, Nigeria, Guinea, the Ivory Coast, and Sierra Leone.[3] Civil and ethnic warfare in Somalia over the past decade caused several hundred thousand refugees to flee to Kenya.[4] The collapse of political order in Albania in 1997 drove thousands of people across the Adriatic Sea to Italy.[5] Even before the crisis in Kosovo, civil war in the former Yugoslavia had already created millions of refugees, of whom "between 500,000 and 600,000 are currently residing in different European countries outside the region of former Yugoslavia, with

Germany, Switzerland and Sweden . . . as the main receiving countries."[6] And in the Kosovo crisis, of course, Serbia expelled roughly a million ethnic Albanians from Kosovo.[7]

Victims of natural disasters, like victims of war, can be included in the category of involuntary migrants. Fires, floods, earthquakes, volcanic eruptions, hurricanes, and similar events can all leave people in search of a new home. Famines are a common example of such events. One of the most famous—or infamous—migrations in history was caused by the Irish Potato Famine. The years of the potato famine produced "a flood of nearly two million emigrants, to be followed in the following decade by nearly a million more."[8] Similar to natural disasters in their effects are environmental disasters, such as the breakdown of the nuclear reactor in Chernobyl, which, according to Klas–Göran Karlsson, produced an "enduring migration flow."[9]

The slave trade is yet another example of involuntary migration. We are most familiar with the enslavement of Africans, and with good reason: as Sowell writes, "Over the centuries, somewhere in the neighborhood of 11 million people were shipped across the Atlantic from Africa as slaves, and another 14 million African slaves were taken across the Sahara Desert or shipped through the Persian Gulf and other waterways to the nations of North Africa and the Middle East".[10] Sowell also points out, though, that slavery, and the corresponding transportation of enslaved peoples, has in fact been a worldwide phenomenon, existing "in the Western Hemisphere before Columbus' ships appeared on the horizon, and . . . in Europe, Asia, Africa, and the Middle East for thousands of years."[11] Sowell's own examples of those carried off to serve as slaves in another land include "thousands of Christians" from the Balearic islands, "a thousand girls and fifteen hundred boys" from Venice, "tens of thousands" of "Europeans living in vulnerable coastal settlements in the Balkans," "hundreds of thousands" of Russians, 10 percent of the Hungarian population each decade of the sixteenth century, "6,000 Greeks" sent to Egypt, and "many thousands" of people from Bali.[12] Quite a few involuntary migrants, to say the least.

Involuntary migrants are also created when a government removes people from its own territory. In 1492, for example, the Spanish government expelled all religious Jews from the country.[13] The expulsion of nonnationals has been commonplace in post-colonial Africa; Aderanti Adepoju lists Sierra Leone, the Ivory Coast, Ghana, Chad, Uganda, Zambia, Equatorial Guinea, Zaire, Kenya, Senegal, Cameroon, Guinea, Nigeria, and Liberia as countries which did this between 1968 and 1983.[14] The same phenomenon occurred on a massive scale in Germany and eastern Europe following World War II. As Heinz Fassmann and Rainer Münz report, "At a rough estimate, which takes into account only the main migration flows, some 15.4 million people had to leave their former home countries." This included enormous numbers of ethnic Germans living in other areas of eastern Europe who were expelled and forced to go to Germany: 7 million people from Poland, 3.2 million from Czechoslovakia, 225,000 from Hungary, and 360,000 from Yugoslavia. The redrawing of international boundaries also resulted in the migration of large numbers of people of other nationalities. About one and a half million Poles and Polish Jews, for example, were forced to leave their homes in areas that became parts of Lithuania, Belorussia, and the Ukraine. Though in smaller numbers, practically every ethnic group in eastern Europe was affected by this process. Including "4.7 million displaced persons and POWs [who] were repatriated (partly against their will) from Germany to eastern Europe and the USSR" and also "'internal' migration flows" (i.e., those occurring within a single country), Fassmann and Münz conclude that the total number of migrants "would probably be as high as 30 million people."[15]

Even if we limit the category of involuntary migration fairly strictly, then, it includes a number of very different groups of people. Within the larger realm of voluntary migrants, the diversity is naturally even greater. Because the list of reasons why people exchange one country for another is practically endless, a discussion of these motives could easily degenerate into a kind of random list. As a way of giving some order to what follows, I borrow a distinction made by social scientists writing about migration between the "push" and "pull" factors causing particular migration streams.[16] Some people, in other words, leave their country and move somewhere else primarily out of a desire to leave where they are (that is, because of "push" factors), others more out of a desire to be in some other particular place (because of "pull" factors). These categories are limited, and I do not endorse them as a universal explanatory model. They oversimplify people's motives, reducing them to the language of economic supply and demand.[17] Furthermore, "pushes" and "pulls" are not mutually exclusive, since in most cases some combination of push and pull factors causes migration. Not always, of course—the "involuntary" migrants described above are, in a sense, responding purely to powerful pushes, while it is also possible to imagine people leaving only because of especially enticing pulls somewhere else. But usually complex combinations of factors are at work, varying with time and place, and calling for more detailed studies of particular historical events rather than insertion into the prefabricated push-pull model.[18] Finally, some motives simply do not seem to fit very well into the push and pull categories. That said, the push-pull model is both ready at hand and useful in a broad, brief survey such as this, so I employ it, like the voluntary/involuntary distinction, as a rough and ready way of identifying and organizing different motives for migration.

First for "push" factors, reasons that might make people wish to leave where they are. Some of these are relatively obvious and leap quickly to mind. (They represent some of those cases in which it is most difficult to distinguish between voluntary and involuntary migration.) One historically important such motive is surely religious persecution. Many of the early American settlers, for example, were members of European religious groups, such as the English Puritans, seeking to escape persecution at home. Jon Gjerde writes of Scandinavian emigrants,

> The very first emigrants from Norway in 1825, for instance, consisted of religious dissidents, a group of Quakers and pietist Lutheran followers of Hans Nielsen Hauge . . . . Likewise, the Janssonists—Swedish followers of pietist Erik Jansson—emigrated in their thousands and formed the Bishop Hill colony in Illinois in 1847. Scandinavians—especially Danes—were among the first Mormon settlers in Utah in 1846 . . . .

These people emigrated because they were "increasingly dissatisfied with the state church and the confines of opportunity at home."[19] The same phenomenon had occurred early in Germany following the Reformation. After the "Treaty of Augsburg . . . had established the principle of 'cuius regio eius religio' . . . the right to emigrate was granted to Lutherans and Catholics, so that individuals not satisfied with the confessional loyalty of their particular state might take up residence under a ruler who professed the same religion as themselves."[20]

Other forms of political persecution also stimulate people to look for a new home. Some groups have formal, second-class status; others are victims of an informal but systematically exploitative application of the law, relegating them permanently to the bottom of the social totem pole. In either case, political persecution and social prejudice mingle to create a hostile climate which people hope to escape. Jews around the world have often found themselves in such situations. Quite apart from the atrocities committed by Nazi Germany—which would certainly qualify the resulting emigrants as *in*voluntary migrants—Jews have faced official discrimination, sometimes spilling over into outright persecution, in many times and places: in Spain during the seventh and eighth centuries, and again during the 14th and 15th centuries, before their expulsion from the country; in the Ottoman Empire and the rest of the Islamic domains as they declined during the 18th and 19th centuries; or in Russia, particularly the Russian area of what had been Poland, during the 19th century, where discrimination culminated in vicious pogroms that between 1881 and 1914 drove one and a half million Jews to leave Russia just for the United States, "one of the great mass exoduses in history."[21] These are among the worst instances, but Jews, whether in Christian Europe or the Islamic lands of the Middle East and northern Africa, have through most of their history faced legal and social discrimination of one form or another.[22] In our own time, official discrimination sparked Jewish emigration from the former Soviet Union. Between 1968 and 1992 several hundred thousand Soviet Jews emigrated, mainly to the United States and Israel, largely due to officially sponsored anti-Semitism.[23] Ironically, the dominant ethnic group in the old Soviet Empire, the Russians, now finds itself in a similar situation, discriminated against in the newly independent ex-Soviet republics, and large numbers of ethnic Russians have returned to Russia in the years since the Soviet Union's breakup.[24]

Mention of the Soviet Union reminds us that some regimes do not merely persecute a particular group, but are just oppressive in general. It comes as no surprise that many people are eager to leave such regimes. For much of Soviet history the government waged "a massive propaganda campaign against emigration," which it also severely restricted.[25] When given the chance, however, people left in significant numbers. Emigration controls were loosened once during the 1970s; Fassmann and Münz report that roughly 340,000 people left the country at the time. During the period of *perestroika* under Gorbachev "a second large wave of emigration took place." The same authors calculate that "[i]n all some 1.5 million people emigrated from the USSR between 1950 and 1991."[26] And in 1991, writes Klas-Göran Karlsson, "over 1.2 million individuals emigrated from the dissolving Soviet state."[27] Another example of such migration, of which the political system would seem to be the most significant, if not the only, cause, is the movement of about 5 million East Germans to West Germany between 1950 and 1990.[28]

Difficult economic circumstances also lead people to migrate in search of a better life. Historically, a variety of factors, such as overpopulation, the decline of feudalism, and the dislocations of the Industrial Revolution, have combined to produce poverty-driven migration. Rudolph J. Vecoli, discussing the "exodus" of emigration from Italy between 1876 and 1915, explains that it resulted from a number of "fundamental changes taking place in Italian society and economy" resulting from "the expansion of capitalism."

A late and immature form of capitalism which affected the various economic sectors and regions of Italy in different ways caused . . . 'uneven development'. Another underlying factor was the growth of Italy's population from 27.5 million in 1871 to 40.5 million in 1931 . . . despite the heavy emigration of those sixty years. Increased population generated demographic pressures on a too slowly modernizing economy . . . . [W]hile capitalist innovations disrupted traditional forms of production and property relations, 'modernization' lagged behind. The industrial sector grew too slowly to absorb a growing underemployed agricultural proletariat, assailed by deep poverty, pellagra and malaria, and reduced to pauperism, vagabondage and brigandage. The agricultural crisis of the 1880s, precipitated by the fall in the price of grain on the world market . . . , spelled disaster for both the small landowner and the *bracciante* (agricultural labourer). Larger families, parcelization of landholdings, displacement of cottage industry by factory production and burdensome taxes all exacerbated the peasants' plight.[29]

Gjerde likewise mentions several interconnected economic factors influencing "early Scandinavian migration to North America," namely "rapid population growth, limited opportunities to own land and a fledgling urban industrial sector."[30] Even in the case of emigration from Ireland during the Potato Famine, which would seem largely attributable to a single factor, Robert Scally suggests that other, related causes were involved as well: peasants' "hold on the land had been wrested loose by poverty and the law; evictions were made easier and mounted; congestion was growing among the poorest classes in the countryside and historically forced dependency on the potato blocked their access to the food chain when the blight struck."[31]

Economic factors can lead the well-off, as well as the poor, to leave their home for another country. Jan Lucassen suggests that, whereas earlier emigration from the Netherlands to America was caused by a need for land among laborers and small farmers hit by successive agricultural crises, later waves of emigration seem to have been triggered by times of relative prosperity, when "labourers...and farmers...were able to acquire enough money to enable them to emigrate."[32] And we are certainly familiar with the graduate of business or medical school who, faced with a discouraging labor market, looks abroad for a place where his skills can be adequately rewarded, as did the more than 15,000 engineers and 15,000 physicians who migrated from India to the United States between the early 1970s and the mid-1980s.[33] Or think of the example I suggested earlier, that of an international celebrity leaving for a land with lower tax rates—as athletes Boris Becker, Steffi Graf, and Michael Schumacher have in recent years become "tax refugees" from Germany.[34]

Local traditions of migration, though perhaps not precisely a cause of migration, are certainly another factor that can influence the decision to migrate. Ida Altman, writing about Spain, refers to "the predisposition of people at practically all levels of society to move around (often several times in a lifetime)" as helping to mold emigration from Spain.

> These forms of mobility suggest that leaving home and family was a commonly accepted, and for many even an expected, occurrence, frequently connected with the achievement of economic independence and formation of new households through marriage. Emigration to the Indies functioned in much the same way, as a life-stage and career choice that took people away from home, temporarily or permanently, to places offering greater economic opportunities and greater social flexibility as well.[35]

Similarly, Vecoli describes the extensive and complicated migratory traditions of Italy prior to the great overseas migrations, and then writes of the latter, "While the magnitude of this emigration was unprecedented, it initially followed the traditional forms of migration, but with constantly engaging [*sic*] larger numbers and dispersal to more far flung destinations."[36] The striking migrations that helped colonize the Americas can thus be seen as the extension of traditions that had developed over centuries in various European cultures, rather than as an entirely new phenomenon. As Walter Nugent writes, "Much of the transatlantic migration was simply an extension of a long-established pattern of labor migration within Europe," an extension made possible largely by advances in transportation technology.[37] It would no doubt be wrong to say that these migratory traditions caused people to migrate, but certainly they made migration a real option for many people to whom it might otherwise not have occurred.

"Pull" factors are motives drawing people toward some particular country. Such incentives can be a particular, concrete reason for moving, like being hired for a job; but more often they are a vague sense of the possibility of improvement, such as "economic opportunity." Nugent, writing of migration to the Americas in the late nineteenth and early twentieth centuries, says that, apart from some particular and proportionately small cases, the pervasive motive for migration was economic improvement . . . . For some, opportunity lay in farmland, anywhere from northern Argentina to northwestern Canada . . . . For others, opportunity lay in factory, mining, or construction jobs; for a few, it meant employment in skilled trades or services.[38]

Britons seeking work in "construction, mining, factories, and certain trades;" young Irish women entering domestic service or taking white-collar jobs as "office workers, shop clerks, or teachers;" Germans families seeking farmland—all were seizing the opportunity to better their lot.[39]

Political liberty, like economic riches, can also be a powerful lure. Many eastern Europeans in the late nineteenth and early twentieth centuries saw America as an enticing land of liberty: "For members of oppressed national or religious minorities, such as Russian Jews, in addition to a promise of material affluence, America symbolized a paradise of civic and political freedom."[40] Nor is America the only land which has attracted migrants because of a tradition of freedom. Gérard Noiriel points out that the French "constitution of 1793 had, in fact, been the first in the world to recognize the principle of the right to asylum."[41] He notes that many Russian Jews fled to France between 1880 and 1890, as did large numbers of Armenians "after the victory of the 'Young Turk' revolution in 1908, which marked the start of their persecution, orchestrated systematically by the new Turkish government."[42] In cases such as these, as in that of the many East Germans who migrated to West Germany, it is difficult to distinguish the "push" of an oppressive political system at home from the "pull" of a freer one somewhere else. That the Russians and Armenians chose France rather than some other destination, though, is doubtless due at least in part to the "pull" of its revolutionary tradition.

Other pull factors are more specific and easier to identify, such as when a person travels to another country in order to join a foreign spouse. In general, the presence of relatives or friends in another country can be a powerful inducement to move there; indeed, the phenomenon in which certain individuals migrate and then encourage others back home to join them, who then do the same thing in turn, is common enough to have received its own name, "chain migration." Writing of emigration from Spain, Altman says

Family and kinship relationships and considerations played a key role in the migration process . . . . [F]amily members on either or both sides of the Atlantic often provided both the impetus and the material wherewithal for a person to emigrate. People commonly went to the Indies accompanied by relatives or expecting to join them, and all through the colonial period they sought out their kin and people from their home towns. Cycles and networks based on family, patronage ties and common origin linked people and places in Spain and America, creating multiple and enduring connections that fostered continuing emigration, often directed to particular places.[43]

Sowell also points out that "particular destination points have tended to be linked to particular points of origin." For example, he writes, "Immigrants from particular towns in Lebanon often settled in clusters together in particular towns in Colombia. Among Lebanese immigrants to the West African nations of Sierra Leone and the Ivory Coast, there was likewise a concentration of people from particular locations in Lebanon in particular parts of the new countries where they settled." Indeed, the phenomenon extends even further:

> The linking of people from specific places of origin in one country to specific destinations in another has in some cases extended right down to the neighborhood level. Jewish immigrants from Poland settled in different streets on the lower east side of New York from the streets occupied by Jews from Russia, Hungary, or Romania, and German Jews lived in very different parts of the city from Eastern European Jews on the lower east side.[44]

The pull of relatives and friends across the ocean could be especially strong when they paid for one's journey. Nugent writes, "In the 1880s and 1890s, prepaid tickets financed one-fourth of the Danish migrants and half of the Swedes. For those hundreds of thousands of people," he quotes another scholar as saying, "' we can almost say that . . . the decision to emigrate was made in America.'"[45]

Sometimes the incentive to migrate is provided in a very direct way by a government seeking to recruit new residents. One of the most prominent such efforts was that by Brazil in the late nineteenth century as it sought new workers for its coffee plantations after the abolition of slavery. Under the Brazilian system, "passage to the New World was fully paid for by the state and federal governments, and a complex wage and piece work payment system was arranged for the immigrant families." These contracts

> provided a fixed payment by the planter for the number of trees cared for by each worker, and a fixed price per weight of coffee harvested, plus salaries for any special day-labour performed . . . . The immigrants were also granted lands to cultivate their own food crops and limited pasture rights to graze

livestock, whose product was for their exclusive use or sale. All housing was provided free.

This program enticed a number of migrating families to choose Brazil as their destination; "from 1889 to 1900," according to Herbert S. Klein, "some 878,000 immigrants arrived in São Paulo alone, of which over three-quarters were subsidized."[46]

France has also at times sought to attract new residents to bolster its workforce. Robin Cohen notes that France, a country which traditionally had a very low birth rate, "is unusual among European countries in wanting to increase its population."[47] In the years between 1880 and 1930, major French industries and landowners together recruited large numbers of workers from Poland and Italy. "By the end of the 1920s, the rising number of foreigners within its population was among the highest worldwide, even surpassing that of the USA . . . ."[48] In addition, after the Russian "civil war and the Bolshevik victory forced millions of 'white Russians' to flee[, s]everal tens of thousands of these refugees were granted asylum in France in the 1920s in order," according to Noiriel, "to boost France's diminished workforce" (diminished because of World War I).[49]

Other reasons fit less easily into the push/pull categories. I mentioned earlier the possibility of an invading army forcing residents to flee elsewhere; but, of course, such an army also brings migrants, as it spreads its native population into new lands. Sowell notes that the conquests of Mongol and Turkish invaders spread those peoples through Europe and the Middle East, and that European conquests brought Europeans into the Western Hemisphere and Australia.[50] Or consider the case of missionaries: they may not be drawn to some particular place because of special "pull" factors; on the other hand, they are probably less "pushed" away from their homes than moved by a desire to preach to people who have not heard their message. Someone might have wanderlust, or a person might travel and simply fall in love with a particular country—pull factors of a sort, I suppose (or is wanderlust a "push"?), but ones operating only at the level of individuals, not masses of people. And what about Eric the Red and his father, whose "departure from Norway . . . 'because of some killings' is an apt illustration of the need throughout the ages for the outlaw to flee to places beyond the reach of ordered government"?[51] Perhaps this is a "push" factor, perhaps even an "involuntary" migration (though the outlawry was presumably voluntary), but it is not the sort of thing that writers using the push-pull model usually have in mind.

Nor should we forget adventurers, people longing to strike out for someplace new—a motive, in the words of Seymour Phillips, "too easily overlooked because it apparently lacks scientific rigour."[52] Many of the first settlers in the New World must have been driven by such highly individual emotions. Yet this particular example pushes us beyond mere individual psychological eccentricities toward larger cultural variables that escape the push-pull categories. For the desire of people to explore new lands can doubtless be influenced by a more general cultural environment of interest in different, far-away places. Indeed, precisely this seems to have happened in Europe during the Enlightenment, when Europeans became ever more "fully aware that they were not alone in the world."[53]

> Interest in foreign cultures did not stem, of course, only from Christian humanitarian concern: it was prompted also by pure curiosity and the keen scientific interest of an enlightened age that was eager to experience anything that was novel or unfamiliar. People were keen to learn as much as they could about the world as a whole. Travel journals became a highly popular form of literature, while 'exoticism' was the fashionable trend in the design of drawing-rooms and gardens.[54]

The encounter with new lands and peoples stimulated not only travel literature and garden design, but also the burgeoning sciences of cartography, botany, zoology, and ethnology.[55] New discoveries helped build a culture fascinated by new, possibly better and purer (the "noble savage"), certainly exotic lands. Was this a "push" or a "pull?" Neither, exactly—but in addition to stimulating explorers and scientists it probably contributed something to the willingness of large numbers of ordinary Europeans to migrate to different lands.

Even when dealing with larger mass movements for which we can list various "push" or "pull" factors, we should not forget the particularity and individuality of each event. Such movements are rarely to be explained by a single "push" or "pull" factor, but rather by a complex combination of causes that necessarily varies from time to time and place to place, lending each migration a character different from that of others. I have listed, one after the other, various reasons for migrating, as though they were separate causes each responsible for different migrations. But that should not disguise the fact that, apart from rare cases, these different causes work together in a multitude of possible combinations. To offer just one example, consider Ong Jin Hui's account of the causes of Chinese coolie migration to the Americas: he mentions overpopulation, which resulted in "heavy pressure on land-use and an inflationary spiral;" drought and floods, which also caused internal migration that "further unbalanced the regional production and consumption patterns of Fukien and Kwangtung;" "political turmoil," together with its "resultant chaos and disruption of the socio-economic fabric[, which] produced large rural-urban migrations and an over-supply of labour in the coastal cities;" a pre-existing "tradition of seeking fortunes elsewhere" in Fukien and Kwangtung; the "end of slavery" internationally, which created a huge demand for labor in the European New World colonies both in their plantations as well as in emerging industries; the willingness of local officials to overlook national laws forbidding emigration; not to mention brute "force" necessary to overcome "disincentives" such as the "tradition of ancestral worship and the need to maintain familial links."[56] Not a cause in the list that I have not already mentioned in one way or another; but, however often factors such as overpopulation, drought, or a demand for labor may appear, their combination in this particular case is different from the concatenations of forces at work in other instances. Thus we see what a diverse phenomenon migration truly is.

Motives of Countries

For whatever reasons migrants leave home, they have to go somewhere. Sometimes countries are happy to have them. We have already seen some reasons why this might be the case in our discussion of pull factors. The large immigrant-receiving countries in the Americas—Argentina, Brazil, Canada and the United States—at one time or another all sought, in various ways, to attract settlers to populate their vast lands, sometimes even actively recruiting them, as was the case in Brazil. Likewise, Canada developed its "National Policy" in the late nineteenth century deliberately in order to populate its western provinces, and it sought European immigrants for that purpose.[57] Immigrants were not only needed to settle vast stretches of fertile land. Mining, the building of railroads and canals, the growth of ports that accompanied the expansion of shipping, and industrialization all created a demand for labor, and cities swelled with masses of newcomers arriving to satisfy that demand. This was obviously true in the United States, which by 1914 "had become the principal New World receiver of urban-industrial, labor-seeking migrants."[58] But it was true elsewhere as well. In Argentina, for example, after the available agricultural land had been settled, immigrants continued to pour into the cities, particularly

Buenos Aires, so that "[b]y 1914, when 53 percent of the native-born lived in cities, 69 percent of the Italian-born and 78 percent of the Spanish-born did so."[59]

Nor was this only a New World phenomenon. I have already noted that France, faced with a declining workforce, sought laborers from other lands. In general, countries are often eager to accept immigrants from whom they expect economic benefits. Even in the early twentieth century, when many respected American academics were calling for restrictions on the "new" and supposedly less desirable immigration from southern and eastern Europe (restrictions which they got in 1921 and 1924), a few people, such as Peter Roberts and Emily Balch, argued that these migrants, even when they came only temporarily and then returned to Europe, were economically beneficial; Roberts wrote that the "Hudson Tunnel is an asset to New York City, [for example]; it is an invaluable agency in the production of wealth; and the Italians who dug it, if all of them had returned to Italy with their savings, would have enriched us by their toil."[60] Such arguments continue to be made today. One of contemporary America's best-known and most vocal immigration enthusiasts, Julian Simon, argues for immigration precisely because, he claims, it is good for the American economy.[61] Even those who are skeptical of such broad claims as Simon's about immigration's economic benefits may be happy to admit immigrants in particular sectors of the economy. American immigration law, like that of many countries, sets aside a certain number of slots for immigration applicants with skills needed in the economy; in 1990, for instance, Congress "nearly tripl[ed] the allotment for importing highly skilled and professional immigrants—up from 54,000 to 140,000 each year."[62]

Migrants may also be welcomed for political reasons. Noiriel, speaking of the Armenian refugees in France, notes that "on the whole the French government retained a positive attitude towards them" largely because of "the rallying of intellectuals . . . fight[ing] to ensure that France kept to the ideals of the French Revolution."[63] During the Cold War, the United States gladly accepted migrants from the Soviet Empire, taking them as concrete evidence of the superiority of the free western democracies to Soviet communism.[64] Similarly, West Germany viewed "migration from the GDR [as] a strong argument in support of the market economy and democratic system. It was often claimed that emigrants were 'voting with their feet'."[65]

Such cases are examples of what Michael Walzer has called "ideological affinity."[66] Other sorts of affinity, such as ethnic or religious, can also lead countries to admit certain outsiders. Germany, for example, has traditionally not only permitted the immigration of but has also offered automatic citizenship to ethnic Germans who were members of the old German Empire. Israel, in perhaps the most striking example of religious affinity, considers itself a national homeland for Jews from around the world. Many countries also recognize the smaller-scale loyalties of individual citizens by making special immigration provisions for the purpose of family reunification, under which spouses, children, or other close relatives may be permitted to immigrate.

When countries are happy to accept migrants, everything works out nicely—people looking for a place to go find a country happy to have them. Problems arise, of course, when countries do not want newcomers. Often this is for economic reasons. Migrants, it is suggested, take jobs that would otherwise go to native citizens, particularly poor citizens. Willing to work cheaply, immigrants are also thought to depress wage levels and allow employers to maintain poor working conditions—again, hurting poorer citizens especially. Other economic objections have arisen with the growth of the modern welfare state, as resident citizens have objected to paying taxes in order to provide welfare benefits for poor newcomers. And every new resident puts extra burdens on systems of education and infrastructure.[67]

Of course, countries often have non-economic reasons for wanting to exclude new migrants. Not all of these reasons are particularly high-minded. Countries can be motivated by racism, as was the case when the United States, beginning in the 1920s and continuing for some time, excluded all Asian immigrants.[68] Or people may simply react against the obvious difference of new groups, perceiving them as dirty, uncivilized, less than fully human. Such reactions need not merely be a cover for bad or racist motives. On the contrary, they can be a natural and understandable reaction to confrontation with a very different way of life. Indeed, a country may object to the introduction of a different way of life not because of any derogatory opinions about it, but simply out of a conscious desire to maintain the particular way of life that it already has.

It can be difficult, of course, to sort out racist motives from the mere desire to preserve one's own way of life. Consider, for example, the notorious "White Australia" policy, under which Australia for many years tried to limit severely its number of non-white immigrants. An Australian minister of immigration defended the policy in these terms:

> We seek to create a homogeneous nation. Can anyone reasonably object to that? Is not this the elementary right of every government, to decide the composition of the nation? It is the same prerogative as the head of a family exercises as to who is to live in his own house.[69]

This sounds like a reasonable defense of a country's attempt to preserve a particular way of life by admitting only those who are thought most likely to share it. Yet, as Joseph Carens points out, many other arguments for the policy at the time "were often quite explicit in their claims about the superiority of the white race."[70] And in fact, quite apart from internal critics, Australia came under a great deal of external criticism for a policy widely regarded as racist. In practice, then, policies intended to protect a particular culture may often be mingled with baser motives. Yet this should not cause us to neglect the fact that genuine concern about cultural preservation often plays a role in people's opposition to immigration. The distinction between racial and cultural motives is nicely exhibited, for example, by Quebec's attempt to regulate immigration in order to preserve its francophone society by giving special weight to knowledge of French as a criterion for admission. As Carens has pointed out in a discussion of these regulations, "Competence in French is not a covert way of reintroducing racist criteria . . . because most of the potential immigrants who speak French come from former French colonies in Africa or Asia . . . ."[71]

As the earth's population has continued to grow, a new kind of fear has emerged in the developed countries: an environmental one. The added population of new migrants increases the demographic pressures on all of a country's environmental resources. It reduces the amount of natural, undeveloped land remaining, leaving it farther away from many people and more crowded with visitors, as well as threatening plant and animal species which rely upon these habitats. And immigration adds more "automobile-using and toilet-flushing residents,"[72] contributing to air and water pollution. Roy Beck, arguing against further immigration into the United States, suggests that the same "plot line" could be applied to "scores of polluted, sick, or threatened natural resources across the country":

> (Act 1) Population grows until the natural resource cannot stay healthy. (Act 2) Lots of money is spent to reduce per capita environmental impact to save the natural resource. (Act 3) Immigration-fueled population growth undermines enough of the improvements to keep the resource threatened.[73]

Immigration, in Beck's words, "makes every bad environmental situation worse."[74]

In addition to these broad reasons for opposing immigration, of course, countries may often have more particular reasons for excluding particular groups of people, or immigrants in general at particular times. Restrictions on criminals, spies, or terrorists, for example, are fairly self-explanatory.

A country wishing to protect specific occupations might not admit applicants practicing those occupations. During times of war, countries may be understandably reluctant to admit members of hostile nationalities. And just as events such as drought, famine, or economic downturn can create emigrants, they can also lead a country to limit immigration.

These, then, are at least some of the reasons why people move, and why countries do or do not want them to come. This catalog may seem like a puzzling way to begin a work of normative political theory. But it is not without a purpose. I offer it in the hope that the reader, faced by such strikingly diverse examples of immigration—real, not hypothetical, examples—will react with skepticism to the idea that the issues raised by such a variety of movements could be adequately considered with reference to any single normative principle or relatively simple set of such principles. On the contrary, it seems, on the face of it, improbable that all of the motives I have described, whether of migrants or of countries, confront us with equal moral claims. At any rate, such skepticism will find a hospitable reception in the argument that follows. How should we react when people in search, perhaps even in need, of a new home find, not a welcome reception, but rather countries with complicated reasons or combinations of reasons for not wanting to accept newcomers into their territory? How should we resolve such a conflict? It is to this problem that I now turn.

Chapter 2

SORTING OUT THE ARGUMENTS

In this chapter I wish to get a handle on the basic opposing arguments that are made about immigration—roughly, that the state may or that the state may not restrict it—noticing particularly how they generally fail to engage one another's underlying presuppositions. Although the historical literature on various migrations is vast, relatively little has actually been written about the philosophical issues posed by immigration. Related topics, such as citizenship and nationalism, have sparked a large and rapidly growing literature, but immigration, at least so far, has been less thoroughly explored. Books addressed to a popular audience appear with some regularity; but it is only a modest exaggeration to say that the scholarly literature—with the exception of the work of Joseph Carens, whose own output practically rivals the rest of the literature put together—consists primarily of two or three anthologies and a handful of other scattered articles.[1] This literature contains some differences of opinion, but on the whole it clearly favors either open borders or something much more closely approximating open borders than the current world situation, in which near-complete control over entry is widely regarded as among the state's sovereign rights.[2]

Because the scholarly literature tends to be pro-immigration, I shall first consider, in order to canvass restrictionist arguments, three recent examples of what one might call intellectual journalism. These books—Peter Brimelow's *Alien Nation,* Roy Beck's *The Case Against Immigration,* and Chilton Williamson, Jr.'s *The Immigration Mystique*—all argue against continued levels of very high immigration.[3] They specifically address the American context, but in doing so they raise issues pertinent to a more general theoretical defense of a country's right to determine its own immigration policy. Their arguments will reveal some assumptions that advocates of such a position often make and that I shall explore more thoroughly in chapter three.

I next turn to the scholarly literature and the argument in favor of immigration. Specifically, I shall focus on the work of Joseph Carens as the best example of this argument. Focusing on Carens as heavily as I do here risks making the existing literature appear somewhat more one-sided than it actually is, since few others are willing to go quite as far as he has or support open borders with quite his vigor. But his position has clearly won general sympathy.[4] Furthermore, Carens's argument represents the opposite pole of the debate from the defense of conventional state sovereignty and thus serves as a useful foil for the presentation of my own views in chapter three. Finally, it has the considerable advantage of being without any doubt the clearest and most exhaustive theoretical argument about immigration that exists, since Carens has developed it at length in a number of thoughtful articles over a period of years.

I shall claim that Carens, like the intellectual journalists whose more conventional views he opposes, ultimately appears to take certain premises for granted. His and their arguments are often quite persuasive, if one accepts those premises. But it is not clear what they have to say to each other. Nor is it clear from their writings how to resolve the resulting stand-off. My own proposal for resolving it comes in the next chapter.

Finally, I shall consider a separate body of literature or approach to political theory, post-modernism. Though I am not aware of much explicitly post-modern treatment of immigration in particular, many of its general themes—such as deliberation about boundaries, oppositions between insiders and outsiders or "us" and "them," and the construction of identity—seem very relevant to a consideration of the subject. And many of the practical issues that immigration raises, about multiculturalism, for example, or ethnic discrimination, are obvious concerns of post-modern thinkers. In the absence of a well-developed post-modern treatment of immigration, therefore, I close this survey of current arguments by considering what such a treatment might look like.

Defending the Nation

Of the three restrictionist books to be considered here, Roy Beck's is the most straightforward. Beck focuses heavily on the economic consequences of immigration. At the end of some introductory chapters, dealing primarily with the history of immigration into America, Beck announces: "The chapters that follow focus on the interests and welfare of the American people after thirty years of unprecedented and unintended immigration" (74). The first of these chapters (chapter five) argues that one of immigration's main results has been a decrease in the size of the middle class. By increasing the labor force, especially the unskilled labor force, immigration has decreased productivity, driven down wages, and increased economic inequalities. Following this are two chapters arguing that immigrants are not needed to fill American jobs. First, in chapter six, Beck argues that there are no "jobs Americans won't do:" Americans will do any job if they are fairly compensated, but they cannot compete with immigrant, Third-World labor forces (especially when the importation of those very labor forces often helped make certain occupations undesirable in the first place by lowering wages and worsening working conditions). In chapter seven he argues that it is also unnecessary to import skilled workers: the number of such workers that we need is relatively small, and America already faces a glut of highly educated workers who could fill the relevant jobs or be easily trained to do so. Chapters eight and nine argue that immigration has always and continues to hurt black Americans in particular, because they are the first group displaced by the arrival of new laborers belonging to other ethnic groups. Even chapter ten, which is devoted to several "quality of life" issues made worse by immigration, discusses a number of problems that are either primarily economic concerns (such as increased pressure on a deteriorating infrastructure) or that have significant economic components (pressure on the educational system or increased levels of welfare dependency).

Grant, for the sake of argument, that Beck is right on all of these counts. Even so, one might well respond, he has proven nothing very interesting. Someone who holds that people have a right to free movement, for example, could simply answer, "I'm sorry this is so hard on you, but I'm afraid that's just your tough luck."[5] It is important to be clear about this from the outset: the economic argument is a secondary one which cannot settle the fundamental questions of whether or to what extent countries may shape their own immigration policies as they will. This is because all the economic matters which Beck raises, important though they are, are relevant only if we already know that a country may justifiably base its decisions on them—may say, for example, "Wages are low right now; let's not admit any more unskilled workers." If, on the other hand, countries have an obligation (for whatever reason) to admit newcomers, the effect of immigration on economic conditions simply doesn't matter. If we already know that we may legitimately tailor immigration policy to our own interests, economic conditions clearly become an important factor in settling on a good one; but they cannot themselves answer that prior question.[6]

So Beck must be assuming that a country does have the right to determine its own immigration policy in accordance with its needs and interests. Indeed, he says as much in his concluding chapter, where he makes his own recommendations for American policy:

> The most important question for Washington is whether a continuing stream of foreign workers and dependents into the country over the next few years will make it more or less difficult to achieve the economic, social, or environmental goals of the American people. In other words, for the first time in decades Washington should consider basing its immigration policy on how many immigrants the nation actually *needs*. Officials should start the process at the zero level and add only the numbers that actually will help the majority of Americans (244; emphasis in original; paragraph division deleted).

Immigration, in other words, should serve "the national interest" (256). But why?

Implicit in Beck's argument is at least a partial answer to this question. To begin with, talk of "the national interest" clearly assumes that there is a nation. And Beck thinks that this nation—"the American people" mentioned above—has a discernible way of life which can not only be changed, but also changed for the worse, by the addition of large numbers of people who do not share it. One aspect of this lifestyle is a certain economic standard of living, and most of Beck's argument, as we have seen, is devoted to showing how immigration can threaten this. But immigration can change that way of life in other ways as well, ways which

> are less tangible but probably more disconcerting to the American people. They involve changes—many of which are considered *losses* by natives—in the quality of life in a community. High immigration tends to lengthen the time it takes people to travel to work; it tends to increase air pollution, to add pressures on already vulnerable environmental resources, and to lower the quality of the schools; and it tends to add transience to a community while diminishing social cohesiveness, decreasing public safety, and generally changing its ambiance and lifestyle (Beck, 203–4; emphasis in original).

Arguing that the ability to enjoy the wonders of nature is central to the American way of life, and noting the congestion and environmental stress caused by increased population, Beck declares that "this country is not simply a set of principles, or a constitution, or a type of economic system, but a nation of particular people living on a particular chunk of land" (228). And, he might have added, living "in a particular way."

This particular people with its particular way of life may have particular moral responsibilities, as well. This, I take it, is the thrust of Beck's chapters on the declining middle class, and specifically of his long treatment of the ways in which immigration, as in the past, continues to harm black Americans especially. Our first obligations, his argument seems to be, are to the members of our own political community, our fellow citizens, and especially to the poorest and least advantaged among them. The claims of these people take precedence over those of strangers—thus we should limit immigration because doing so will help those of our compatriots who need it most.

Finally, Beck sometimes suggests a democratic argument for limiting immigration. At one point, he combines this suggestion with the claim that immigration threatens Americans' way of life: "[Immigration] is transforming communities throughout the United States into something their residents often don't like or quite recognize as their own" (18). That they can no longer recognize their own communities suggests the previous existence of a particular way of life; that they don't like the changes implies that those changes have been wrought (illegitimately) without their consent. The same argument appears when he writes that immigration "creates sweeping changes for communities that never request them and seldom approve of them" (105). Beck also states that much lower immigration levels would be "far closer to what the American people most desire" (19) and that "[p]olls showed that a large majority of Americans agreed" with proposals "to reduce legal immigration toward more traditional levels" (73). Finally, he writes, "In 1924, [when it drastically reduced immigration,] Congress halted the power of immigration to change the social landscape of communities or to obliterate lifestyles of the American people without their permission. Thoughtless federal policies since 1965 have removed that protection" (241). The clear implication: only the American people's "permission" can justify such changes in its way of life.

A people with an identifiable way of life, moral obligations toward its members, and the right to determine its own future—these seem to be the implicit elements of Beck's argument in support of a country's right to decide on its own immigration policy, a right which underlies and allows us to make sense of his other economic arguments. Like Beck, Brimelow devotes some time to discussing economic issues, and he also assumes that

America is entitled to set immigration policy in accord with its own interests.[7] But he also deals more directly with some of the issues that remain
implicit in Beck's book. For example, he raises the democratic issue right at
the start. Citing a *Time* magazine article claiming that American policy is
"for the first time in its history . . . truly democratic" (xviii), Brimelow
responds that current American immigration policy is actually "unusually
undemocratic, in the sense that Americans have told pollsters long and loudly
that they don't want any more immigration; but the politicians ignore
them" (xviii; emphasis in original). He then writes, "Their [*Time's*] notion
of democracy, in other words, has degenerated to the point where it is
assumed to require invalidating the right to an independent existence of
the very *demos,* people, community, that is supposed to be taking decisions
on its own behalf. Democracy becomes self-liquidating . . ." (xviii).
Democracy, Brimelow is saying, logically requires that there be a distinct,
defined people, able to make decisions about its own identity; otherwise, it
cannot even ensure its own continued existence.[8] Similarly, Brimelow
writes of two American soldiers whom he had met as a child in Britain: "I
don't know what they or their children think of the unprecedented experiment being performed—apparently by accident and certainly with no
apprehension of the possible consequences—upon the nation they so
bravely represented. I do know, however, that they ought to be asked"
(21–2; paragraph division omitted). As Beck suggested, sweeping changes
in a democratic community require that community's permission. In a
democracy, "public opinion" is "ultimately the only legitimate arbiter" of
how many immigrants a nation ought to accept (Brimelow, 262). High levels of immigration have "robbed Americans of the power to determine
who, and how many, can enter their national family, make claims on it . . .
and exert power over it" (Brimelow, 4–5).[9]

Democracy, then, entails the existence of a distinct people or nation,
which Brimelow defines as "an *ethno-cultural community*—an interlacing of
ethnicity and culture" (203; emphasis in original).[10] Thus, in presupposing
the existence of a people, the American democracy rests upon a particular
"interlacing of ethnicity and culture." This is Brimelow's response to those
who claim that "America isn't a nation like the other nations—it's an idea"
(208). Like any nation, America represents a particular "interlacing of ethnicity and culture." Americans share a common European, and more
specifically Anglo-Saxon or British, ethnic and cultural heritage, a fact
which could hardly have been questioned before the most recent surge in
immigration (206). Indeed, the concept of a "universal nation," based on

an idea, is really "a contradiction in terms. A nation cannot be universal because it is, of its essence, specific—ethnically and culturally" (206). America is no exception.

The temptation "to abandon the bonds of a common ethnicity so completely and to trust instead entirely to ideology to hold together their state . . . is an extraordinary experiment, like suddenly replacing all the blood in a patient's body" (208). Not only would Americans be voluntarily relinquishing the concrete stuff that makes them a people, they would be risking dangerous consequences by ignoring human nature and the importance of national identities.

> History suggests little reason to suppose it [this experiment] will succeed. The political form of the Estados Unidos Mexicanos is essentially that of the United States of America. But the content is Mexican, and the result very different. Conversely, the universalisms of Christendom and Islam have been long ago sundered by national quarrels. More recently, the much-touted "Soviet Man," the creation of much tougher ideologists using much rougher methods than anything yet seen in the United States, has turned out to be a Russian, Ukrainian, or Kazakh after all. (208)

Brimelow cites numerous examples to demonstrate that multi-ethnic societies have been either despotic or remarkably unsuccessful (123–7). Internationalists who favor large-scale immigration overlook this "need for homogeneity" and its consequences: "Given enough diversity, only [the] exercise of raw authoritarian power can possibly hold the warring tribes together" (232). Brimelow concludes:

> At the end of the twentieth century, the central issue in American politics is what might be described as "The National Question"[:] Is America still that interlacing of ethnicity and culture we call a nation—and can the American nation-state, the political expression of that nation, survive? (232; bold print omitted)

The test for future immigration into America must be how it affects the answer to this question (259).

Brimelow thus emphasizes more explicitly than Beck an existing people's democratic right to determine its membership and identity. He also repeats Beck's argument that our moral obligations to our fellow citizens take precedence over ones we may have to others. Receiving immigrants is, in any case, a hopelessly ineffective way of using our wealth to help people; it can help only a relatively small number, and at the cost of overwhelming the very economic system which is producing that wealth in the first place (244–6). More importantly, though, Brimelow argues that moral obligations are only intelligible if they are restricted, referring to "the impossibility of rational and meaningful moral action if our responsibilities are viewed as limitless" (249). He writes:

> The only way to navigate in the sea of human pain is to make distinctions. The moral market will fail unless some equivalent of property lines is speci- fied. Our rights and duties have to be put in some sort of priority. And there is an ordering principle in the modern world: once again, it is our old friend the nation-state. (249)

The nation-state, then, provides a way of identifying those people to whom we are first and foremost obligated, and by doing so it enables us really to help some people, instead of being simply buried beneath problems which are beyond our ability to solve.

Unlike Beck and Brimelow, Chilton Williamson, Jr. devotes little time to the economic arguments for and against immigration.[11] He does, how- ever, recognize the centrality of the nation-state to the debate over immi- gration.

> [T]he present stalemate on immigration is the result of differences in stress and emphasis regarding the component parts of the consensus, immigration being in reality not a single issue but a congeries of subordinate ones, includ- ing nationalism and national sovereignty, free trade, freedom of movement, economic freedom and economic growth, democratism, and human rights, to name some of them. What these issues have in common is an intimate rela- tionship to the question of the legitimacy of the modern nation-state . . . . (13)

Williamson also shares the view that American immigration policy is something which America has a right to determine for herself. Thus he suggests as a "concrete question" for American legislators to consider, "What should the goals of an *intelligent American* immigration policy be?" (75, my emphasis) The choice of words here is telling: legislators should seek an "intelligent" policy, not, for example, a "just" or "moral" one; and it should be American, not universal. They should seek, that is, a prudent policy for a particular people, not an abstract principle which could appro- priately be applied by all peoples everywhere. Thus Williamson castigates legislators for not having, among their various exhortations and moral tru- isms, even "the smallest consideration for the national interest, including such pragmatic concerns as the likely effect of expanded immigration on population growth and natural resources" (85). Democracy, he suggests, entails a people's right to determine its own make-up: "The submersion of American culture by another, or others, is of itself not necessarily a good thing, or a bad one. The issue is simply, Is it something that the American people wish to have happen?" (136) The same view of democracy is evident when Williamson criticizes those pro-immigrationists who insist "that mere *preference*, however widespread and deep-seated, is insufficient ground on which to base immigration policy" (6; emphasis in original).

Williamson defends the American people's right to determine its own fate through an attack on two related beliefs: American exceptionalism and the notion (to borrow Brimelow's phrase) that America is an "idea, not a nation." The two beliefs are related because exceptionalists hold that America's exceptionalism lies in its being united, not by common bonds of ethnicity, culture, or history, like other nations, but by a shared commitment to certain abstract principles of government. In a pointed jab at Lincoln, Williamson notes that

> in composing his address on the battlefield at Gettysburg [Lincoln] discovered that the Declaration had dedicated the nation to a proposition. Despite there being no mention in that document of any such dedication, Lincoln's poetic reading raises the philosophical question of whether a nation can in fact be dedicated to a proposition of any sort, and whether, if it could, it ought to be. (29)

Williamson, it is fairly clear, is doubtful that it can be, and certain that, if it can, it shouldn't be.[12]

The belief in America's special commitment to liberal, democratic ideals encourages a feeling of moral purity and a crusading attitude which do more harm than good. When it does not produce isolationism, Williamson suggests, this belief leads either to the attempt to "export Democracy" to the world, or to the immigrationist position, which seeks to bring in lots of immigrants so that they can become like us. Williamson criticizes such a view fiercely: "Exporting American democracy . . . . By importing the world? This is tantamount to a demand for universalism on the ground of American exceptionalism, which is really a contradiction in terms" (94). The sense of a special, American moral mission, Williamson argues, is deeply hubristic in its refusal to recognize that no one country has a monopoly on goodness, justice, or even uniqueness. And, he concludes, "a civilization that believes destruction to be the just reward of a society that fails to achieve moral perfection is certain, sooner or later, to gain that reward" (108).

Not only does the exceptionalist vision of America carry the danger of a crusading moralism, it also offers a distorted image of American identity. Of those who believe American identity to be defined around a few abstract principles of political theory enshrined in the Constitution (and whom he calls, in another reference to Lincoln, "propositionists"), Williamson writes, "[Their] arguments are less remarkable for the thinness of their historical sense than they are for their determination to deperson-alize the United States, by reducing it from an historical presence to an intellectual abstraction whose concrete reality is that of a democratic machine" (112–13). He continues: "The propositionists assert their claim for America's uniqueness in the history of the world by denying the Amer-ican nation a coherent personality, the attribute most wholly unique to any human individual or group" (113). Such a view is obviously well-suited to the admission of large numbers of immigrants, who cannot disrupt an identity which is held not to exist. Williamson points out, though, that such an approach is not only self-perpetuating but also self-fulfilling:

> Given the degree to which a common commitment to a democratic ideal has helped to bind an ethnically heterogeneous nation together, this unifying ideal will become even more critical in the future as America becomes still more heterogeneous. Multiculturalism, then, strengthens the concept of the United States as a political idea. But a political idea, no matter how good a one, is not the same thing as a moral system, a national conscience that can only evolve historically, through time and cultural development. An enhanced concept of America as a political ideal can only lead to the grow-ing conviction that the solution to the myriad problems associated with immigration, multiculturalism, and every other problem facing the nation is indoctrination in the right political ideas—what Claes Ryn calls the civics-class understanding of national history. (136–7)

Williamson thus seeks to emphasize that there is more to American identity than only abstract ideals (though they too are a part of that identity [28]). Universal ideals, after all, can be embraced by anyone. That we would not recognize everyone who does so as thereby obviously "American," how-ever, indicates that American identity has a concrete texture which those ideals do not fully capture.

Whereas the belief in America's exceptional commitment to democra-tic principles ironically results in a kind of universalizing moralism,

Williamson recommends instead attention to the needs of our fellow citizens: "Love of the unique civilization that constitutes one's patrimony is itself a conscientious act, and so is the motto that would have us take short views and trust in God for the rest" (164). As Brimelow did, Williamson emphasizes the need for moral duties to be limited in order to be meaningful: "While indiscriminate generosity may be itself a sort of immigration policy, indiscriminate benevolence is not an ethic" (151–2). Instead, real love must attend first to those to whom we are most closely bound.

> Universalists tend to believe that love of one's own is selfish, though in truth it is the only *real* love—and true love is never selfish. The most selfish act imaginable would be to pull down the gates and let them all come in, thereby assuring that our children and grandchildren—and our friends, neighbors, and compatriots, and *their* children and grandchildren—will be subjected to the equal distribution at home of the poverty and misery that were formerly the world's. (154; emphasis in original)

Together with Beck and Brimelow, Williamson argues that our first duties are to be found at home.

Where a distinct people with its own way of life exists, these authors argue, it has both a right to determine its own constitution and policies as well as a duty to care for its own members, and these carry greater weight than duties it may have to non-members. Finally, national identity plays an important role for these authors in the determination of immigration policy. Williamson, for instance, points to this component of the argument as that which makes immigration such a difficult topic:

> [T]he immigration issue has finally to do with the identity of the American nation, and thus, in small, with the identity of every American. Immigration, at both the national and the individual level, is a gigantic, unsightly, confusing, and infuriating blot, a kind of national Rorschach test. (15)[13]

Sometimes the three advance the identity argument in a positive sense, as when Brimelow argues that the United States shares a common, basically British, ethnic and cultural heritage. Williamson makes the same argument, saying of the founding generation, "If no one at the time appeared to notice the fact of their British Protestant culture, it was because that culture was taken entirely for granted" (28), and adding later, "[A]t the end of the twentieth century the old WASP culture remains the only national culture worthy of the name; not solely on account of its primary and defining role in creating the country and the nation, but because it represents today the inherited culture of an elite, an informal aristocracy of talent, learning, and accomplishment . . ." (115).

More often, though, all three authors make a negative argument about American identity, saying what the American nation is *not*—in particular, that it is not, as the popular myth would have us believe, a "nation of immigrants." They do this by addressing the history of immigration into America. They show that this history, rather than being one of continuous mass immigration welcomed by a nation happy to have the newcomers, was one of bursts of immigration followed by lulls during which the immigrants could be absorbed; one in which the Great Wave of the late nineteenth and early twentieth centuries was an aberration, rather than the norm; one of significant ethnic homogeneity; one which, despite its apparent success, entailed great hardship for those, especially newly freed blacks, displaced by new arrivals; and one which was often opposed by large numbers of native Americans, who gained a positive impression of immigrants for the first time only during the period of restricted immigration between 1924 and 1965.

Beck and Williamson each devote a chapter to describing this history; Brimelow spends several doing so.[14] Clearly, they must view the question of national identity as very significant. Why? They evidently consider a country's identity an important and legitimate factor in determining its immigration policy. If America really *were* a nation of immigrants, really did have a tradition of continually accepting large numbers of newcomers with open arms, then perhaps current policy would be understandable; otherwise, there would be no need to go over the history so carefully in order to refute this myth. Thus there is an argument about the meaning of being "American" and the place of immigration in that meaning. Our understanding of who we are and of immigration's role in forming us into that people shapes and ought to shape—or so these authors' arguments suggest—the policies we choose for ourselves in the present.

Though this position is implicit in their arguments, they do not try to justify it at a deeper level. Assuming that we can identify a particular people with a certain way of life, why is it entitled to choose the immigration policy that suits it? Beck, Brimelow, and Williamson essentially take this right for granted, without providing a fundamental argument for it. In the next chapter, I shall attempt to provide roughly such an argument. My argument will not be specifically about America, as theirs are, nor will it be an argument for immigration restrictions. It will, however, seek to defend a country's claim to craft immigration policies that reflect its particular identity, even if those policies prove, as they surely sometimes will, to be restrictionist. Thus I shall be arguing not so much for the restrictionist conclusions of authors such as these three as for the premise necessary to get those arguments off the ground. This is itself a significant step, because prevailing scholarly opinion, to which I now turn, generally denies that restrictionist views such as these can be morally acceptable. Under my theory, by contrast, they are potentially as legitimate as other policy recommendations and may compete with those alternatives to offer a compelling account of a given people's political and cultural identity.

Liberalism and Open Borders: The Argument of Carens

Prevailing scholarly views on immigration tend to be diametrically opposed to Beck, Brimelow, and Williamson. In their more radical forms, they argue for open borders; even more restrained versions are sharply critical of existing state practice, defend extensive limitations on sovereign control over immigration, and thus point towards a world of much greater immigration that currently exists. Occasionally, of course, a more moderate voice, seeking to balance a right of individual mobility against claims of communal autonomy, can be heard. Frederick Whelan, for instance, has suggested that "[t]he current practice of Western countries"—in which exit or emigration is relatively free while states exercise considerable control over entry or immigration—"seems to represent a reasonable compromise between competing, extreme conceptions."[15] But he offers no positive argument in favor of this plausible suggestion. Indeed, by referring to this compromise as "a middle position between two theoretically more consistent extremes,"[16] he appears to concede that the case for open borders (like that for the other extreme, complete state control over exit and entry) has a certain intellectual heft that the compromise, reasonable though it may be, lacks—a concession I would not be so quick to make.

Nor is this impression altered by a later essay in which Whelan does specifically argue that even liberal principles, which are "typically opposed [to] protectionist policies" such as "restricted access to positions and careers," can justify immigration restrictions that are designed to protect liberal institutions themselves.[17] If one believes that liberal government is desirable, he argues, then one must seek to ensure the survival of a "liberal base" within which liberalism can flourish and from which it can over time be shared with more and more people: "the preservation of liberal institutions where they exist must be the first priority, even if this means restricting some of the operations that liberal principles would have in a more ideal world."[18] Such an argument, however, does not necessarily justify very extensive immigration restrictions, as Whelan himself recognizes:

> The practical bearing of this argument, finally, depends on prevailing circumstances—on the actual number of potential immigrants and their political or cultural attitudes, and on the assimilative capacity of the liberal society. It is outlined here as a potentially restrictive argument with regard to immigration, since it qualifies the tendency of pure liberalism (from which it is derived) toward openness and free mobility in a restrictive direction, but given some actual state of affairs, it might well turn out to justify rather extensive immigration. In fact, it might well be consistent with much higher volumes of immigration than the United States and other advanced countries presently experience. Indeed, arguments of the form suggested here might actually favor—even require—openness to immigration to the maximum level.[19]

Notice, too, that this argument, like the earlier description of immigration restrictions as part of a "reasonable compromise," appears to view "pure" liberalism as requiring, in principle, open borders, even though conditions in a non-ideal world might make them currently unattainable. This concession becomes explicit when Whelan closes his argument by elaborating upon three "hybrid" perspectives—liberal statism, liberal democracy, and liberal communitarianism—that can provide more robust justifications for immigration restrictions. Whelan's treatment of these perspectives indicates his sympathy for them, as does his claim that they "perhaps come closer to ordinary beliefs and lead to policy conclusions that are less paradoxical than does liberalism alone."[20] But he again offers no positive argument for such a "reasonable compromise." The cumulative effect of his arguments is thus to suggest that liberalism itself can sustain only fairly minimal restrictions on free movement, and that other compromise positions, however reasonable they may be, represent less a coherent intellectual point of view than a jumbled hodge-podge of unrelated and even opposing considerations.[21]

Another attempt to strike a balance between the competing claims of national sovereignty or political community and individual rights is Mark Gibney's *Strangers or Friends*. Indeed, Gibney explicitly announces his intention of taking a middle path in his opening sentence: "My aim is to frame an alien admission policy for the United States that will meet certain duties to those who live outside of the United States, and, at the same time, maintain the autonomy of the U.S. community and its subcommunities."[22] In constructing his argument, however, he emphasizes duties to outsiders much more than communal autonomy, leaving the moral status of the latter unclear. He writes, for example, that "[m]embers *can* be differentiated from nonmembers and they *should* be distinguished" (16, emphasis in original). Nowhere, however, does he tell us *how* they can be differentiated or *why* they should be distinguished. As a result, his justification for preserving autonomous political communities is not nearly so well articulated as his arguments in support of duties to outsiders.[23]

Reflection on the two principles that Gibney recommends as rules for immigration policy, the Harm Principle and the Basic Rights Principle (which he calls the HP and the BRP), confirms the suspicion that his balancing act tilts in the direction of significantly more open immigration. The Harm Principle holds, first, that "individuals have a duty not to harm others," and, second, that "those who have caused harm have a special duty of restitution to the victims of this harm" (80). Thus, countries who cause harm to individuals in other nations—through war, for example, or through economic or environmental exploitation—have a duty to make good on the harm they have done, and some of these responsibilities may have to be met by admitting harmed individuals as immigrants. The Basic Rights Principle, which supplements the HP by aiding people who are disadvantaged in ways for which no specific harm-causing nation can be identified and held responsible, "attempts to honor the basic rights of subsistence and security that individuals possess" by obligating "nations to play some part in meeting the basic rights of individuals in other societies even if they were not the cause of this need" (103). These principles do reflect a genuine attempt to balance Gibney's stated goals of individual rights and communal autonomy, because they are limited in scope and, as Gibney rightly emphasizes, "avoid open-ended obligations" (107). The Harm Principle is inherently limited because it seeks only to correct specific wrongs that countries have committed, and Gibney limits the Basic Rights Principle through what he calls the idea of the Fair Share, a formula based on GNP and population that establishes the amount a country must devote to meeting its obligations under the BRP.[24]

Despite these limits, however, the operation of Gibney's principles seems likely to reduce the sphere of state sovereignty in this area considerably, as Gibney himself notes. "[T]he proposed system," he admits in conclusion, "could bring political, economic, and social disruptions by the numbers of individuals admitted" (145). This is especially true of the Harm Principle, which under some circumstances "will obligate very large-scale alien admissions to the nation causing harm" (145).[25] And the BRP—though the numbers of admissions it requires may sometimes be less than those under the HP—represents a theoretically more significant limitation on state autonomy; in effect, it transforms what would have been regarded as Good Samaritanism into an obligation. That Gibney's proposals are a serious challenge to conventional assumptions (a fact he recognizes) becomes even clearer when we realize that he actually envisages alien admissions as the means by which a state fulfills only a small part of its duties to others, most of which are to be met through foreign aid (85, 104–5). Although Gibney views this feature of his theory as an illustration of its attempt to recognize communal autonomy—because countries will often be able to meet their obligations through foreign aid rather than alien admissions—the scope of these combined duties shows clearly that, in comparison with accepted practice, his principles represent a considerable curtailment of that autonomy.

Two theoretical considerations add force to this description of Gibney's argument as pursuing less of a middle path than his formal presentation indicates. The first is the normative basis adduced for his two principles. They are founded, he suggests, upon the duty to protect individual autonomy. His introductory argument that citizens have international moral obligations relies tentatively on autonomy as its justification (75–6), and this is confirmed explicitly by Gibney's description of the Harm Principle— "The HP seeks to protect the autonomy of the individual" (79)—and implicitly by his elaboration of the Basic Rights Principle (123).[26] If individual autonomy is the fundamental principle of his theory, then his defense of communal autonomy, were he to present it, would presumably follow the lines of Will Kymlicka's liberal argument for group rights. I doubt that individual autonomy can provide the starting-point for any very robust defense of community; but since I address Kymlicka's more fully elaborated argument at length in chapter five, I pass over the point for now. Here I note simply that the emphasis on autonomy gnaws at the foundation of Gibney's larger argument. For example, if the primary wrongs to be corrected are infringements of autonomy, then it is not clear why we should regard the BRP as subordinate to the HP, as Gibney suggests. It is easier to allocate responsibility for wrongs occurring under the HP, of course, which is practically useful, but the nature of the injustice appears the same under either principle. And if the BRP is coordinate with the HP, it becomes a matter of considerable interest whether Gibney's limiting device of the Fair Share can stand up to the corrosive influence of individual autonomy as a master principle, about which there may be some doubt.

The second theoretical consideration relates to Gibney's presentation of the conventional view, opposed to his own, that "sees governments acting in the purported best interests of [their own] society" (75), which Gibney dubs the "trustee" view (i.e., government is the trustee of its own society's national interests). Gibney suggests that this "trustee" view can be combined with his insistence on certain moral duties; that is, a nation can fulfill its moral obligations to outsiders and still seek to pursue the particular interests of its own members. This seems reasonable enough. But the way in which he refers to the trustee view is quite revealing. He writes, for example, that "there is no logical reason why the moral component should be removed when a nation acts as a trustee for its citizens" (75). Similarly, in a telling remark, he says that "the 'trustee' argument should not be without a moral component" (141). The clear implication of such formulations is that the trustee view, though it can and should be accompanied by a moral "component," is not in and of itself a moral view. In other words, this way of describing the opposing views excludes the possibility that the trustee view might itself be the *product* of moral argument, that moral reflection could lead us to the conclusion that a country's or government's *primary* duty (even if it has additional secondary obligations that it also seeks to fulfill) is towards its own citizens. This conclusion would, of course, be the opposite of Gibney's: "I am not against the pursuit of such national goals and concerns. However, they have their proper place, and their proper place is after a nation has met its *deeper* obligations under the HP and the BRP" (146, emphasis his).

This presentation of the trustee view, combined with the absence of any justification for preserving communal autonomy on the one hand and an emphasis on individual autonomy on the other, confirms the suspicion that Gibney's argument does indeed present quite a challenge to conventional practice. Certainly it does not amount to an argument for the current state of affairs, in which states maintain substantial control over their own immigration decisions, as a kind of "reasonable compromise," in Whelan's phrase, between extreme competing positions. It would be more accurate to say that Gibney characterizes current practice as a compromise, but not a reasonable one. The argument that I shall develop in the following chapters, by contrast, might appropriately be thought of as an attempt to provide an explicit and coherent defense of what Whelan describes, without defense, as a reasonable compromise between competing but more coherent extremes.

Indeed, it is only within the context of an intellectual debate already skewed heavily against the claims of the nation-state that Gibney's argument appears as moderate as it does. Far more typical than the balancing act he attempts are claims such as Bruce Ackerman's that "[t]he *only* reason for restricting immigration is to protect the ongoing process of liberal con-versation itself" and that politicians must strive to respect "an immigrant's prima facie *right* to demand entry into a liberal state."[27] Or Veit Bader's argument that "there are strong moral reasons in favor of policies of 'fairly open borders.'"[28] Or Onora O'Neill's claims that "actual boundaries are often impediments to justice," that an "account of just borders which takes account of these issues . . . must deny that they [nations or national identi-ties] create claims to bounded states which exercise absolute internal or external sovereignty," and that recognizing this has "very serious implica-tions . . . for the justice of legislation that selectively restricts boundary crossing, whether for asylum, travel, migration, abode, work, settlement, or to take up citizenship."[29] These citations illustrate the dominant intellectual consensus in favor of a markedly restricted view of state sovereignty over immigration.

Given the ubiquity of such views, it is especially important to focus carefully on the case for open (or, in Bader's phrase, "fairly open"—which is to say, very open) borders, since this argument reveals with particular clarity the assumptions commonly made in scholarly treatments of the sub-ject. Joseph Carens, who has written more than any other scholar on the theory of immigration, makes this case with special force.[30] His article, "Aliens and Citizens: The Case for Open Borders," is surely the clearest and best-known statement in the literature of the case for free movement, and he has refined his argument in a number of subsequent writings. His detailed treatment demands careful analysis, particularly because it differs so sharply from the conclusions that I will reach in the next chapter.

1. The Argument

In "Aliens and Citizens" Carens argues that three popular but very differ-ent contemporary theories—those of Nozick and Rawls, and utilitarian-ism[31]—all lead to open borders. This argument is worth summarizing briefly. Because property rights play a central role in Nozick's theory, Carens suggests, one might be tempted to think that it could generate a defense of immigration restrictions based upon some collective property right held by citizens in their country. But, Carens points out, Nozickian theories emphasize individual, not collective, rights. Collective rights have no place in, and indeed undermine the very foundation of, a theory such as Nozick's. "According to Nozick the state has no right to do anything other than enforce the rights which individuals already enjoy in the state of nature. Citizenship gives rise to no distinctive claim" (AaC, 253). In such theories, the state's function is limited to enforcing the rights of individuals; it cannot prevent them from exercising those rights in ways that would admit foreigners, nor can it deprive foreigners of their rights. "[T]he control that the state can legitimately exercise over [its] land is limited to the enforcement of the rights of individual owners. Prohibiting people from entering a territory because they did not happen to be born there or otherwise gain the credentials of citizenship is no part of any state's legitimate mandate" (AaC, 254). So Nozick's approach, Carens concludes, cannot support restrictions on migration.

Turning then to Rawls, Carens argues that, although Rawls himself assumes a closed society for the purposes of his theory, the same reasons that make his approach compelling for thinking about justice within a state also make it attractive for thinking about international justice. In particular, the original position with its veil of ignorance, which is supposed to prevent factual contingencies that are (in Rawls's phrase) "arbitrary from a moral point of view" from influencing our choice of principles of justice, seems well-suited to thinking about international relations. This is because facts such as who one's parents are or where one is born are morally arbitrary and therefore precisely the sorts of things ruled out by the veil of ignorance. Thus we should "take a global, not a national, view of the original position" (AaC, 256). Given this, people in the original position would select a principle of international justice that protected the right to free movement, because migration might prove essential to their life plans. Thus a Rawlsian perspective also suggests that free movement is a fundamental liberty.[32]

Utilitarianism permits more arguments in favor of immigration restriction than either the Nozickian or the Rawlsian position, because it considers any interests citizens have in excluding newcomers. Nevertheless, Carens argues, utilitarianism, despite internal disagreements about the best utilitarian approach, also points toward considerably more open borders. This is because—regardless of whether one considers only economic factors or also other ones, such as cultural interests or even mere prejudices—the utility of aliens must be weighed equally with that of citizens, which would undoubtedly tip the scales in the direction of free movement. "Under current conditions, when so many millions of poor and oppressed people feel they have so much to gain from migration to the advanced industrial states, it seems hard to believe that a utilitarian calculus which took the interests of aliens seriously would justify significantly greater limits on immigration than the ones entailed by the public order restriction implied by the Rawlsian approach" (AaC, 264).[33]

Carens argues, then, that these three very different contemporary theories all point toward open borders. Let us grant, for the sake of argument, that he is right about the theories' implications. Nevertheless, all three theories share something fundamental in common: all are forms of liberalism. Indeed, as Carens himself writes at the beginning of the essay, "Each of these theories begins with some kind of assumption about the equal moral worth of individuals. In one way or another, each treats the individual as prior to the community" (AaC, 252). Or as he writes later, "Each is rooted in the liberal tradition" (AaC, 265). If they view the individual as prior to the community, though, it is not surprising that these theories "provide little basis for drawing fundamental distinctions between citizens and aliens who seek to become citizens" (AaC, 252). This liberal basis of Carens's argument appears especially in his discussion of Rawls, where he writes,

> [T]he effect of immigration on the particular culture and history of the society would not be a relevant moral consideration . . . . [This] follows from what Rawls says in his discussion of perfectionism. The principle of perfectionism would require social institutions to be arranged so as to maximize the achievement of human excellence in art, science, or culture regardless of the effect of such arrangements on equality and freedom . . . . One variant of this position might be the claim that restrictions on immigration would be necessary to preserve the unity and coherence of a culture (assuming that the culture was worth preserving). Rawls argues that in the original position no one would accept any perfectionist standard because no one would be willing to risk the possibility of being required to forgo some important right or freedom for the sake of an ideal that might prove irrelevant to one's own concerns. So, restrictions on immigration for the sake of preserving a distinctive culture would be ruled out. (AaC, 262)

One might note, in passing, that there is considerable distance between Carens's statement of the perfectionist principle ("to maximize the achievement of human excellence" in some respect) and his "variant" of it ("to preserve the unity and coherence of a culture"). Of more concern, however, is the sweeping reach of this radical statement of individual right. For taken seriously, it would grant individuals a veto power over their entire culture's right to exist, or, more precisely, its right to take steps to ensure its continued existence. This follows necessarily from Carens's statement that "no one would accept any perfectionist standard." For this entails more than simply that an individual may reject some particular culture or way of life, which, after all, might not have significant social consequences.[34] Rather, the claim is that people would reject the general perfectionist principle itself (along with Carens' variant of it)—the principle, that is, that would permit social institutions to be organized so as to further some important communal goal, even at some cost to individual freedom and equality. But the consequence of rejecting this general principle is that any individual who is not "willing to risk the possibility of being required to forgo some important right or freedom for the sake of an ideal that might prove irrelevant to [her] own concerns" can deny to the community the ability to order its institutions and collective life around *any* particular ideal (precisely because the principle, rather than merely the particular way of life, has been rejected). This is the "priority of the individual over the community" with a vengeance, and it is hardly surprising that such a line of thought leads to open borders.[35]

This is not to say, of course, that distinct communities would cease to exist in a world of open borders. Even though the rejection of the perfectionist principle entails an individual veto over collective attempts to preserve a particular way of life, it does not follow that, in the absence of such measures, distinct communities could never survive. Perhaps after the borders are opened no one will show up. And even if they do, distinct regional identities obviously can be compatible with free mobility—consider the persistence of regional differences within the European Union or the United States. The point, rather, is that these distinct communities would not be entitled, should the need arise, to take the steps they thought necessary to preserve themselves in existence. Such action would be simply illegitimate, because it would involve a reliance on the perfectionist principle, something "no one would be willing to risk."[36]

Perhaps, though, Carens does not really endorse such a thorough rejection of the perfectionist principle; perhaps, that is, his elucidation of the consequences of Rawls's argument goes beyond what he himself actually believes. His essay "Immigration and the Welfare State" seems to raise this possibility. There, relying on a principle of collective responsibility, Carens argues that equally affluent communities that satisfy minimum standards of welfare provision for their citizens may legitimately impose at least some limited restrictions on immigration from one another. This is because they may legitimately decide to provide varying levels of welfare support, and unrestricted movement would undermine their ability to do so more generously. They can rightly insist that other, comparably situated communities take responsibility for their own members, leaving them all free to provide the levels of support they choose. Without the right to restrict migration, communities lose the capacity for making such collective decisions.

It is not clear, however, exactly what we should make of this line of argument. For Carens clearly intends this possible restriction on free movement to apply only in the case of comparably situated liberal egalitarian states fulfilling all of their minimal obligations in terms of domestic welfare responsibilities and foreign aid. Thus he writes, "[F]reedom of movement is in fact an important personal liberty and . . . any restrictions on freedom of movement (even residency requirements) entail the subordination of an important liberal value to other concerns. We thus have a case for limited forms of exclusion by comparably situated communities under some circumstances" (IWS, 227). In other words, a country may be entitled to impose some restrictions on immigration—as long as it is already sufficiently liberal.[37] This argument, then, far from weakening the reliance on liberalism at the heart of Carens's case for open borders, indirectly confirms that reliance.[38]

The same difficulty appears in a later essay, in which Carens considers whether one could construct a hypothetical defense of immigration restrictions in a country like Japan, highly homogeneous and with very different traditions in this respect from ours in North America. Carens suggests that in such circumstances a plausible case for restriction could be made. But here too he is clearly speaking of a liberal Japan which is meeting all its international obligations in other ways (MigaM, 37). Indeed, he writes, "Appeals to diversity and pluralism carry no weight when it comes to the violation of basic human rights. From a liberal egalitarian perspective all states are obliged to respect such rights regardless of their history, culture or traditions" (MigaM, 36). Once again, then, even the possibility of making a case for restrictions on movement arises only in the context of states which are already liberal.

Still, Carens does write in the piece on "Immigration and the Welfare State," "I think it is possible to make more persuasive arguments for exclusion, arguments that do not focus primarily on the preservation of the welfare state but on the claims of communities to preserve their identities and distinctive ways of life" (227–8). What, then, might such arguments be? If Carens is to admit some form of the perfectionist principle, this would seem to provide the opening for it. Carens examines this possibility most thoroughly in his very interesting and subtle article "Democracy and Respect for Difference: The Case of Fiji."[39] Here he defends certain political arrangements—such as policies designed to maintain land ownership in the hands of native Fijians, or to preserve the authority of chieftains in Fijian society and politics—intended to help preserve traditional Fijian culture, even though those arrangements impose some costs on the large group of Indians (about half the island's total population) also living in Fiji. Considerations of space permit only a brief summary of Carens's lengthy and complex discussion, but I think it is fair to say that his support for these arrangements rests upon two main claims. The first is a positive argument: that these illiberal practices have in fact been good for native Fijians. Thus he writes that "it seems plausible to suppose that policies more in keeping with liberal individualism—for example an insistence on individual, alienable title to land as opposed to the collective, inalienable form of ownership adopted in Fiji—might have had disastrous consequences for native Fijians as such policies did elsewhere" (576). In other words, the practices adopted, despite (or rather because of) their departure from the liberal ideal, truly did preserve at least some aspects of the native Fijians' traditional way of life, and in doing so helped to shield them from the depressing fate of so many indigenous peoples subjected to colonialism. Although the practices involve restrictions of individual rights, native Fijians have, on the whole, genuinely benefited from them.

The second prong of Carens's argument is negative: the political arrangements designed to preserve traditional Fijian culture do not involve serious violations of moral requirements. They are not, as Carens puts it, "dependent on the subordination of any other group" (594). Thus, for example, although native Fijians have secured their continued ownership of the vast majority of land, "Fijian dominance in this area is balanced by the dominance Indians have achieved in other areas of economic life" (595). In more general terms, Carens suggests that policies designed to preserve cultural differences may be legitimate as long as they do not violate what he calls "minimal moral standards" (628). Though Carens does not define in great detail what these minimal standards might be, he does suggest that at least one of them is equal citizenship, claiming that "at a minimum, anyone born and brought up within the borders of a modern state is morally entitled to citizenship in that state" (581) and that "citizenship in the modern state must be treated as a threshold concept [so that o]nce over the threshold, one is entitled to be treated as an equal" (582).[40] On these grounds, Carens criticizes the 1987 military coup "whose goal was . . . the firm establishment of native Fijian political hegemony" (574). By contrast, Fiji's political system before the coup, including the arrangements designed to protect traditional Fijian culture, was not "dependent on the subordination of any other group" and so did not, Carens argues, deny Indians equal citizenship. Thus he writes,

> In sum, minimal moral standards set significant constraints on morally permissible cultural variation. If the institutions and policies of independent Fiji before the coup seem morally permissible, as I have generally argued that

they do, that is because they generally respected basic individual freedoms and political rights. Within the limits set by minimal moral standards, there can still be an important range of cultural variation. (628)

Or, as he puts it near the end of his article, the position he has sketched "should open up a space within democratic politics within which people are morally free to choose among competing visions of how society ought to be organized" (629).

Here Carens, in terms reminiscent of his earlier discussions of immigration and welfare and of hypothetical Japanese restrictions on immigration, endorses a limited version of the perfectionist principle. Is this endorsement sufficient to support more significant restrictions on immigration than those discussions did? I think not, for two reasons. First, even in the passages just cited, Carens insists that deviations from the liberal norm are only acceptable when minimal moral standards are met, so that the Fijian policies are legitimate "because they generally respected basic individual freedoms and political rights" (Fiji, 628). This suggests, however, that if free mobility is regarded as a "basic individual freedom," then it would constitute part of the minimal moral standards that must be respected. Though Carens does not, I think, anywhere declare that mobility *must* be so regarded, he certainly suggests in various places that this ought to be the case. In "Aliens and Citizens," for example, in considering Rawlsian theory, he writes that people in the original position "would insist that the right to migrate be included in the system of basic rights and liberties" (258). Elsewhere he repeats the argument that, from the Rawlsian perspective, "[f]reedom of movement would be a basic element in the global system of basic liberties" (IWS, 215); and he also writes, speaking now in his own voice, that "freedom of movement is in fact an important personal liberty," limited restriction of which is occasionally acceptable only among relatively prosperous liberal states meeting the various obligations of justice (IWS, 227). Elsewhere he writes, "Liberal egalitarianism entails a deep commitment to freedom of movement as both an important liberty in itself and a prerequisite for other freedoms" (MigaM, 25).[41] This consistent line of argument raises the distinct possibility—I am inclined to say probability—that Carens includes free mobility among the "basic individual freedoms and political rights" that must be respected by even the limited perfectionist position that he develops in his consideration of Fiji.[42]

A second consideration, reinforcing this interpretation, is the crucial qualification Carens attaches to his support for Fiji's perfectionist policy, which was permissible because it "was not dependent upon the subordination of any other group" (Fiji, 594). Yet Carens quite clearly does not consider this to be true of contemporary restrictions on migration. In "Aliens and Citizens" he writes that the argument for open borders "is strongest, I believe, when applied to the migration of people from third world countries to those of the first world. Citizenship in Western liberal democracies is the modern equivalent of feudal privilege—an inherited status that greatly enhances one's life chances" (251–2). Restrictions on migration on the part of wealthy countries are simply an unfair means of protecting inherited privileges against demands for equality by those less fortunate— much less fortunate, in fact. Carens makes the same point in both of the other instances where he considers possible perfectionist restrictions on immigration. In the case of restrictions to protect different levels of welfare provision, he writes,

> [V]ast economic inequalities undermine the argument that it is fair to restrict entry in order to preserve the capacity for collective self-determination . . . . Exclusion then becomes a means of protecting differences in resources rather than preserving the ability to make different choices . . . . Therefore, despite my sympathy for the project of preserving the welfare state, I am driven back to the conclusion of my analysis of liberal theory. Preservation of the welfare state does not justify restriction of immigration from poor countries to rich ones. (IWS, 227)

Similarly, in discussing the possible legitimacy of restrictions to preserve Japanese culture, Carens quite clearly states that the case in favor of such restrictions succeeds "in a context where we have temporarily assumed away the most urgent concerns (desperate poverty and fear of oppression) that motivate so many of those who actually want to move and that make their claims so powerful" (MigaM, 39).

Thus, even if free mobility were not to be regarded as a fundamental right, the protection of which would be demanded by minimal moral standards, the requirement that perfectionist policies not be "dependent upon the subordination of any other group," in conjunction with the great economic inequality currently existing among nations, strongly suggests that the only perfectionist restrictions on immigration that might win Carens's support would be ones between comparably situated countries already satisfying all the demands of a liberal conception of justice.[43] It should be clear, then, that Carens's defense of open borders really does rest fundamentally on his commitment to liberalism. Does he offer any other argument that might broaden the theoretical foundations of his position and be potentially persuasive to those who do not already share this commitment?[44]

2. The Communitarian Objection

If such an argument is to be found, one might well expect it in the section of the "Aliens and Citizens" article entitled "The Communitarian Challenge" (264–70). Here Carens responds to Michael Walzer's argument (in *Spheres of Justice*) that states are entitled to restrict immigration—"[t]he best theoretical defense of the conventional assumption."[45] As Carens briefly but accurately puts it, "Walzer's central claim is that exclusion is justified by the right of communities to self-determination" (AaC, 266). Carens raises, I think, some very important questions about this claim, but not in such a way as to expand or strengthen the underlying presuppositions of his own position.

First, Carens questions Walzer's argument about the state's need to exclude by raising the example of freedom of movement among cities and states within the United States. These smaller units maintain distinct and often quite different identities, Carens points out, although they are not permitted to restrict freedom of movement. "So, these cases call into question Walzer's claim that distinctiveness depends on the possibility of formal closure. What makes for distinctiveness and what erodes it is [*sic*] much more complex than political control of admissions" (AaC, 267). Furthermore, even when internal migration does have the potential to cause great changes in local communities, we do not grant them the right to restrict it, because we consider internal freedom of movement more important. But, Carens asks, "If freedom of movement within the state is so important that it overrides the claims of local political communities, on what grounds can we restrict freedom of movement across states? This requires a stronger case for the *moral* distinctiveness of the nation-state as a form of community than Walzer's discussion of neighborhoods provides" (AaC, 267; emphasis in original). This is certainly an important question to raise against Walzer. But it does nothing to establish the correctness of Carens's argument, for it need not point in the direction of free movement. Rather, we could grant Carens's point but decide that the proper response is to limit internal movement as well, to grant local communities the power to enforce and maintain particular identities against intrusions from outside.

Carens's more important argument against Walzer uses Walzer's own method—reflection upon the shared meanings within a particular political community—to challenge his conclusion. As Carens puts it, "Any approach like Walzer's that seeks its ground in the tradition and culture of *our* community must confront, as a methodological paradox, the fact that liberalism is a central part of our culture" (AaC, 268–9; emphasis in original). Of the three theories he has discussed, he writes that

> their individualistic assumptions and their language of universal ahistorical reason makes [*sic*] sense to us because of *our* tradition, *our* culture, *our* community. For people in a different moral tradition, one that assumed fundamental moral differences between those inside the society and those outside, restrictions on immigration might be easy to justify. Those who are *other* simply might not count, or at least not count as much. But we cannot dismiss the aliens on the ground that they are other, because *we* are the products of a liberal culture. The point goes still deeper. To take *our* community as a starting point is to take a community that expresses its moral views in terms of universal principles. (AaC, 269; emphasis in original; paragraph division omitted)

This view, however—even if true—is simply not an argument against Walzer's larger claim that communities may determine their admissions policies based upon their own, particular conceptions of membership; on the contrary, it effectively concedes that claim. It is an argument about the character of America, about the understandings Americans share, the beliefs they are committed to, and the consequences of those beliefs. Such an argument leads to open borders only if Carens is right about our tradition and our self-understanding. Perhaps Carens has described them accurately; if so, then he has a powerful argument that America (and possibly, by extension, other similarly liberal countries) ought to open its borders.[46] But it is not an argument that other countries ought to do so. In other words, Carens has, in a sense, opened precisely the kind of conversation that Walzer suggests a country ought to engage in when trying to design an immigration policy. He has raised the questions, "What kind of a people are we and what kind of a people do we want to be?" But the answers to these questions, obviously, apply only to the people in question. The implication of this line of argument, then, is that only societies with the liberal universalist identities that Carens describes here are committed to open borders. Other societies, with different views, will arrive at correspondingly different policies.

This is in no way to belittle the importance or the strategic effectiveness of Carens's argument. It is merely to point out that by its very nature it cannot call into question Walzer's larger claim about communal self-determination. On the contrary, to argue that Americans are committed to open borders because they share certain liberal beliefs is to argue within the boundaries established by Walzer's argument. Of course, Carens's argument is a very important one—perhaps the most important one—for Americans (and again, by extension, liberals elsewhere) trying to decide upon a fair immigration policy. But the correctness of his conclusion depends entirely upon whether he has accurately described their beliefs, and about that they must argue and decide for themselves. And if they decide that his description is inaccurate, Carens apparently has nothing further to say to them—or, if he does, he does not say it. So we are left where we started, confronted by the circular character of the argument: People (and countries) who think the individual is prior to the community—who subscribe, that is, to some version of the universalist liberalism that Carens describes—should support open borders. Other people do not appear to have a reason to do so.

In concluding the argument of "Aliens and Citizens," Carens notes that open borders would indeed prevent certain ways of life from continuing. But this, he says, does not completely destroy local, collective self-determination and control over a way of life; rather, it only constrains it. "Moreover, constraining the kinds of choices that people and communities may make is what principles of justice are for" (AaC, 271). This is a lot of constraint, though—it concedes the right to exist (or, more precisely, to attempt to preserve themselves in existence when necessary) to only a few, liberal forms of political community. Surely members of others sorts of communities are entitled to an argument that only liberal societies are legitimate before they open their borders as recommended by Carens here. But "Aliens and Citizens" does not provide such an argument.

Nor, I think, do Carens's numerous other writings on the subject, in which he most often accepts (for the sake of argument) conventional assumptions about the state's right to regulate immigration but within that context offers arguments pushing toward more open borders. Most of these I have already touched on in considering the scope of Carens's rejection of the perfectionist principle; here I simply note briefly one additional article. In a piece on the infamous White Australia immigration policy, Carens characterizes his approach in the earlier "Aliens and Citizens" article thus: "to ask whether the exclusion of peaceful immigrants can be justified in light of fundamental principles of justice and morality" (Austr, 41). Using this method, he had concluded, as we have seen, "that exclusion is not justified" (Austr, 41). In the article on Australia, however, he proposes to use a different approach:

> To argue for or against open borders on the basis of fundamental principles is perhaps to go too deep too soon. We may learn more about the ethics of

immigration by trying to explore the moral views embedded in the political practices and policies of different states. The assumption behind this second approach is not that morality always determines policy or that the best moral view always triumphs, but that we can understand these issues in politics best by being sensitive to the moral understandings of the participants themselves as reflected in debate and in action. In this view, any important question of political morality is bound to have complex, local dimensions tied to the history and culture of particular communities. We need not accept local understandings uncritically, but we should begin with these understandings if we wish to inhabit the same moral world as those about whom we write. (Austr, 42)

Using this approach, which of course takes for granted the nation-state and its right to control admissions, Carens argues that the White Australia policy, which sought to preserve an ethnically and culturally homogeneous (white and British) Australia, constituted an impermissible restriction on immigration.[47] This, of course, is the same form of argument Carens used against Walzer in "Aliens and Citizens," for it seeks to show that the immigration restrictions imposed by Australia were incompatible with the liberal beliefs broadly shared among Australians. As an internal critique, one which accepts its opponents' premises but disputes their conclusions, it is a highly effective argument against defenders of the White Australia policy, just as the argument from "Aliens and Citizens" about American liberalism is an important one for Americans to consider. But it does nothing to broaden the foundations of the earlier case for open borders, nothing to make it potentially persuasive to a wider circle of people who do not already share its basic presuppositions.

3. New Developments?
In several recent writings, Carens has clarified his argument in a variety of ways. He has become more open towards considerations of culture even in liberal politics, and accordingly has not emphasized the anti-perfectionist argument as strongly as he did in the "Aliens and Citizens" article; he has explored in greater depth the moral and theoretical significance of obstacles to open borders posed by political realities such as the global system of sovereign states; and he has described the relationship of his argument to liberalism and the primary audience to whom that argument is addressed. These clarifications, however, as he himself has emphasized, have not altered his central claim: that, however distant we may be from achieving the goal, our ultimate moral obligation is to have open borders. I here address these recent writings briefly, both to stress their underlying consis-

tency with the works already considered and, in conclusion, to indicate what I believe is an important shortcoming of Carens's argument.

One important theme of Carens's recent writings is his development of a distinction between two different approaches to morality, which he calls realistic and idealistic. The realistic approach focuses on minimizing the gap between ought and can, on avoiding a morality which would require of people things which there is no likelihood of their actually doing. "[B]y insisting in various ways on the need to avoid too large a gap between the is and the ought, a realistic approach to morality aims to focus moral discussion on issues that are actually up for debate in society, and thus to maximize the opportunity for reasoned moral reflection to have an impact in public life" (RealIdea, 164). An idealistic approach, on the other hand, recognizes that focusing on present possibilities may simply legitimate injustices. It therefore takes nothing for granted and insists on searching out what is right in principle, regardless of whether people are likely to do it or not.

> The basic presupposition of this sort of approach is that our institutions and practices may not be all that they should be. We want a more critical perspective than the realistic approach allows. We do not want to build the flaws and limitations of existing arrangements into our moral inquiry. So, we try to abstract in various ways from the status quo. We try to avoid limiting presuppositions as much as possible. (RealIdea, 166)

Both approaches, Carens suggests, are important for practical ethical reflection.

He has also tried to show how both might be employed in thinking about immigration. In an essay entitled "The Rights of Immigrants," he first outlines the demands of idealistic moral theory, repeating his by-now familiar argument in favor of free movement. He then suggests that this approach may not seem helpful in solving the problems of the world we actually face, and then turns to realistic moral theory as a way of addressing issues such as refugees, family reunification, and appropriate criteria of admission. In doing so, he accepts (for the sake of argument) "the conventional moral view . . . that states are largely free (in a moral sense) to admit or exclude immigrants," but argues that "[t]here are some important moral constraints on and qualifications to this general right," which limit how states can exercise it and push in the direction of greater openness (RoI, 152). Carens makes much the same argument, using only slightly different labels, in a later essay where he distinguishes between engaging in moral and political reflection from the standpoint of either a "just world" or a "real world presupposition" (ROB, 1084–88). The former asks "what justice requires in some sort of absolute sense;" by doing so, it "enables us to focus more sharply on fundamental principles and opens up the possibility of our gaining a critical perspective on unjust arrangements that are deeply entrenched" (ROB, 1084, 1085). The latter, by contrast, is aimed at guiding our immediate, practical action, and it therefore "take[s] into account all of the factors that we excluded with the just world presupposition, because we want to know how we should act in the world as it is" (ROB, 1086).

It would be wrong, though, to mistake this elucidation and, perhaps, modification of Carens's views for a fundamentally new approach or a partial abandonment of the case for open borders. For Carens nowhere backs away from—on the contrary, he continues to defend—his earlier claim that justice, in principle, requires open borders. Indeed, he still writes, in discussing the realistic and idealistic approaches,

> The assumptions we adopt should depend in part on the purposes of our inquiry. Moral inquiry can provide a guide to action, and it can assess the fundamental legitimacy of our institutions and practices (and of alternatives to them). Both purposes are important, but there can be a deep tension between them in contexts where existing arrangements are fundamentally unjust yet deeply entrenched. That is precisely the case, in my view, in the area of migration. (RealIdea, 169)

Similarly, he ends the essay contrasting the "just world" and "real world presupposition" approaches to morality with a vigorous reaffirmation of his views: "The challenge of open borders continues" (ROB, 1097).

Thus the discussion of realistic approaches to morality and migration represents less a principled concession to critics of open borders than a willingness, as a kind of strategic move in an ongoing process of political dialogue, temporarily to adopt assumptions held by others in order to achieve important gains (in, for example, the admission of refugees, or family reunification), even though Carens in fact regards those assumptions as mistaken and intends to challenge them at other times.[48] Such argumentative flexibility on Carens's part should come as no surprise, for the complex relationship between theory and practice, as well as the effect that relationship has on the kinds of arguments one makes and the manner in which one makes them, have been concerns of his from very early on. In an article published well before even the "Aliens and Citizens" piece, Carens discussed the role of compromise in politics. There he argued that compromise is illegitimate when questions of principle are involved, fundamental matters of right and wrong. But because "[i]nterests and morals are often intertwined in politics" (CiP, 130) and because people disagree about which principles are right and wrong (as well as about the relative weight to be given different principles), it is not always obvious where compromise is or is not legitimate. In such circumstances, an open attitude and willingness to see the reasonableness of opposing beliefs help widen the realm of possible agreement and increase the likelihood of finding a solution. Something like this, I think, is what Carens hopes to accomplish through his recent contrasts between realistic and idealistic approaches to morality and migration. Without changing his view of the theoretical merits of free movement, he has simply recognized the wide disagreement on the issue, even among intelligent people of good will, and, without abandoning his earlier position, he simultaneously pushes for policies that approach that ideal but are still real political possibilities.[49]

4. Taking Liberalism for Granted

Carens's argument, then, has remained fundamentally consistent throughout his writings on immigration: justice requires open borders (or at any rate something very close to open borders). Nor has the basis of this argument—an appeal to liberalism—changed. Indeed, in his recent work, Carens has been quite explicit in recognizing this: "[A]s I have constructed it, the open borders argument does indeed presuppose a commitment to liberal principles" (ROB, 1093).[50] But he has not attempted to defend that underlying commitment to liberalism itself. Thus one might describe his overall argument as a kind of broad-scale communitarian one: people who accept fundamental liberal principles ought to support open borders. Carens's most recent book, *Culture, Citizenship, and Community,* while not specifically restating his views on immigration (though it does consider a number of closely related topics), lends credence to this way of approaching and assessing Carens's work. There, in a discussion of Michael Walzer, he lays out an interesting and promising framework for thinking about problems of political ethics, a framework that is intended to reconcile universalist and particularist accounts of morality. Carens suggests that we think of liberal justice in terms of three concentric circles (CCC, 32–6). The outer circle includes those principles we are prepared to apply to all human beings; the middle contains those principles that we think apply to all liberal democracies; and the inner consists of judgements about a particular liberal democracy in light of its own history and culture. As we move outward through the circles, our moral judgements lose specificity and richness of content, but they apply to more contexts; similarly, as we move inwards, our judgements become thicker in the sense of settling more details and specific problems, but they apply to fewer places.[51]

Of particular relevance for us here is the description Carens gives of the outermost concentric circle. For although this circle contains the moral norms that *we think of* as universal, Carens does not in fact view them as constituting a universal morality. On the contrary, he states clearly that they are also a part of *our* morality. We believe that they apply to all people, but that does not mean that all people do or would accept them as their own moral norms. "I am perfectly prepared to acknowledge that the outermost circle of our morality, the one in which we apply our critical standards universally, is a feature of *our* morality. Indeed, what is so striking about this part of our morality, in my view, is that we *are* prepared to apply it even to people who may not share it, whereas we have many moral norms that we think should apply only to people who share our commitments" (CCC, 47; emphasis his). Indeed, Carens consciously sidesteps the question of whether or not "there are any moral standards universally shared by all human societies" in favor of the "internal, interpretive" question of when we *believe* we should apply our standards to others and when not (CCC, 47). This broad account of moral reflection underscores my description of Carens's open borders argument as a necessarily liberal one. Even at his most universalistic moments, and even when reflecting upon a fundamental value like equality, Carens is doing no more—and, to do him justice, claims to be doing no more—than spinning out the implications of values to which some people (we liberals, broadly speaking) are committed, but others are not. It is in this sense, I suggest, that the argument for open borders is appropriately characterized as a kind of broad communitarian argument for liberals.

But this broad liberal communitarianism, as we have seen, is one that applies at least some of its standards to outsiders. Carens does not explicitly say, as far as I know, that the open borders argument is among those "universal" standards, but the weight of evidence suggests to me that he would include it with them. He does, after all, call the "Aliens and Citizens" argument (in its subtitle), not just "a" case for open borders, but rather "*The* Case for Open Borders" (my italics).[52] More significant than that detail, however, is his undefended (perhaps necessarily so, given the concentric circles framework described above) claim in *Culture, Citizenship, and Community* that "liberal democracy is the only just political order, at least under modern political conditions" (120).[53] And it would seem to follow that, if all people ought to be liberal, and if open borders are the logical outcome of liberal commitments, then all people ought to have open borders (keeping in mind, of course, that Carens's distinction between realistic and idealistic approaches leaves flexibility for contingently adopting policies that fall short of the actual moral requirement). My own sense is that the general tone of Carens's body of work supports this reading, so long as it is understood as a statement of fundamental moral principle towards which we should conscientiously strive and not as an insistence that all people must immediately throw their borders open today, without any regard for circumstances. A final consideration in support of this view is that an argument for open borders, or free movement, seems by its very nature to address all people, in all countries, and with all their different beliefs, not just some subset of people already committed to certain values. Normally, when we speak about open borders, we mean just that: a world of open borders, not a world in which a few countries open their borders while the rest refuse to do so. Immigration, after all, is an issue that can be faced by any people, not only a liberal one, and there would be something misleading in presenting an argument as the case for open borders if all that one really meant were that some countries, with certain beliefs, were morally obligated to open their borders, while other countries, with different beliefs, were not.[54]

This presents a problem, however, especially in the context of immigration. For immigration policies are not just like any other kind of policy a government may consider. Because they shape membership itself, they inevitably have a profound effect upon the identities of the countries that adopt them. Thus countries can be expected to choose immigration policies that reflect their understandings of themselves. Yet, as we have seen, Carens's argument for open borders is closely linked to liberal political theory. Thus, insofar as it is indeed addressed to all countries, it appears to require them, in the name of moral principles considered universal from the standpoint of one particular point of view, to adopt policies that will inevitably transform them in a liberal direction. In other words, his argument, put most bluntly, appears ultimately as a kind of indictment: Only liberal states—and perhaps only some liberal states (of the sorts that Carens discusses in "Aliens and Citizens")—are legitimate.[55] Surely, though, other kinds of polities, embracing different political beliefs that point toward different immigration policies, are entitled to some broader defense of the liberalism underlying Carens's arguments—the kind of defense from which he deliberately abstains—before they render themselves vulnerable to the kind of fundamental transformation that open borders seem to invite.

Carens, in his reply to an earlier version of this argument, specifically denies that his argument should be received in this manner. "[I]t is not," he suggests, "a demand to 'other kinds of polities' to 'render themselves vulnerable to . . . fundamental transformation.' Instead, it should be seen as a way of starting a conversation" (ROB, 1094), a conversation between people who must address each other across the divide of their different beliefs and commitments. In this, I believe, he is entirely sincere, and there is an admirable humility and openness, a willingness to engage others on equal terms, in this description of the argument. Yet it is striking that, a mere page and a half after issuing this conversational invitation, Carens characterizes his open borders argument as follows: "[W]hen I say that free migration should be regarded as a human right, I am claiming that all states are morally obliged to open their borders whether the populations or authorities of those states accept the premises from which my arguments are derived or not. The reach of the claim is universal even if the source of the argument is particularistic (in the sense that it is rooted only in the liberal tradition)" (ROB, 1095–6). I'm not sure how other conversationalists will react to such a declaration, but that certainly sounds like a demand to me. And as long as the underlying commitment to liberalism is left undefended—and, as we have seen, Carens's most recent statements raise doubts about whether it even *can* ultimately be defended—it will, I think, almost inevitably be regarded as an unjustified demand.

It is important to be clear about exactly what the problem is. It is not that universal claims can never arise from a within a particular moral tradition.[56] Obviously, it is possible for people within a given tradition to discover truths that are universal. Indeed, if this were not the case, we could never have access to any universal moral norms, since there does not appear to be any place else for them to originate. Thus there is no difficulty in conceding that we could justifiably be held to moral standards that were derived, in the first instance, from premises we regard as mistaken. In such a case, however, we will necessarily regard the moral obligation in question as justified *in spite of* its original derivation, presumably because we think it is also justifiable on some alternative basis other than the one we consider mistaken. In other words, what is immediately of interest to us when confronted by a claim of moral obligation is not the premises from which others might have derived it, nor is it whether they thought themselves to have discovered a universally applicable standard; it is, rather, whether we ourselves, for whatever reasons, should regard it as a true statement of our moral duties. To state this more clearly in terms of the argument for open borders: A non-liberal confronted by the purely liberal case for open borders will reasonably want to know whether the argument can be justified in any other way, and it is hard to know why he would perceive the mere reiteration of the liberal chain of reasoning as anything more than a demand. To the question, "Why should I, who reject your premises, feel bound by your conclusion?" it can never be very persuasive to answer, "Well, *I* think you should."[57]

There are, of course, some possible ways of answering the question that would not necessarily appear as a demand and that could conceivably lead to a more persuasive answer. I can imagine three general strategies. First, one could attempt to appeal to some universal moral perspective transcending the two particular traditions or viewpoints confronting each other (however the precise relationship between universal morality and particular tradition is understood). As we have seen, Carens explicitly declines to pursue this strategy. He writes, "I am inclined to leave open the question of whether there are any moral standards universally shared by all human societies," because "I'm not sure this is a fruitful question" (CCC, 47). In light of this, it would be unfair to speculate about whether Carens thinks this question has an answer or what it might be; clearly, though, he does not wish to buttress his arguments through such an appeal. Second, one could look for reasons within the other's tradition that would also support the conclusions one has derived from one's own. But Carens cautions against this approach, on the plausible grounds that it "creates powerful incentives to interpret that tradition in ways that satisfy our desire to criticize" (49). It is thus more likely to distort the other tradition than genuinely to engage its otherness and is unlikely to be persuasive. So Carens appears to reject this way of seeking additional support for his arguments as well.

The third possibility would be to argue that one's own tradition, or the premises from which one argues, itself embodies universal moral truth, and that all peoples, therefore, should accept it. There is some reason to think that this is in fact Carens's view and that he might find it an attractive strategy for broadening the appeal of his open borders argument. As noted earlier, Carens does claim that "liberal democracy is the only just political order, at least under modern political conditions" (CCC, 120). An argument in defense of this claim would help immensely in preventing the open borders argument from appearing simply as a kind of demand for acquiescence by non-liberals. In fact, it would make it much more possible to have a genuine argument about the merits of the open borders proposal. As long as that proposal is confined within the walls of the kind of broad communitarian liberalism I have described, it is hard to know how someone who rejects its premises should respond, or even why he should bother. As long as Carens has "not offered any reasons why those who are not liberals should accept" (ROB, 1093) the open borders argument, they need offer no reasons for not doing so. It will always suffice to reply, "How curious that you see things that way; we don't."[58] An actual defense of the liberal tradition as itself embodying a universal moral standard, by contrast, would call for an equally reasoned response. But since Carens has not—not yet, at any rate—attempted to defend the claim that all peoples (at least in the contemporary world) should be liberal democrats, it can hardly broaden the appeal of his argument among those skeptical of his premises. On the contrary, left undefended, it seems likely to have almost the opposite effect, amplifying the sense of being confronted with an unjustified demand for homogeneity. Should Carens pursue this question further, of course, that would be another matter.[59]

Doing so, however, would raise a different problem, for it would require Carens to explain why we should agree that liberal principles are what he thinks they are. I have deliberately refrained from raising this point and have instead simply argued as if Carens were right about the implications of liberalism—not necessarily because I agree with him about those implications, but rather because I have been interested in pursuing a different problem here, the problem of whether Carens's argument, the most forceful case for open borders that I know of, holds any promise of persuading people not already committed to its fundamental premises. It should go without saying, however, that not all liberals agree with Carens that open borders are the logically necessary result of their own principles. To pick only an obvious example, John Rawls, in his essay on "The Law of Peoples," has argued that the original position should *not* be applied globally—a move which was the basis for Carens's extension of the Rawlsian view in "Aliens and Citizens"—but should rather be used for selecting domestic principles of justice. Rawls notes, in fact (though, in fairness to Carens, it is a throwaway remark, offered without further elaboration or defense), that one consequence of his approach is that "a people has at least a qualified right to limit immigration."[60] To pick even more obvious examples, all three of the writers considered in the first part of this chapter—Beck, Brimelow, and Williamson—would generally be regarded as writing within the broad tradition of liberalism, despite the significant differences among their views (Brimelow and Williamson are on the right, Beck on the left). Yet if Carens were to make it clear that the open borders argument is derived from a liberalism for which he thinks he can provide a universal justification, it would become a matter of considerable importance to explain either why authors such as this trio reason invalidly from liberal premises, or why they should not be regarded as defending a form of liberal politics at all.

None of what I have written here is intended to belittle the significance of Carens's argument, which is both provocative and thoughtful. He makes a significant contribution to an ongoing debate within liberalism. Even if he has not offered an argument that might persuade non-liberals, he has certainly challenged liberals to re-examine the implications of their own beliefs in innovative and radical ways. As the next chapter will make clear enough, my own arguments owe much to his efforts to think normatively about immigration. Indeed, I think that Carens was entitled to write, in his earlier response to my argument, "I think the open borders argument poses an important challenge to liberal theory that still has not been met" (ROB, 1096). Though I do not appeal specifically to liberalism, the present book was written at least in part out of a sense that he is right about this. And certainly he was also entitled, in an article like "Aliens and Citizens," to argue that liberalism leads to open borders without having to offer a full-blown defense of liberalism itself. But something like that is, ultimately, what the argument requires. And, ironically, it has come to require it more, not less, urgently as it has become clearer that Carens's argument arises not from a crusading, hegemonic liberal universalism but from a cautious liberal communitarianism—precisely because people will reasonably want assurance that they are not being offered the former in the humble guise of the latter.

Postmodernism and Borders

The views that I have discussed constitute the two basic sides to the immigration debate. But another body of literature is at least relevant to that debate: postmodernism. All postmodern thought is, in a sense, about borders, their construction, contingency, and permeability. This is true not only at an abstract level, where postmodernists busily expose false dichotomies or the suppression of the Other by restrictive, ungrounded, and essentialist conceptions of identity; it also appears in the concrete problems which often engage such thinkers. The familiar issues of identity politics—racism, sexism, gay and lesbian activism—are precisely about the contestable borders drawn up between various groups, as well as the privileges accruing to those who are on the "right" side of such borders. One could easily translate the argument against immigration restrictions into this kind of language: borders between states are highly contingent constructions which conceal and protect enormous forms of privilege. The movement of people across these borders destabilizes them, especially when large illegal migrations create culturally ambiguous areas—much of the southwestern United

States, for example—that highlight the essentially arbitrary nature of state boundaries. These borders are perhaps the most potent force in the world today for labeling "Us" and "Them," and for keeping Them separate from Us.[61]

Immigration would thus seem to be a topic tailor-made for a postmodern treatment. It is therefore noteworthy that it has received relatively little such treatment. To be sure, there are discussions of related issues, such as Julia Kristeva's treatments of nationalism.[62] Similarly, discussions of multicultural societies, race relations, or ethnic group rights are often attempts to tackle problems resulting from migration. Calls for international redistribution raise some of the same issues that arise in the mainstream theories of immigration that I have considered. And migration does at times appear as an explicit theme in postmodern writing. Thus Iain Chambers, in *Migrancy, Culture, Identity,*[63] uses the idea of "migrancy" in at least three ways: as a general metaphor for the condition of contemporary life, characterized by a feeling of ceaseless movement, transition, and shifting identities; as, through its production of diversity in actual cities and countries, an important cause of the contemporary world thus characterized; and as the proper stance of the cultural critic, who possesses "a migrant intellectual disposition," crossing boundaries and speaking in a "travelling voice."[64]

Since this does not quite amount to a focused treatment of immigration in particular, it may be worth asking what a postmodern approach to the subject might look like.[65] I propose, therefore, to reflect upon works by two prominent postmodern scholars, William Connolly and Iris Marion Young, with this subject in mind. I choose them not only because of their prominence and the attention their arguments have drawn, but also because of the differences between them. One might call Connolly a kind of postmodern individualist, fiercely suspicious of all collective identities, critical of the way they distort reality, oppressing and confining those to whom they are applied; indeed, he extends his critique even within the individual self, showing how it too is fragmented and internally diverse. Young, by contrast, offers a theory that explicitly gives various groups an important, even institutionalized, role in society and government. Thus one might expect their theories to lead in rather different directions. My suggestion that, in the realm of immigration at least, they in fact produce quite similar results may therefore be of some interest, both in illuminating premises shared by different postmodernist thinkers and also in raising the possibility of a general postmodernist critique of contemporary immigration practices.

I should emphasize that I do not claim to be enunciating a position on immigration to which these thinkers, or others like them, are necessarily committed. I hope only to explore the implications of their arguments for immigration. Indeed, I should state at the outset that I consider myself neither a postmodern nor any kind of expert on postmodern thought. What follows is thus, as it were, the view of an outsider looking in—a small act of border-crossing of my own, so to speak, but one to which insiders can hardly object. I offer no definitive account and suggest no solution, but seek only to probe questions from a new perspective and encourage the "insiders" to take the matter up themselves.

1. Identity\Difference and the Contestability of Borders

William Connolly's *Identity\Difference* could well be described as a book about borders. His argument is this: Identity is a necessary part of human life, without which there is no possibility of meaningful action.[66] Yet identity carries with it significant dangers, for we have little reason to believe (he thinks), and good reason to doubt, that our identities are normatively grounded in nature, truth, being, or some such entity. In Connolly's view, on the contrary, being is a kind of abundance, an excess which always evades the limits of any particular identity. Identities are thus complex and important, but contingent, human constructions. Precisely because of identity's ontological vulnerability, however, people are constantly tempted to reinforce it, "to congeal established identities into fixed forms, thought and lived as if their structure expressed the true order of things" (ID, 64). But this is only possible at the cost of considerable injustice. For every identity is understood as such only in contrast to some Other, which is different from it.[67] And the construal of our identity as natural labels the Other as unnatural; of ourselves as good, of the Other as evil; of our way as right, of the Other's as wrong. Thus the attempt to ground a fixed identity does harm to the Other, who is both demeaned through the imposition of a degrading identity and whose own being can never be fully captured by the labels bestowed upon it. As Connolly puts it, "Identity requires difference in order to be, and it converts difference into otherness in order to secure its own self-certainty" (ID, 64).[68] To use one of Connolly's own favorite examples, heterosexuality is maintained as a cultural norm through the construction of homosexuality as an opposed and unnatural other. Such constructions of identity through differentiation are thus vulnerable on two counts: (1) they falsely claim an ontological foundation in being, which in truth always exceeds their inevitably partial and limited definitions; and (2) they injure other human beings through the imposition of unjustified and demeaning counter-identities.

Though Connolly for the most part explicitly restricts his analysis to domestic politics,[69] one can readily imagine how it might be extended to challenge conventional patterns of international relations and in particular assumptions supporting the traditional sovereign right of a country to determine its own immigration policy. One might begin by exposing the arbitrary nature of national boundaries and national identities. Often enough, boundaries have been the result of force and concessions to force. But even when this is not the case, when they coincide with "natural" borders such as rivers or mountain ranges, the groups they enclose and separate (or create?) do not correspond to any natural entities. We are often presented with an ideal in which each state corresponds to "its" particular nation. Yet this is patently false. For practically all states contain various, sometimes hostile, "nations," or a mosaic of intermingled ethnicities, or some hybrid resulting from years of contact and intermarriage. The "nations" we see in the world today are historical constructions, "imagined communities,"[70] often created through policies deliberately designed to encourage a particular national orientation or strengthened in response to such processes elsewhere, as different identities become more clearly defined in opposition to each other.[71]

Yet these contingent national identities become the basis of considerable privilege, operating in accord with Connolly's model. For countries define themselves in terms of each other; whatever Americans are, for example, Mexicans, Haitians, Cubans are something else. And these opposing self-definitions become the basis for policies that pursue the "national interest." In the realm of immigration, such policies seek to preserve a country's distinctive "national identity" by keeping out others who do not share it and could present a challenge to it. The construction of a national identity seeks to halt the play of difference and prevent challenges to the established order. It becomes self-legitimating and self-perpetuating, permanently saddling those not fortunate enough to belong to more favored nationalities with identities that are arbitrary, unchosen, and often portrayed as inferior.

This represents, as it were, the negative pole of a critique of nationalist immigration policies, sufficient grounds for challenging them. But a positive response is needed, some way of making boundaries porous. In domestic politics, Connolly suggests "agonistic democracy" as a way of achieving this. In agonistic democracy, which "opens political spaces for agonistic relations of adversarial respect" (ID, x), people have identities, to be sure, but they recognize their contestability, are sensitive to the ways their identity impinges on those of others, and remain open to the challenges posed by alternative possibilities. "When democratic politics is robust, when it operates to disturb the naturalization of settled conventions, when it exposes settled identities to some of the contestable contingencies that constitute them, then one is in a more favorable position to reconsider some of the demands built into those conventions and identities" (ID, 192). Agonistic democracy does not abolish identity, but it seeks to keep it from becoming settled and fixed, closed to the elements of arbitrariness and the imposition of difference that constitute it.

How might such a model apply to immigration policy? To begin with, perhaps we should note what it does *not* imply: that states will cease to exist. I see nothing in this ideal of political relations that would rule out some form of territorial government.[72] Nor does it imply, I think, that states, in whatever form they might exist, would never have any identifiable characteristics. But it does undermine attempts to solidify, to nurture and preserve, those characteristics. In other words, Connolly is opposed to the rigidification of identity wherever it may appear. And collective identities can pose the same dangers as individual ones.[73] This points, I think, in the direction of a policy of open, or at least nearly open, borders. Such a policy does not mean that no groups will continue to exist or that they will have no discernible features. But it does mean that they cannot be ensured against contestation, penetration, and transformation; that they cannot present themselves as rooted in nature or being; and that they cannot embody themselves in policies that would trap others in identities they would themselves choose to question or even reject.

Open borders help accomplish these goals in several ways. Newcomers present challenges to the hegemony of identity by confronting us with a dazzling array of different human types. This abundance reminds us of the constructed nature of those types as well as of the vast potential for other, new possibilities. Migrants who take up residence in a new land disturb and unsettle its identity, even gradually transforming it—perhaps they cannot help doing so—and, presumably, are transformed themselves. The possibility of movement, travel, and resettlement exposes people—those who move as well as those who stay—to the variety of human experience. Furthermore, the very tensions which are produced by contact with different ways of life are, for Connolly, desirable. He strikes a distinctive note when he writes of the "orientations" of agonistic democracy, "At best . . . they support new possibilities of strife among dispositions in the self and the polity, a strife that enables a peculiar respect for difference to compete on more even terms with attachment to personal and collective identities" (ID, 167). Strife within the polity carries dangers, to be sure, but it also presents new opportunities for agonistic democracy to take root. Connolly criticizes those "contemporary theorists" who "worry about relativism, atomism, egoism, nihilism, and estrangement" (ID, 172). At one level, he writes, their theories contain an element of truth, for they recognize a kind of vague unease in contemporary life.

> But at the most fundamental level these interpretations do not make sense to me. The standards of unity and harmony they presuppose seem closer to death than to life. The difficulty resides not primarily in a fragmentation of identity and the concomitant loss of a common identity. It resides . . . in a fixing and consolidation of a set of contending identities, each of which takes itself to be the true identity deserving harmony. (ID, 172)

A policy of open borders, fostering the confrontation not only between different identities within a polity but between even more widely divergent ways of life as well, seems to be an especially well-suited way of preventing this "fixing and consolidation" of identity, of creating the kind of "strife" within the polity that gives agonistic democracy a toehold.

Though *Identity\Difference* does not say a great deal about international relations, Connolly does criticize traditional conceptions of state sovereignty.[74] A number of familiar factors, such as "[n]onstate terrorism, the internationalization of capital, the greenhouse effect, acid rain, drug traffic, illegal aliens, the global character of strategic planning, extensive resource dependencies across state boundaries, and the accelerated pace of disease transmission across continents" (ID, 24), have combined to form a "worldwide web of systemic interdependencies" (ID, 23) that "call[s] the sufficiency of sovereignty into doubt" (ID, 216).[75] To respond to this situation, Connolly calls for "supplement[ing] and challeng[ing] *structures of territorial democracy* with a politics of *nonterritorial democratization of global issues*" (ID, 218; emphasis in original). It is not clear to me whether this "nonterritorial democratization of global issues," by itself, has any particular implications for immigration.[76] But the weakening of the claims of sovereignty, combined with the positive case for open borders sketched above, create a powerful argument that Connolly's theories of identity and difference point in this direction.

Connolly's more recent work develops these themes in a way that lends plausibility to the interpretation and extension of his thought suggested here. In *The Ethos of Pluralization*,[77] issues of international relations are clearly subject to a politics of identity and difference. Thus factors such as "the acceleration of population flows," "the experience of contingency, porosity, and uncertainty in territorial boundaries and national identities," and "transnational mobility" (xi) are explicitly included—and on the first page of the introduction!—among those contributing to late-modern pluralism and the "globalization of contingency."[78] What Connolly calls "fundamentalizing" responses to these phenomena (in contrast to his own politics of "pluralization") seek to restore "a unified . . . nation and/or territory that never was secure" through means such as the "intensification of state border patrols" (xii). Clashes between fundamentalization and pluralization occur over (among other things) "the pace and composition of immigration . . . the policing of territorial boundaries . . . [and] the sovereignty of the state" (xii). He charges that conventional pluralism has "bound diversity by the territorial state" (xiii) and "has not proceeded deeply enough into dominant presumptions within Euro-American culture about the character of the state, the nation, identity . . ." (xix). And he insists upon the need "to *pluralize the modern territorial imagination* that, to exaggerate just a little, maps a nation onto a state, the nation-state onto preexisting subjects, the subject onto the citizen, and the citizen onto the nation-state as its highest locus of political allegiance" (xxiii, emphasis in original; see also p. 167).[79] Clearly, immigration and the cluster of issues surrounding it now engage Connolly's attention, and he views them as legitimate subjects for his theory.[80]

Connolly comes closest to addressing the question of immigration directly in chapter five, "Democracy and Territoriality."[81] Here he makes his most extensive argument for loosening the tight connection between democratic practice and the institutions of the territorial state. Democracy, he argues, is not only a "mode of governance," but also "a cultural medium of the periodic denaturalization of settled identities and conventions" (EP, 155; original in italics). Thus understood, democracy can give birth to "[c]ross-national, nonstatist democratic movements" (EP, 157) that challenge the sovereign authority of the territorial state on various issues.[82] Citizens can, in this view, express allegiance to a democratic way of life that is not simply identical with allegiance to a particular territorial state or set of institutions.[83]

In the course of making this argument, Connolly responds to Michael Walzer's *Spheres of Justice*.[84] He criticizes Walzer's language of "shared understandings" and "internal logics" for concealing a number of "fundamental divisions . . . [that] disrupt the Walzerian spheres both as descriptions of actuality and as norms capable of integrating outcasts, abnormals, marginal workers, and aliens" (EP, 143). These hidden divisions rest upon one central division which Walzer relies upon heavily: "the spatial division . . . between the inside and the outside of the state" (EP, 147). Of this, Connolly writes:

> Inside the wall of walls there is the rich, warm world of we, community, primary goods, membership, internal understandings, our morality, meanings, distributive mechanisms, mechanisms of state security, democratic accountability, obligations, and obediences. On the other side there are alternative worlds of strangers, danger, external principles, uncertain obligations of mutual aid, and conceivable moralities. Many of these others live in other states (with, conceivably, their own warm meanings that are only tepid to us), while others of these exist in the infinite coldness of statelessness. But not very much connects either set to us politically, morally, temporally. That's just the way it is, baby. (EP, 147)

By "overcoding the boundary of the territorial state" (EP, 149) in this way, Walzer implicitly limits the reach of democratic politics to domestic affairs. Beyond state boundaries are only "interstate and state/stateless relations, but not democratic politics" (EP, 148). This inhibits any adequate democratic response to the globalization of contingency that marks late-modern time.

This is relevant to a consideration of immigration because of the purpose of Walzer's argument. His discussion of membership focuses on questions of immigration and citizenship.[85] Walzer bases a state's right to exclude foreigners and determine conditions of membership upon the existence within its boundaries of a people sharing a certain way of life and a particular self-understanding. By attacking both the notion of a shared way of life (because of the divisions and exclusions it conceals) as well as the sharp distinction between those inside a state and those outside of it, Connolly seeks to undermine the very foundations of Walzer's defense of a state's right to impose immigration restrictions. Once again, here where he most explicitly discusses questions of sovereignty and the conventional state system, Connolly's argument points in the direction of open borders.

2. Immigration and the Politics of Difference

In *Justice and the Politics of Difference*,[86] Iris Marion Young seeks to promote justice for oppressed groups such as blacks, women, and homosexuals.[87] In doing so, she argues for a politics of group representation.[88] Central to the coherence of her project, therefore, is the ability to define the concept of a social group. "A social group," she writes, is a collective of persons differentiated from at least one other group by cultural forms, practices, or way of life. Members of a group have a specific affinity with one another because of their similar experience or way of life, which prompts them to associate with one another more than with those not identified with the group, or in a different way. Groups are an expression of social relations; a group exists only in relation to at least one other group. Group identification arises, that is, in the encounter and interaction between social collectivities that experience some differences in their way of life and forms of association, even if they also regard themselves as belonging to the same society. (43)

These groups are "socially prior to individuals" (9) in the sense that they "constitute individuals. A person's particular sense of history, affinity, and separateness, even the person's mode of reasoning, evaluating, and expressing feeling, are constituted partly by her or his group affinities" (45). An individual experiences these groups "as always already having been" (46), and thus in a very existential way; at the same time, they are "multiple, cross-cutting, fluid, and shifting" (48), because they are defined "only in relation to other groups" (46).[89] Young's proposal of group representation is intended to protect and empower oppressed groups, to give them a voice as a way of countering the tendency for "the perspective and interests of privileged groups to dominate" (184). Such a politics views group differentiation as a positive and valuable force and considers its public expression "liberating and empowering" (166).

It is tempting to suggest that a similar account could be invoked in defense of the contemporary international system of nation-states. National identities are clearly defined to a large extent relationally, as various ethnic conflicts continually remind us, though the process need not be as crude as that: any American will immediately notice it simply by crossing the border to Canada and recognizing the extent to which his northern neighbors understand themselves in relation to the United States below. As long as two and a half millennia ago, the Greeks were distinguishing themselves from the surrounding barbarians. These identities are fluid and changing, as evidenced (for example) by the movement from more local to more national affiliations in modernizing Europe. Nevertheless, any given individual is deeply shaped by the chance acquisition of a national identity that she experiences as "always already having been." And the system of sovereign states gives these various national identities, even small and less powerful ones, a public voice in international affairs. Recognition as a sovereign state assures that one's national group can not, at least, be simply ignored or treated as nonexistent. Young suggests the possibility of applying this theory to national groups when, in responding to individualist theories, she lists "nationality" among various factors that ought to be understood as partially constitutive of people's identities (45).

If this extension of Young's argument were valid, it could lend support to a state's claimed right of regulating immigration in the name of group (national) identity. Without this right, national groups would find themselves subject to a kind of systemic domination—which Young defines as "institutional conditions which inhibit or prevent people from participating in determining their actions or the conditions of their actions" (38)—that could slowly erode their very existence as groups.[90] This suggestion gains credence because migrants are not, according to Young's definition, oppressed. "[O]ppression is a condition of groups" (40), she writes. Yet migrants do not seem to form a social group. Recall that members of a group share a certain affinity for and identification with other members of their group. Yet it is surely implausible to think that migrants taken as a whole, including all the various types of people described in chapter one, feel these kinds of sentiments toward each other. Rather, migrants seem to fall into a category that Young contrasts with social groups. They are an "aggregate[, which] is any classification of persons according to some attribute" (43). And if migrants are not a social group, then they cannot claim to be oppressed (as long as "oppression is a condition of groups"). So they seem unable to press the kind of claim that national groups can.

Although this may be a plausible use of Young's theory of the social group, however, it is clearly not the direction in which she herself would develop these ideas. Indeed, Young at one point explicitly criticizes the idea of a unitary national identity rather fiercely. It is, she says, "unrealistic," in that it ignores large minorities who do not fully share in that identity; "oppressive," in that it requires cultural "[s]elf-annihilation" through assimilation into the dominant, mainstream identity; and self-defeating, in that it creates factional strife and division rather than unity (179).[91] That she should take this position is ultimately unsurprising, for two closely related reasons: (1) the central motivation for her book as a whole is to achieve justice for domestic minority groups oppressed by a majority that portrays itself as impartial and universal (e.g., 107–11); and (2) underlying her argument is a theory of identity and difference similar to the one we saw in Connolly's argument:

> The irony of the logic of identity is that by seeking to reduce the differently similar to the same, it turns the merely different into the absolutely other. It

inevitably generates a dichotomy instead of unity, because the move to bring particulars under a universal category creates a distinction between inside and outside . . . . Because the totalizing movement always leaves a remainder, the project of reducing particulars to a unity must fail. Not satisfied then to admit defeat in the face of difference, the logic of identity shoves difference into dichotomous hierarchical opposition: essence/accident, good/bad, normal/deviant. (99)

Given these fundamental beliefs, it is to be expected that Young would oppose proposals to grant national identity a fixed, formal, and privileged status capable of suppressing subordinate, supposedly non-"national" identities: "In the twentieth century the ideal state is composed of a plurality of nations or cultural groups, with a degree of self-determination and autonomy compatible with federated equal rights and obligations of citizenship" (180).

So Young is hardly likely to adopt this hypothetical defense of national identity. In fact, the closing chapter of *Justice and the Politics of Difference,* entitled "City Life and Difference," gives some indication that Young too, despite her theory of social groups, might be sympathetic toward a policy of open borders. Here she proposes "a normative ideal of city life" (237).

By "city life" I mean a form of social relations which I define as the being together of strangers. In the city persons and groups interact within spaces and institutions they all experience themselves as belonging to, but without those interactions dissolving into unity or commonness . . . . City dwellers are thus together, bound to one another, in what should be and sometimes is a single polity, but they do not create a community of shared final ends, of mutual identification and reciprocity. (237–8)

The first reason Young gives in support of such an ideal is that city life, at its best, allows "social differentiation without exclusion" (238; original in italics). In a city, in other words, countless different groups and identities live together, side by side, in a kind of productive tension. They respond to differences among but do not repress one another. Indeed, there is a continual interchange and reciprocal influence among various groups. In describing this ideal, Young makes the suggestive remark, "In the normative ideal of city life, borders are open and undecidable" (239).

In this political ideal, different groups continue to exist. Yet they are always in flux, intermingled with each other and responding to these close and continuous contacts. That borders are "open and undecidable" means that it is impossible to draw any sharp line distinguishing one group from another. "Many city neighborhoods have a distinct ethnic identity, but members of other groups also dwell in them. In the good city one crosses from one distinct neighborhood to another without knowing precisely where one ended and the other began" (239). A world of such neighborhoods, or of such cities, would be a world in which contingent borders of some sort existed, but in which border-crossings were not only constant but also desirable.[92]

Young closes her book with a brief epilogue on "international justice." Here she cautions against extending her argument indiscriminately: "The principles, categories, and arguments I have developed in the preceding chapters cannot be simply extended or applied to the context of international relations . . ." (257). But this does not mean it has nothing to teach us: "Many of these principles, categories, and arguments, however, are also not irrelevant to understanding social justice in these parts of the world ['the Southern and Eastern Hemispheres'] . . . within and between nations" (257). She notes favorably such phenomena as "the worldwide breakup of . . . nationalist and state-fostered unities" (259) and "movements . . . toward greater international federation, breaking down the exclusions and separations that hitherto have defined state sovereignty and autonomy" (259–60). And she concludes the book with this very intriguing sentence: "Only psychological dispositions, cultural expressions, and political institutions able to loosen but not dissolve borders, make them permeable and undecidable, at the same time that they create guarantees of group self-definition and representation in the public, can hold the hope of a more peaceful and just future for the world" (260). Borders which are loosened but not dissolved, permeable and undecidable—that sounds like a description of a world in which borders exist but people are free to cross them. Though it may be less clear than in the case of Connolly, I suggest that Young's "normative ideal of city life" also points toward a world of open borders.[93]

3. Borders and the Rediscovery of the Familiar

Because Connolly's and Young's arguments do differ in important respects, it is interesting that they both, if the readings offered above are persuasive, point us in the direction of open borders (Connolly perhaps more so than Young). This convergence should alert us to the plausibility of—what in any case should probably not be surprising—a more general postmodern critique of national identity and national boundaries in the name of difference.[94] For those, like me, who are skeptical about proposals for open borders, it is worth considering what might be said in response to these arguments. There are, of course, a number of reasons why one might potentially oppose open borders, some of them better than others. But here I seek in particular a response that could appeal to postmodern thinkers, one that draws upon the concerns with identity and difference that motivate the arguments of writers like Connolly and Young. How might we defend national identity and immigration restrictions—or at least a right to impose some such restrictions—in a way that responds to these concerns?

An obvious place to start might be with the suggestion that diversity (pluralism, the play of difference) is embodied precisely in the international system of states. In the words of Alexander Solzhenitsyn, "The disappearance of nations would impoverish us no less than if all peoples were made alike, with one character, one face. Nations are the wealth of mankind, they are its generalized personalities: the smallest of them has its own particular colors, and embodies a particular facet of God's design."[95] In this view, it is precisely the existence of distinct nations which ensures the existence of and confrontation between different identities and ways of life. Immigration restrictions might thus be valuable as a way of preserving distinct ways of life that would otherwise be threatened with disintegration.

Unfortunately, this is little different from the possibility that I already considered in discussing Young's thought, only to conclude that she decisively rejects it. Nor is it more likely to appeal to Connolly. It is in fact quite reminiscent of the distinction he draws between pluralism and pluralization. "A conventional pluralist celebrates diversity within settled contexts of conflict and collective action" (EP, xiii). This, in a sense, describes the international system of states. But the problem with such a "conventional" view, according to Connolly, is that it does not permit challenges to the underlying "settled context." Pluralization represents challenges to that basic framework itself. A theory of pluralization recognizes the need for "preexisting pluralism," but also the way in which it "engenders obstacles to new drives to pluralization" (xiv). A state system which allowed national identities to congeal and crystallize into a permanent and exclusive set of possibilities would thus embody for Connolly the shortcoming, rather than the promise, of pluralism. Pluralization would continually contest and challenge such a system, seeking to create space for the emergence of new possibilities.[96] Solzhenitsyn's suggestion, then, whatever its merits, is unlikely to appeal to writers of Connolly's or Young's bent.

What we need, then, is a way of considering national identity as real, meaningful, and valuable without making it permanent or absolute; a way of giving it a content that does not seek to obliterate the diversity and multiplicity that it conceals. G.K. Chesterton—perhaps an unexpected source—has provided an insight into how we might do this. He writes, "The chief case for old enclosures and boundaries is that they enclose a space in which new things can always be found later, like live fish within the four corners of a net. The chief charm of having a home that is secure is having leisure to feel it as strange."[97] Chesterton's own illustration of this is delightful enough to be worth quoting:

> If a man must get to Brighton as quickly as possible, he can get there quickest by travelling on rigid rails on a recognised route. If he has time and money for motoring, he will still use public roads; but he will be surprised to find how many public roads look as new and quiet as private roads. If he has time enough to walk, he may find for himself a string of fresh footpaths, each one a fairy-tale. (20)

The point is that this rediscovery of the familiar, as we might call it—a discovery of new and different aspects of that which one thought one already knew—is only possible when one has a certain leisure, some time for exploration. Chesterton calls this the "law of leisure needed for the awakening of wonder" (20).[98] And it is precisely boundaries that make this possible, that maintain a kind of stability without which things change more rapidly than we can keep up with, preventing us from probing beyond the superficial and "merely" familiar. Boundaries thus serve to set off an area in which "new things can always be found" (21).

This is, I think, an idea with which we are familiar in other areas of life—not least of them the academy. Why do we ask college students to choose a major? Why do graduate students continue studying a single (often even narrower) field at greater length? And why do scholars generally devote their careers to the pursuit of a single discipline? In part, at least, the reason is that limiting ourselves in this way enables the acquisition of a certain depth of understanding, a depth that requires time and that would be impossible were we to spread our attention more thinly. A semester's introduction may suffice to give one a shallow and all too temporary understanding of a topic; but for an appreciation of the deeper attractions of a field, of the nooks and crannies of its unique personality, more time is needed. This is not to say that no one can or should delve into multiple disciplines. I suspect that many intelligent people can attain considerable proficiency in two, perhaps even three, disciplines; and every now and then an extraordinary individual comes along who seems to master everything she tries. And some topics—immigration is one, I think—seem to bridge disciplinary boundaries by their very nature. For the most part, though, we are fortunate to achieve a real understanding of the complexities and special problems in a single field. When we devote ourselves to the study of a single field, and pursue that study over an extended period of time, we are often surprised to discover new insights, new perspectives, problems (perhaps even an occasional solution?) which had not occurred to us before. And this difficult, valuable, and rewarding experience is made possible precisely through submission to disciplinary boundaries.

Of course, this may not be the most fortuitous choice of example—postmodernists are not exactly known for their love of disciplinary boundaries! So consider another example with which many of us are familiar: marriage. It is, on the face of it, rather puzzling why we human beings should so consistently be willing to limit ourselves to a life-long relationship with a single person, when there are, after all, so many pleasant people around. Yet surely one of the great delights of married life is the opportunity to develop a relationship of unique depth with someone, to get to know (and be known by) another person in an often unexpectedly close way, unnerving and exciting at the same time. The mysteries and continued newness of another human individual are only rarely revealed to us, and that only after much time and attention—indeed, they are undoubtedly never exhausted. Spouses both know each other extremely well and are constantly surprised by each other. But such a deep experience of the endless diversity within each human being is only possible when we limit ourselves, giving up various possible relationships for the sake of building this special one. Again, boundaries enable the rediscovery of the familiar.

Finally, this notion should be perfectly comprehensible to the political theorist. Consider Hobbes's account of the transition from the state of nature to civil society. In the state of nature, "every man has a Right to every thing; even to one anothers body."[99] Yet without any laws, there can "be no Propriety, no Dominion, no *Mine* and *Thine* distinct; but onely that to be every mans, that he can get; and for so long, as he can keep it" (90). Thus a person has a right to everything, but secure possession of nothing. Similarly, people in the state of nature may be entirely free to do as they please, but in fact they are condemned to a life either of perpetual fear and defensiveness, seeking to preserve themselves against others, or of perpetual warfare, launching preemptive strikes against those who will attack them if they don't act first, since "there is no way for any man to secure himselfe, so reasonable, as Anticipation; that is, by force, or wiles, to master the persons of all men he can, so long, till he see no other power great enough to endanger him" (87–8)—which time, of course, remains always the day after tomorrow. Hobbes's own description of this state of nature as "solitary, poor, nasty, brutish, and short" is justly famous, but for our purposes here the first part of that description may be more telling: "In such condition, there is no place for Industry; because the fruit thereof is uncertain: and consequently no Culture of the Earth; no Navigation, nor use of the commodities that may be imported by Sea; no commodious Building; no Instruments of moving, and removing such things as require much force; no Knowledge of the face of the Earth; no account of Time; no Arts; no Letters; no Society . . ." (89). The great diversity of human life and activity, all that raises it above a mere animal scramble for existence, is possible only through the restrictions of law, boundaries which prove liberating rather than limiting.[100] To put it in something more like Chesterton's terms, boundaries like these provide us with a kind of time, with leisure to explore the multiple possibilities of our humanity. My point, of course, is not to endorse Hobbes's particular account—which I select here from numerous possible examples only because of its clarity—nor to pretend that postmodernists will find much that appeals to them in it. I use it simply to illustrate the fact that, peculiar though it may at first sound, we are in fact quite familiar with the notion that boundaries can be a way of nourishing, rather than destroying, plurality, not simply externally, as in the earlier example of the system of nation-states, but internally as well.

What implications might this line of thought have for immigration policy? I suggest that it offers us a way of thinking about national identity as other than monolithic, as a force which can sustain and enable healthy internal diversity rather than suppressing it. It offers a perspective from which less-than-open borders could be seen as preserving broad national identities without insisting upon complete closure. Consider in this regard Roy Beck's claim that Americans have been most favorable toward immigration (and immigrants) precisely when it was moderate. "Partly because of the low immigration from 1925 to 1965," he writes, "Americans developed a whole new attitude toward immigrants, becoming substantially positive about them for perhaps the first time since the country's birth."[101] Immigration regulations which preserved some form of national identity, he suggests, allowed Americans the leisure to understand the newcomers, rather than feeling overwhelmed or threatened by waves of rapid change. To some degree, of course, that was because the small numbers of newcomers had to assimilate. But it is implausible to suggest—and surely no good postmodernist would maintain!—that their arrival left America unchanged. Stable (though not rigid or impermeable) boundaries allowed a process of mutual transformation and self-discovery to take place. This process can be adjusted, of course, to allow for more or less (in)stability, a faster or slower rate of change, but the basic point illustrates Chesterton's observation: that appreciation of internal diversity, the rediscovery of the familiar, occurs within, not in spite of, settled boundaries and identities.[102]

None of this, of course, constitutes a knock-down case against the post-modern argument for open borders. And, I should perhaps emphasize, it is in no way intended as an argument for *closed* borders. Nothing in the Chestertonian dictum implies rigidity or permanence. Its goal, after all, is the "awakening of wonder" (20) and creation of "a space in which new things can always be found later" (21). Thus it may encourage people attracted to the open borders line of argument to think about national identity in a new light, as a means for helping us see "things superficially familiar as well as . . . things superficially fresh" in new and different ways. Such a perspective draws upon the values underlying Connolly's and Young's accounts to give partial and qualified approval to "old enclosures and boundaries" (21). It invites such thinkers, in the name of their own commitments, to an appreciation of a surprising virtue of these boundaries: "The chief charm of having a home that is secure is having leisure to feel it as strange."

Some, no doubt, will remain unconvinced. I will seem to have sought inspiration in peculiar places. What kind of postmodern argument invokes Chesterton? Who would seek to marshal postmodern values in the name of national boundaries and identities? To them, I respond that I have promised and delivered only the view of an outsider looking in, peeking through the windows as it were. I await with interest their response. In the meantime, though, I offer them an invitation: to feel their secure theoretical home as strange.

What does this review of the current state of the debate over immigration reveal? Setting aside my hypothetical postmodern explorations, we have two opposed sets of claims that to a significant degree fail to engage one another. On the one hand are several public intellectuals who, from different points on the political map, defend the traditional right of sovereign states to control immigration, but who—perhaps (in fairness to them) necessarily so, given the constraints of the genre—say little in defense of the premises which appear to underlie their arguments. On the other hand is an argument, best exemplified in the writings of Joseph Carens, in support of a right to free movement (or, at least, much freer movement than currently exists). Ironically, this argument too appears to have little to say to those who do not share the particular liberal principles upon which it rests. This fundamental impasse is not bridged by the occasional appearance of apparent moderate voices; Whelan, for example, makes no attempt to defend his suggestion that current state practice (relatively open emigration, state control over immigration) represents a "reasonable compromise," whereas the implications of an argument like Gibney's do not, upon reflection, seem as moderate as his stated intention suggests, pointing instead at a considerable opening of current state practice.

I attempt to bridge this gap in the next chapter. My hope is to provide a more thorough normative defense of the premises that are the undefended foundation of the arguments by Beck, Brimelow, and Williamson, and thus to justify Whelan's "reasonable compromise." My aim is not to show that countries in general, or any specific country in particular, ought to restrict immigration. It is to defend the state's claim, in most circumstances, to decide whether it wants to restrict immigration and how restrictive it wants to be, and to do so based upon its own history and identity as a particular political community. To that broader question I now turn.

Chapter 3

"THIS IS MY OWN, MY NATIVE LAND":

IMMIGRATION, NATIONAL IDENTITY, AND THE PROBLEM OF PREFERENCE

In Chapter 2 I suggested that Carens's argument for open borders, if it is meant to apply generally and not only to liberal states, amounts to the claim that only liberal polities–perhaps only certain kinds of liberal polities–are legitimate. Now I want to broaden that suggestion and argue that no single immigration policy, whatever it might be, can be claimed as the "correct" one for all countries; one result of this, of course, is that the argument for open borders fails. To begin, I suggest that we ask what a people confronted with the task of designing an immigration policy does. As we shall see, this is not the deepest question we shall ultimately face; nor is it yet a normative question, though it may have normative implications. As a starting-point, though, it has the merit of reflecting people's own experience and reactions, of beginning where we begin. Confronted by significant numbers of strangers wishing to enter our country, how do we respond? The first question that a people faces in these circumstances, I want to suggest, is this: Who are we? What common bonds or shared beliefs constitute us as this particular people? In other words, a people considering immigration policy first confronts the question of national identity.

Now it seems perfectly clear that different peoples will give different answers to the question of national identity. Some peoples may locate their identity in a thick shared culture. Others may be united by the common pursuit of economic prosperity. Still others may identify themselves by a shared religion, ethnic heritage, or common language. Some peoples may coalesce around a particular set of political principles, be they those of constitutional democracy, hereditary monarchy, or a traditional aristocracy. Possibilities abound, especially when one considers the potentially endless variations on these basic themes or conceivable combinations of different factors, as well as the way in which the identities of different peoples, whatever their central elements may be, will have been shaped by particular historical events that are fundamental for the people in question but of little if any significance for other peoples with their own histories.

It seems equally clear that these different answers to the question of national identity have different implications for immigration policy. In general, it seems safe to assume that a people will rarely welcome immigrants who would undermine the fundamental features of its identity and radically alter its character. This means more than that a people will object to immigrants who are actively hostile to its identity; in practice, it also means that a people will oppose large numbers of migrants who do not share at least important parts of that identity's core. Different identities will, of course, lead to policies of varying restrictiveness. A people united simply around certain political principles ought in theory to be open to anyone willing to adopt those principles.[1] A people motivated by the desire for economic wealth would presumably welcome anyone who would contribute to that wealth[2] (though precisely how restrictive such a policy would be is a matter of some dispute). Peoples for whom a shared language or religion is central, on the other hand, might potentially favor policies with significant restrictions: think of Quebec's desire to limit the influx of English-speakers, or imagine Israel adopting a policy which required admission of any Muslim who wanted to come![3]

But it is not only extreme cases of religious or linguistic unity (for example) that can provide a basis for restrictive policies. I suggested that a people united around a set of political principles ought in theory to be open to migrants willing to adopt those principles. Yet the practical adoption of such principles, so that they become effective components of a person's being, may involve more than an abstract intellectual commitment. It may involve the absorption of various habitual modes of thought and action. Consider the argument of Thomas Jefferson, reflecting, early in the United States's history, upon the wisdom of seeking to increase the new land's population by attracting immigrants:

> Every species of government has its specific principles. Ours perhaps are more peculiar than those of any other in the universe. It is a composition of the freest principles of the English constitution, with others derived from natural right and natural reason. To these nothing can be more opposed than the maxims of absolute monarchies. Yet, from such, we are to expect the greatest number of emigrants. They will bring with them the principles of the governments they leave, imbibed in their early youth; or, if able to throw

them off, it will be in exchange for an unbounded licentiousness, passing, as is usual, from one extreme to another. It would be a miracle were they to stop precisely at the point of temperate liberty. These principles, with their language, they will transmit to their children. In proportion to their numbers, they will share with us the legislation. They will infuse into it their spirit, warp and bias its direction, and render it a heterogeneous, incoherent, distracted mass.[4]

In other words, the success of a fair and stable polity may rest upon certain cultural preconditions. And the relative scarcity of such polities throughout world history may recommend caution in deciding exactly which cultural factors have played important roles in those polities' success.[5] So even an identity which seems in theory to be quite inviting may include elements that would support various restrictions on immigration.

But why should we accept this starting-point? Why should we think that a people considering immigration policy first confronts the issue of national identity, or that it will be so unwelcoming towards those who do not share its identity? The reason lies in the fundamental nature of immigration and its centrality to political and social life. Michael Walzer has written, "The primary good that we distribute to one another is membership in some human community."[6] Immigration is one of three fundamental ways in which a polity does this (the others being naturalization and the attribution of citizenship at birth). By determining or changing the very composition of a people, questions of membership go to the heart of its basic character or identity. And because it is unrealistic to think that people will exhibit a cavalier disregard for the preservation of the culture they share, they can be expected to desire immigration policies which nurture and protect that culture. Immigration triggers these deep responses because it forces a people to address the question, Who are we and who do we want to be?

Doing so, of course, need not be any specially philosophic enterprise. The point is not that immigration sparks a kind of national liberal arts seminar, an episode of deep soul-searching and intense self-examination. I don't want to exclude the possibility of a somewhat reflective process, but often—probably most of the time, I imagine—the response will be much more immediate and straightforward, perhaps even rather crude: "We don't want to live next to *them;* they smell funny!" My point is simply that insofar as a people experiences newcomers as different, it necessarily calls upon not only ideas of what "they" are like, but also readily available understandings of who "we" are. It is in this sense, I suggest, that immigration, at least in any significant numbers, inevitably compels a people to confront, at least implicitly, the question of its own identity. Indeed, without *some* conception of "who we are," however minimal, it would seem impossible to conceive of immigrants as a separate group of people in the first place–immigration as an issue would simply vanish from sight.

Here, though, a rather pointed objection may be offered: that no such thing as "national identity" truly exists at all. Such an argument often takes the form of the postmodern critique I discussed in the previous chapter, though it need not be based upon postmodern philosophical assumptions. One might simply point out that almost all existing states in fact contain people of multiple nationalities; that those "nationalities" which appear to exist rest upon earlier uses of brute force at worst, and upon continued belief in historical myth at best; and that invocations of "national identity" thus serve only to oppress people who do not share the central characteristics of an entity which is only a subjective construction–a fiction–in the first place.[7] Policies designed to construct and strengthen supposed national identities might thus be suspected of only encouraging hostility among nations and oppression within them.

David Miller, in his book *On Nationality,* offers a response to this objection.[8] He describes the critique of national identity this way:

> A number of people find themselves tied together politically, either because they are subjects of the same state or because it is in their interests to acquire a state of their own. In either case, it is helpful for them to conceive of themselves as forming a community with its own distinct national character, traditions, and so forth. There is an incentive both to produce and consume a literature that defines such a common identity. But we have no reason to think that the identity so defined corresponds to anything real in the world; that is to say, there is nothing that marks off this group of people from those around them other than their *wish* to think of themselves as forming a distinct community. National identities are, in a strong and destructive sense, mythical. (32–3)

But in spite of the considerable element of historical myth involved in any national identity, Miller replies, the concept remains both valid and valuable. For one thing, national identities can serve worthy purposes: "they provide reassurance that the national community of which one now forms part is solidly based in history, that it embodies a real continuity between generations; and they perform a moralizing role, by holding up to us the virtues of our ancestors and encouraging us to live up to them" (36). In these ways, they support effective and ethical collective action on the part of their corresponding political communities. Furthermore, Miller points out, it is too easy simply to say that national identities are founded upon historical myth, for this overlooks differences in the way various identities have been formed.

> To the extent that the process [by which a national identity has arisen] involves inputs from all sections of the community, with groups openly competing to imprint the common identity with their own particular image, we may justifiably regard the identity that emerges as an authentic one. No national identity will ever be pristine, but there is still a large difference between those that have evolved more or less spontaneously, and those that are mainly the result of political imposition. (40)

Miller suggests, that is, that we can think of national identities being created in more or less democratic fashions. In some cases identities may simply be imposed on the people from above; in others, however, the people may themselves have played an important role in creating those identities. In other words, there is a difference between the partially mythical nature of many national identities and their illegitimate or authoritarian imposition. If the people who profess a particular identity have themselves participated in the creation and consolidation of the myths that they believe, then it seems somewhat arbitrary to reject that identity as invalid simply because it is a less than perfectly accurate historical account.

But surely this defense is rather disingenuous. After all, few, if any, of the powerful national identities in our world were produced through any kind of democratic process. On the contrary, in countries such as England, France, and Germany, national identities were the creation, often the self-conscious creation, of relatively small political or intellectual elites who then sought through a variety of means to spread those identities to ever-wider circles of the population, usually with the deliberate intention of suppressing and replacing pre-existing local identities. Such identities can hardly be legitimated as the product of a collective act of democratic creation. And even if a case could be made that such identities had been more or less popular creations, an equally pressing problem would still remain: What about us? *We* had no say in creating those identities; *we* do not create them anew for ourselves today. Rather, we find them simply given to us, an inheritance created and passed on by our predecessors. We are born into nations whose identities were largely formed well before we arrived on the scene, and if we share those historical identities, it is because we accept what others have created and handed on.

Perhaps, though, this points toward a reformulation of Miller's point that can meet the objection in a more satisfactory manner. I suggest that we look for the popular element in national identity not in its creation, but rather in its continuing acceptance over time. In other words, a national identity is legitimate—in spite of its elements of historical fiction or its less-than-democratic manner of original creation—as long as people continue to accept it as describing, more or less accurately, who they are, and as long as it thus continues to give meaning to their lives. As Joseph Carens has written, in defense of certain policies designed to preserve the traditional culture of native Fijians,

> [A]ll cultures are subject to exogeneous influences. That does not, however, prove that there are no legitimate cultural commitments or attachments. What makes something a legitimate part of people's culture, regardless of its origins, is the fact that they have internalized it, made it their own, integrated it with other aspects of their culture.[9]

In other words, if people accept a national identity as theirs, that in itself provides a powerful reason for believing that it really is theirs. This is not to say, of course, that a people could somehow "choose" any national identity it desired. Presumably a real national identity ought to have some basis in actual fact, and to that extent it should be possible to do a better or worse job of describing a nation's identity.[10] For example, Americans might think that their identity is determined primarily by allegiance to a set of liberal democratic political principles, or alternatively by the shared English language and a broadly Anglo-Saxon cultural inheritance (or yet some other factor). Either of these accounts seems at least plausible (though one might in fact be more correct, historically, than the other). By contrast, the claims that American identity is defined primarily by an allegiance to monarchy or by the shared use of the Chinese language are obviously preposterous. The point, then, is not that national identity is simply a matter of some peculiar kind of decisionistic process of existential self-definition in which historical truth carries no weight. It is rather that such identity is not exhausted by questions of historical truth, such that mythical elements would automatically discredit it. A national identity's ability to win continuing popular support and acceptance over time should therefore be taken as good evidence of its legitimacy.[11]

The most important response to the critique of national identity, though, is even more direct than this: that critique vastly underestimates the concrete reality of such identity in everyday life. I can remember lying in bed as a boy, falling asleep listening to the Cleveland Indians on the radio. One particular commercial from that time has remained vividly in my mind to this day. This advertisement informed the listener that Chevrolet vehicles were "as American as baseball, hot dogs, and apple pie" (I quote from memory). Now, the cynical reader will regard this recollection as merely evidence of the depressing power of advertising and the media; and Ford loyalists will no doubt view it as practically treasonous. But the point, of course, is that this commercial somehow resonated with me. Even at that relatively young age, the trio of "baseball, hot dogs, and apple pie" did indeed strike me as distinctively American. This is not to say, of course, that someone who drives a Chrysler—or even a Honda!—is not American, or that a person who doesn't like hot dogs is a fellow traveler. Nor does it imply that no members of other nationalities enjoy a baseball game or a good slice of apple pie. But something about that particular trio—quartet, if you throw in Chevrolet (or Ford)—does capture part of the flavor of American life, in a way that it would not capture that of some other nationality. As Miller puts it,

> For in such a [national] community people are held together not merely by physical necessity, but by a dense web of customs, practices, implicit under-standings, and so forth. There is a shared way of life, which is not to say that everyone follows exactly the same conventions or adheres to the same cul-tural values, but that there is a substantial degree of overlap in forms of life. One can't detach this way of life from the national identity of the people in question. (41)

He goes on to offer an example of his own: "Even the physical landscape bears the imprint of the historical development of the community: roads may meander round fields in deference to the property rights of landown-ers, or they may be driven in straight lines to serve the needs of the state and its armies" (41–2). My Chevrolet commercial may be a less sophisti-cated example, but it remains in my memory today precisely because it really did invoke a set of characteristics I recognized as American; indeed, had it not been able to do that, it would have been just a bad—even non-sensical—advertisement.[12]

Another objection may be made at this point, however: that my argu-ment succeeds only by ignoring an important distinction, namely, that between political culture and culture more generally. I have been speaking rather vaguely of a people's unwillingness to accept threats to its "way of life," and using that phrase interchangeably to refer to threats to its culture or to its political system or to both. Perhaps my argument's power rests only upon its emotional appeal to people's understandably strong desires to preserve their own, familiar way of life. Maybe, though, I am justified only in considering the implications of a people's political culture, rather than its way of life as a whole, which would not give it such free rein to attempt the preservation of its entire culture. By moving back and forth too easily between "polity" and "culture," I may be eliding important distinctions.

Consider two different ways in which such an argument might be made. First, one could call upon this distinction in response to the criticism I have suggested of the open borders argument: that it admits the legitimacy of only liberal polities (perhaps, even, of only certain kinds of liberal polities). Perhaps this is not the case. For the claim that justice requires open borders, even if based upon liberal theory, is not the same as a claim that all countries must be liberal. It is certainly possible that polities of various sorts could decide, no doubt for various reasons, to adopt a policy of open borders. The derivation of open borders from liberalism may be particularly clear, but perhaps other theories also contain principles or ideals that could justify free movement. In other words, to borrow an image from John Rawls, it is possible that various countries could reach an "overlapping consensus" on the matter of immigration, all settling upon the same policy of open borders despite differences of opinion about broader theoretical issues.

Put this way, the objection may seem somewhat implausible. After all, it is not sufficient to show that different theories have resources that *could* be used to support open borders; rather, one would have to show that they *necessarily* result in open borders.[13] More obviously, it just does not seem terribly difficult to imagine polities for which such a policy would be quite unnatural. But the more subtle point of the argument is to claim that I have not sufficiently distinguished between political culture and culture more generally. I have suggested that large-scale immigration inevitably alters a country's identity, that the argument for open borders is based upon liberalism, and thus that a world of open borders would force all countries to become liberal. But this may not follow, for it is not clear that one can move back and forth in this way: just because one can argue from liberalism to open borders does not mean that open borders automatically take one back to liberalism. In other words, it may be indisputable that massive immigration works changes in a people's culture generally, but also possible that different kinds of polity, liberal and non-liberal alike, can continue to exist despite the changes occurring in cultural life at large. Because political culture and culture at large are distinct, with a certain amount of slack between them, changes in the one need not entail corresponding changes in the other. To return to the image of the overlapping consensus: since any national culture already contains some amount of diversity, it is reasonable to think that a stable political culture represents an area of agreement within that diversity, and immigration might affect the particular mix of cultural diversity without changing the consensus on a certain form of polity.[14]

A second way of making this objection is rather different. It is simply to claim that differences in political culture alone are sufficient to support my argument that different polities will select different immigration policies. In other words, it is perfectly reasonable to think that free-market liberal democrats will be inclined toward immigration policies different from those which classical republicans would support, and that Marxist-Leninists might well favor yet different policies. There is no need, on this argument, to appeal to deeper differences in national identity. Doing so only arouses intense emotions on a subject which is controversial enough to begin with. Nor need this view insist that we look only to bloodless, abstract principles in thinking about a given people's immigration policy. The kinds of differences referred to by Jefferson in the passage quoted earlier, for example, presumably fall within the scope of "political culture" without requiring a wide-ranging discussion of national identity at large.

The points of these two arguments are obviously very different. The first tries to show that cultural changes caused by immigration need not imply political homogeneity; the second that one need not rely on broad cultural differences to defend diverse immigration policies because differences in political culture alone are sufficient to produce that result. But both arguments share in common the claim that in arguing about the immigration policies appropriate for different peoples one can and should distinguish between political culture and culture in general. As a way of assessing this argument, let us begin by supposing that any given polity can be divided into three elements: the specific form of the political system itself (democracy, oligarchy, monarchy, etc.) as it is embodied in concrete institutions such as a king, constitutional court, or state legislatures; the political culture, that is, all those elements of the broader culture—encompassing areas such as art, literature, philosophy, religion, and economics—that buttress and support (or potentially undermine) the specific form of political system (what Tocqueville called "mores"[15]); and the remaining cultural elements, which may contribute to a people's "national identity" but are, from the point of view of the political system itself, irrelevant—they could change one way or another without altering it.[16]

It is tempting to think that a people's justification for protecting these different elements of the polity steadily decreases, so that it is fully entitled to protect the basic form of its political system, faces a greater burden of proof in protecting elements of the political culture, and has little if any justification for protecting those aspects of the culture which are irrelevant to the political system. Thus, to put it in terms of immigration, a people does nothing wrong by preventing immigration that would threaten the specific form of the political system itself.[17] Presumably, of course, this particular threat is relatively rare, but it would, for example, justify a polity's refusal to admit those who had explicitly declared their hostility to its political system, or perhaps those for whom there simply existed considerable evidence of such hostility. It might not always be necessary for such hostility to involve the violent overthrow of the political system—a democracy, for instance, might claim on these grounds the right to restrict the influx of non-democrats, since their entry in large numbers could eventually contribute to the formation of an anti-democratic majority capable of transforming the system from within.[18] Few, I think—including advocates of far greater freedom of movement than currently exists—would deny polities this form of what is essentially political self-preservation.[19]

When we consider the desire to protect the political culture, however, we see quickly that the proposed hierarchy of levels of justification is inadequate. For if we accept the description given above of political culture (those moral, artistic, economic, and other elements of the culture that buttress the political system), and if we also accept a people's right to preserve its specific political system, then it seems logically necessary to permit a people to protect its political culture against erosion. For example, if one accepted Tocqueville's argument that the general belief in Christian religion helped support and strengthen American democracy, then one would also have to concede that Americans at that time would have been entitled, in constructing immigration policy, to take into account immigration's effect on the vitality of Christianity.[20] In general, if a people is entitled to preserve its political system, then it must also be entitled to preserve cultural elements that are necessary to that system's continued functioning—to preserve, that is, its political culture.

But what of the remaining elements of the culture, those that are irrelevant to the political system itself? Perhaps we have simply a two-fold division, in which a people may take steps to protect its political system and political culture, but not, for example, its preference for baseball over soccer. Since these "irrelevant" or arbitrary elements of the culture arguably constitute much if not most of a people's concrete national identity, this seems to be roughly the position urged by the objection under consideration, that I have insufficiently distinguished between culture in general and political culture in particular. Yet this suggestion too seems inadequate. For it seems to rest upon an assumption that only those political systems are legitimate that adopt a fairly strict division of this sort; it rules out, in other words, those polities in which there is a tight fit between politics and culture. But by assuming this distance between culture at large and political culture in particular, it clearly begs an important theoretical question. In the case of the first of my hypothetical counter-arguments along these lines, this seems to be merely another way of repeating the requirement that polities be liberal, since this distance between politics and culture is a central element of the kinds of liberalism leading most obviously to open borders.[21] With regard to the second hypothetical counter-argument, that the move beyond political culture is unnecessary, one might say that it is correct but moot, because one of the crucial matters to be determined by the political culture is, of course, precisely what relationship is to exist between politics and culture.

So it does not seem possible to limit in advance a people's consideration of its identity for the purposes of constructing immigration policy by restricting its debate to items of political culture. For the same reasons, it does not seem preferable in this context to draw a sharp distinction between political culture and culture in general; on the contrary, the attempt to do so subtly weights the debate against certain forms of polities. By using the language of national identity in a broad sense, then, we leave room not only for peoples who distinguish sharply between politics and culture, but also for those for whom the two blur together. And the point is important, because it is precisely these latter peoples who have the most obvious reasons to oppose open borders, or indeed any policy not carefully tailored to their particular identities. By discussing the issue at the level of different national identities, we refuse to prejudge the question of how close a fit is permitted between a people's political culture and its culture in general.[22]

Many different kinds of polities exist, then, embracing very diverse national identities. Different kinds of polities, containing different relationships between the political system and the general culture, call for different kinds of immigration policies. Even if this is true, though, it does not yet take us to the heart of the matter. For the argument thus far has been largely descriptive, and it is not obvious that it can really generate the normative conclusions I am suggesting. It may be true that countries possess very different national identities, and that the implications of these identities point towards very different immigration policies. But this does not by itself demonstrate that countries are entitled to enact those policies. Merely determining that peoples with different national identities will incline towards different immigration policies does nothing to help us discern the range of such policies that peoples may *justifiably* enact. How might we go about answering this deeper, clearly normative question?

The first point to make, I think, is that the vast majority of these different potential political *cum* national identities are legitimate. By calling them legitimate, I mean simply that they are entitled to exist. Illegitimate is thus, in my view, a very strong term: to call a government illegitimate is to say that it has no right to continued existence, that the rest of us would be justified in overturning it—conceivably even obligated to do so. Nevertheless, some governments will merit the epithet "illegitimate." This might provide a rough normative guideline to help us narrow the range of justifiable immigration policies: insofar as those policies are a way of protecting, preserving, and shaping a particular people or its character, it seems reasonable to deny such powers of self-preservation and self-determination to a government which is simply illegitimate.

We might deny them for at least two different reasons. Sometimes we might think that a given government and its policies genuinely reflect the identity of its people, but believe that the identity itself is illegitimate. Thus, for example, if we thought that German national identity during the rise of Hitler were centered around an ethnically-defined German *Volk* whose existence required the extermination of corrupting Jewish influences,[23] we might claim that an identity requiring large-scale murder is itself illegitimate and cannot justify policies designed to preserve it. Alternatively, we might also reasonably claim that some regimes, ones that utterly fail to pursue the proper ends of government, cannot plausibly be thought to reflect their people's identity at all. Thus a government that engaged in the massive slaughter of its subjects could be called illegitimate precisely because such slaughter could never be in the people's interest or part of their identity. The same could generally be said of those practices we easily identify as the worst or most serious forms of oppression: campaigns of random imprisonment, routine torture, or the systematic and arbitrary confiscation of people's goods. Because one cannot really imagine a people's identity calling for such severe self-inflicted punishments, a government that imposed them could not very persuasively pose as representative of the national identity when that seemed useful as a justification for some policy.[24]

Denying that illegitimate governments or identities are entitled to use immigration policies as a means of perpetuating themselves is a way of pruning the set of all possible immigration policies down to the range of those that are morally defensible. Obviously, though, since I have employed such a demanding definition of illegitimacy, the pruning done under this approach is pretty modest—more like shaping a few outer branches to define the bush's shape than a radical cutting-back to escape some serious disease. Why adopt such a permissive view of the distinction between legitimate and illegitimate? Why such a low hurdle for acquiring the status of legitimacy? Drawing the distinction as I have here reflects my sense that we should imagine the realm of political morality divided roughly into two spheres, in which different kinds of judgements are appropriate. Dividing these spheres is a kind of baseline, representing the minimal purposes that any morally valid government needs to serve. Below this line are those regimes that engage in the sorts of severe oppression described above. They have no claim to moral validity and are simply unjust, and we therefore identify them as illegitimate.

Above the line, however, is the broad range of regimes that are morally valid, or legitimate, and here the judgements we make are of a different sort. Whereas the line itself marks a basic distinction between just and unjust, legitimate and illegitimate, we judge the various minimally just, morally tolerable regimes simply as better or worse. Note that there are still judgements to make and that all regimes above the baseline need not be viewed as morally equivalent: precisely because the "legitimate" encompasses so much variety, we can continue to argue about better or worse polities (and even, I think, reach correct, if not universally shared, opinions on such matters) and to strive to improve our own. But the judgements we make are less certain, the room for disagreement is wider, people can produce plausible arguments in support of different views under different circumstances, and the alternatives we regard as worse are ones we should concede that people are entitled to pursue if they want to, even if we think them poor choices.[25]

I do want to emphasize that this broad range of legitimate regimes, as I envisage it, contains lots of room for regimes that we might find relatively unsavory. Non-democracies, military rulers, benevolent despots—all can meet the minimal standard for a just regime, if they do not engage in the worst sorts of oppression. The basic insight here is that, as thinkers such as Hobbes or Augustine have stressed, simply preserving basic political order and stability is an extremely important and, historically, often a rare achievement. A polity that does these things, that sustains the minimal conditions for decent human lives, is meeting the minimal standards of political justice, even if we think it could do better—and, indeed, even if we are right. The criterion of legitimacy has less to do with approaching any particular ideals of justice than with avoiding the worst forms of injustice.[26]

This two-tiered distinction between legitimate and illegitimate regimes is important to the argument over open borders precisely because the range of legitimate polities will necessarily include ones in which there is considerable overlap or blurring between political and national culture. Complete overlap is, I think, indefensible—it would be the invasion by politics of all of life, the totalitarian state. But short of that is an extensive continuum of ways in which various features of national identity slide in and out of political culture to a greater or lesser degree, and the different points on this continuum, I suggest, fall within the realm of the legitimate. Consider, for example, recent proposals in America to make English the official language, either of a particular state or at the national level. Such proposals clearly represent an attempt to lodge a significant aspect of the national culture within the political culture, and it seems equally clear that, whatever one may think of such proposals, their success would not make the United States an illegitimate government. Opponents of these laws might argue that they would be unconstitutional; but that is an argument about what America is, about American national identity, and not about the qualifications of legitimate government in general.

One could come up with numerous other examples of ways in which national identity and political culture merge, even in a liberal country like the United States, where there is presumably more of a distinction made between political culture and culture in general than might be the case elsewhere. Attempts to use the tax code to support home-ownership, the nuclear family, or entrepreneurship would be examples; so would the use of so-called "sin taxes" on alcohol and tobacco to finance large public projects like sports stadiums. Americans love their automobiles, and this manifests itself within the political culture in a deep unwillingness to raise gasoline taxes. Zoning regulations commonly try to create particular kinds of areas or neighborhoods. Indeed, it is almost impossible to imagine a polity in which such overlap were not common—it would seem to require people to support a government utterly indifferent to the preservation of its particular way of life. So national identity and political culture are intertwined, and together they influence policy decisions.[27] But if the range of acceptable manifestations of their merger is extensive, so must be the corresponding range of acceptable policy outcomes. And this is true of immigration policy as well. Such an outcome can only be forestalled by declaring the political and national identities upon which they are based illegitimate, and that does not seem defensible.

The argument thus far, then, is this: Different polities will exhibit differ-ent national identities, and these identities will in turn shape political cul-ture in various ways. These different amalgams of political and national identity will inevitably point towards different kinds of policies, in immi-gration no less than in other areas. Thus no single immigration policy—and certainly not a policy of open borders—can be claimed as the correct pol-icy for all polities to adopt. If policies are closely related to particular understandings of politics and its purposes, and if a large variety of such understandings is legitimate, then there will also necessarily be a large vari-ety of legitimate immigration policies, and countries will choose ones that reflect their particular identities.

This, however, may still be a bit hasty; another question is necessary to complete the normative inquiry. For even if it is true that the range of legitimate political and national identities is as broad as I have argued, and even if it is also true that these various identities call for different sorts of immigration policies, it still might not be true that different countries are entitled to enact these various policies. For it does not follow from the legitimacy of an end that any means used in pursuit of it is also legitimate. And restrictive immigration policies, conceived as a means toward the end of preserving legitimate national identities, raise an important and familiar ethical dilemma about the relationship between particular and universal duties. A people's use of immigration policy to protect its own way of life seems to rest upon a view that we are at least permitted (and perhaps, depending upon the formulation, required) to give a kind of preference to our compatriots as opposed to other, random human beings throughout the world. It assumes that we may justifiably give special weight, in ethical and political matters, to "our own," broadly speaking—our own people, our own way of life, our neighbors, friends, and fellow citizens. But this, of course, might not be true. Perhaps we should not prefer one group of peo-ple to others in this way. Perhaps our moral obligation is to treat all human beings equally, showing no preference for our compatriots—who, after all, are only those who happened to be born in the same territory—and the way of life we share. Thus a new question arises: To what extent may we prefer ourselves and our own way of life? And by "prefer" I mean, of course, *actively* prefer, that is, back up our preference with the power of the state, at a cost to others with different ways of life. Even if we grant that a group of people shares a common life that might be threatened by new-comers, may they legitimately act to preserve it?[28]

Existentially, I think, people first face the question I initially considered, the question of national identity. Faced with the prospect of admitting strangers, we first ask what their arrival will mean for us and our way of life. Only then do we confront the question of permissible preferences as a challenge. It is for this reason that I have arranged the argument in the order I have. Logically, though, this question of preference is really prior to the question about national identity. Thus the simple solution of answering "no," we may *not* prefer our own way of life to those of others, renders the whole discussion of national identity offered above, as well as that of legitimacy, simply irrelevant. Indeed, one could interpret Carens's early argument for open borders in the "Aliens and Citizens" article as an attempt to resolve the issue in precisely this way: his three varieties of liberalism all effectively deny the possibility that a segment of humanity might have a common way of life deserving this kind of protection. Utilitarianism, of course, explicitly denies that we may prefer one person to another, and this strategy of equally weighing each individual's interests makes any particular group identity a minority in the face of collective humanity—as nation-states, for example, are outweighed by those innumerable migrants who would benefit from the freedom to move. Similarly, the extension of the Rawlsian original position to the realm of international relations makes the relevant political community humanity as a whole, thus negating any particular identities that might serve as grounds for restricting movement among polities. And the Nozickian argument's individualism dissolves the possibility of any collective identity that could determine policy.

Settling the question of whether or to what extent we may actively prefer our fellow citizens and the way of life we share with them would clearly be a large endeavour, requiring a book of its own,[29] and I shall not try to accomplish that here. Fortunately, though, my purposes do not require me to make the attempt. Rather, I merely hope to indicate a few of the questions that would need to be definitively answered in order to establish the claim that countries may not give special preference to their own members and ways of life. The very complexity of these questions and the possibility of plausibly answering them in a variety of ways, I shall argue, make it appropriate to allow countries, in constructing immigration policy, to engage in the kind of reflection upon their own identities that I have already described.

Consider a first question that would need resolution in order to establish the untenability of preferential policies. I have asked whether we *may* prefer our own way of life; but surely it is also important to ask whether we sometimes *ought* to prefer it. If this were the case, of course, it would go without saying that a country's protection of its own culture would sometimes be permissible. And surely there is a reasonable case to be made that, indeed, countries should at times seek to preserve aspects of their cultures. In defense of this, one need only believe that cultures often contain features—ideas, accomplishments, or traditions in areas as diverse as politics, art, philosophy, religion—that are of universal worth, the disappearance of which would be a loss for others as well as for themselves. Few, I think, would want to deny this. Cultures as diverse as the ancient Chinese empire, the Arabic world of the early Middle Ages (which, in addition to its own accomplishments, was also responsible for preserving and transmitting some of the great achievements of classical Greece), and Renaissance Europe have made lasting contributions to human history and knowledge. These are clearly among the more striking and obvious examples one could think of, but it is not far-fetched to suggest that many cultures contain elements worth preserving, elements upon which others could profitably reflect. What is lost when such things vanish?[30]

Another way of putting this question is to ask whether diversity is valuable in and of itself. Do different cultures represent diverse forms of human flourishing, different ways in which the latent potentialites of humanity play themselves out? If so, they may well deserve protection for that reason alone. These different human possibilities present us with alternatives to our own way of life, alternatives which may at times attract us and at others confirm our preference for our own culture. At the very least, they can help us see the contingency of our particular way of life, and especially of the fact that we happen to share it rather than another, without denying that it (like others) may be valuable and worthy of defense. Such a view seems quite plausible. Thus a rejection of preferential policies would require a showing that diversity is not intrinsically valuable in this way, or at least that the value of preserving a given culture's offerings for the world can never be overriding.

In addition to asking whether diverse cultures may contain elements worth preserving because of their universal value, we must also confront another difficult question: Are some cultures superior to others in certain respects? Once we entertain the possibility that different cultures represent different forms of human flourishing, we can hardly avoid asking whether some of them do a better overall job of promoting that flourishing or allow broader scope, in more areas of life, for its occurrence. Indeed, this question seems particularly pressing in the context of migration, since the very circumstances that often prompt people to leave one place for another—terrible oppression, political collapse, utter poverty—practically compel one to ask whether better and worse forms of civilization have arisen in different places. This need not, of course, involve a blanket judgement that one culture is simply superior to others, in all respects. But surely some systems do a better job than others of providing for the basic economic needs of their members; some create stable political systems that endure through ages; others provide greater freedom and autonomy to individuals; still others better satisfy their members' desires for fraternity and belonging. By the same token, though, blanket judgements can hardly be ruled out from the start. After considering various standards by which one might gauge the accomplishments of a given culture, it is certainly possible that some ways of life might appear relatively successful at achieving a broad range of human goals, and might in that sense deserve to be called broadly superior to other alternatives. As good liberal people, who dislike making potentially critical assessments about others and their ways of life, we tend to shy away from such judgements. But I do not think their possibility can be ruled out *a priori,* particularly if one takes into account a variety of possible standards for measuring human success.

Obviously, establishing the superiority (or superiority in some respect) of a given culture would not in itself determine in detail the consequences for immigration (or other kinds of) policy, since such a finding might have different implications in different times and places. Should a superior people reject immigrants to preserve its culture from being overwhelmed or simply diluted by newcomers? Or should it seek to accept many immigrants as a way of spreading its culture and sharing it with ever more people? Such questions call for political judgement in light of particular circumstances. Nevertheless, regardless of the specific form that policy takes, the conclusion that a given culture is in some respect superior to the available alternatives surely calls for policies designed to preserve the culture in question, however precisely they may go about doing it. Thus the rejection of preferential policies denies that the superiority of a given way of life could ever be a politically decisive factor.

Another question raised by the denial of preferential policies is whether human beings require a relatively stable culture as a precondition for their own development. Regardless of one's own conception of human flourishing, that is, and even if one were wary of possible threats to individual freedom arising from the legal enshrinement of a common culture or national identity, one might nevertheless think that all human beings, precisely for the sake of their individual development, require a coherent cultural context in order to form their own views and make sense of the world in which they live.[31] People will respond to this context in various ways, of course, ranging from whole-hearted endorsement and internalization to conscious and far-reaching rejection. Similarly, cultural contexts themselves may vary widely from place to place. Some cultures are characterized by stability or even rigidity; by contrast, fluidity and change (within limits) are themselves the distinguishing marks of other cultures. Any of these cultures, however, can provide the necessary background against which individuals can reach some understanding of the world and their place in it.

If one thought that some such context were necessary for individual development, this would also provide limited grounds for at least some preferential policies. It would, of course, be a rather different justification from the other possibilities discussed above, relying neither upon the superiority of a given culture in some respect nor even upon the wider value of some of that culture's achievements. Instead, it sets aside the question of a culture's content and focuses simply on the possibility that all human beings need *some* culture, even if only to react against.[32] In so doing, it provides even those with a very individualistic view of human nature with a potential reason for supporting policies designed to protect a culture in at least some places at some times. Thus a flat rejection of preferential policies would seem to require the view that human flourishing is possible even in the absence of any stable cultural context.

A fourth important question involves the status of human sociability. Are social and political life simply a part of what it is to be a human being and lead a human life? Do they arise from human nature? If so, then it would seem to be a violation of human nature not to let people participate in such activity and develop their own societies; some measure of collective self-determination, in other words, seems the natural consequence of such a view.[33] The precise boundaries of that self-determination may be hard to gauge; but one could reasonably expect that they would permit some attempts at cultural self-preservation, of which immigration restrictions might well form a part. Another likely consequence of the view that people naturally form societies and live together with their fellows is that the various interactions and relationships that spring from this common life give rise to certain bonds and obligations among members that do not exist, or not in the same degree, between members and non-members. This possibility might provide a foundation for at least sometimes preferring members and their shared way of life to outsiders. On this view, to neglect the communities that human beings naturally form and the special bonds which these communities inevitably produce is to lead a less than fully human life, a life that ignores important parts of what it is to be human.

One could make such an argument in a variety of ways, of course. One might claim, with Aristotle, that "man is by nature an animal intended to live in a polis" and that political association is the appropriate culmination of humans' social instincts.[34] St. Augustine gave a Christian view of human sociability when he described all of human history in terms of the metaphor of two cities, the City of God and the earthly city; even the members of the earthly city, he wrote, driven by pride and the lust for domination, desire some kind of peace with their fellow human beings.

> What tigress does not gently purr over her cubs, and subdue her fierceness to caress them? What kite, however solitary as he hovers over his prey, does not find a mate, build a nest, help to hatch the eggs, rear the young birds, and, as we may say, preserve with the mother of his family a domestic society as peaceful as he can make it? How much more strongly is a human being drawn by the laws of his nature, so to speak, to enter upon a fellowship with all his fellow-men and to keep peace with them, as far as lies in him.[35]

And David Hume, from yet another perspective, placed great weight upon the "social disposition of mankind," claiming that the "propensity to company and society is strong in all rational creatures." [36] The argument that social life is intrinsic to human nature might thus take different forms. But any of these forms could support the view that special bonds exist between fellow members of a society. In order to rule out the possible legitimacy of preferential policies, then, it seems that one would have to reject either the claim that communal life is a vital part of human nature or the claim that this life can give rise to special kinds of moral relationships and obligations.

These are some of the difficult questions involved in asking whether policies designed to prefer a particular people and its way of life might ever be legitimate. Presumably there are more that I have not raised. I have not attempted to answer these questions here. I would not want to be understood as denying that they could have answers—indeed, the reader may be forgiven for suspecting that I do have opinions about these matters. Here, though, I have sought only to suggest that all these questions could plausibly be answered in ways that would potentially justify preferential policies. Unless we can settle them definitively, then—unless we can determine that peoples are never justified in seeking to preserve valuable elements of their cultures, that no cultures are ever superior to others and thus worthy of protection, that individuals can develop and flourish without a stable cultural context in which to begin, that social life is not integral to human nature, giving rise to special bonds and obligations—we cannot rule out the possible legitimacy of policies designed to preserve and protect specific cultures.

These different questions are obviously related. They are all ways of raising one of the most fundamental questions of political theory, namely, the proper weight to be given cultural or communal concerns in political life.[37] It is therefore not too strong a claim to point out that the rejection of policies which actively prefer a given culture to others presupposes a resolution to this fundamental problem—presupposes, that is, a fairly well-developed conception of the nature and purposes of politics. I have argued in chapter two, for example, that the most carefully argued scholarly approach to immigration, Joseph Carens's case for open borders, rests upon the undefended endorsement of a certain variety of liberalism. In the same way, other positions on immigration—positions that necessarily seek to answer questions about how many or what kinds of immigrants polities should or should not admit—also rest upon certain assumptions about the nature of political community.[38] Thus to insist that justice requires all countries to follow the same immigration policy, be it open borders or something else, is to insist that all countries adopt the view of political community that underlies and ultimately justifies that policy.[39]

But this kind of agreement can hardly be expected. I have already suggested, in discussing the relation between political culture and national identity, that precisely this question of the extent to which culture is viewed as intertwined with politics is one of the most fundamental aspects of a people's identity, about which different peoples will certainly disagree. And I have further shown the improbability of an argument that might persuade them all to set aside their own conclusions on such matters and abandon their culture's survival to the winds of fate; on the contrary, I have suggested, perfectly plausible arguments exist for thinking that peoples are entitled to preserve what they consider the distinctive elements of their culture. In light of this, it seems unreasonable to hold that a single approach to immigration is the correct one for all countries. To do so is to demand that they set aside their own conceptions of political life for some other one, even if they remain unpersuaded that their own vision of political community is inferior to the proffered alternative. The unreasonableness of such a demand is even more striking in light of the fundamental nature of immigration itself, which is one of the basic ways in which a community takes shape. Thus to insist on unanimity in immigration policy is to insist on agreement about vital questions about political community not simply in some peripheral regions of policy but in the very creation and maintenance of that community itself.

In light of this lack of consensus regarding those matters which might justify a single immigration policy as universally valid, it seems appropriate to leave countries considerable leeway in constructing policies that reflect their own identities, their own visions of political community—to permit them, that is, to engage in the kind of self-reflection I described in the first half of this chapter.[40] The only alternative to this would be finding some way of implementing a selected universal immigration policy even in countries that reject its premises. This would require some form of world government or empire, some governing structure with the power to enforce its decrees on recalcitrant members. And since the prospects for such a body's arising through consensus among nations seem rather dim, it would also presumably require the use of considerable force. In the absence of broad agreement on the principles of some single immigration policy, and given the plausible arguments in favor of diversity and preferential treatment, this seems unjustifiable.

But here, one might object, there is a distinction to be made, for surely I am blurring the difference between armed intervention and moral judgement or criticism. After all, we might accept the necessity of permitting different countries with their different policies to exist and concede that they will not all throw open their borders tomorrow, without ever intending to invade them or take them over in order to force the issue, but also without justifying those policies in principle. Criticism would be an alternative to a world government designed to bring delinquents into line. But insofar as it is precisely the point of my argument to justify a broad diversity of policies in principle, I am worried not simply about armed intervention (which few, presumably, envisage on these grounds) but also about certain *kinds* of criticism. If my argument about the broad range of legitimate regimes is correct, then there seems to be something intellectually unfair, unjustified, in calling an immigration policy reflecting a legitimate national identity unjust or illegitimate. This kind of "moral intervention" (or "moralizing" intervention), as we might call it, a tendency to issue strict judgements on matters where there appears to be room for reasonable disagreement, exerts a form of moral pressure that is less obvious but no less real than the military force employed in conventional intervention. This pressure matters, and if it is improperly exerted, that seems every bit as unfair as, even if less overtly dangerous than, armed intervention. My suggestion here is that the combination of three factors in particular—the fundamental importance of immigration for a political community and its identity; the wide range of legitimate regimes; and the entirely plausible arguments in support of preferential policies—ought to chasten our judgements about different immigration policies and restrain the kinds of criticisms we are prepared to make. In this sense the argument is directed not simply at armed intervention, but also at moral intervention, at unjustified (or insufficiently justified) forms of criticism.

Because different immigration policies are closely related to correspondingly different conceptions of the proper relationship between culture and politics, then, insistence on any single policy as correct for all peoples presupposes a degree of consensus on such matters that does not exist and cannot be expected. Attempts to overcome this disagreement exact a high cost. This cost might involve some form of outright intervention, the erection of a world government able to mandate the replacement of policies that can be plausibly justified and that reflect a given people's own understanding of political life with other, alien conceptions of whose superiority they remain unpersuaded. Or it might be more subtle, involving the exertion of a kind of moral pressure exceeding what can be justified in light of the reasonable range of disagreement about these matters. In either case, the cost is sufficiently high that the task of adopting an appropriate immigration policy to fit a specific country is best left to the people of that country themselves, reflecting upon who they are and who they hope to be.

Chapter 4

IMMIGRATION POLICY AND NATIONAL IDENTITY:
TWO CASE STUDIES IN PRACTICE

In the last chapter, I argued that different immigration policies rest upon different assumptions about the nature of political community (which are themselves connected with different national identities, particularly with respect to the relationship between politics and culture), and that as a result we should be hesitant to restrict the kinds of immigration policies peoples may enact and pursue, because in doing so we restrict the kinds of political communities they are able to create, inhabit, and preserve. In this and the following chapter, in two different ways, I want to illustrate and reflect upon the important first aspect of that claim, the close connection between conceptions of political community and immigration policies. In chapter five I shall do this at the level of theory; but here I want to begin at the level of practice, of actual policy. This follows roughly the movement of the previous chapter, starting with a more descriptive account and proceeding to a more normative one (not that the two are ever perfectly separate and distinct). So I offer here an examination of two countries, the United States and Germany. This examination should provide us with a more concrete understanding of the close connection between immigration policy and national identity, and thus, I hope, buttress the suggestion made in the previous chapter that any attempt to declare a given policy, whatever it might be, the "correct" one for countries to follow inevitably involves claims about the legitimacy or illegitimacy of the cultures and polities, broadly understood, of the countries in question.

Both the United States and Germany have in recent years engaged in significant debates about immigration policy. The United States has experienced annual immigration at levels unseen since the massive population flows at the turn of the century, while also facing enormous tides of illegal immigration, which have provoked a significant backlash—California's Proposition 187 being the most notorious example—in the most affected parts of the country. Germany has found itself home to large, and not always welcome, immigrant minorities, the legacy of past economic policies, at a time when the collapse of the Soviet empire also exposed it to large influxes of ethnic German migrants from the east. Indeed, one of the central campaign pledges of Gerhard Schröder's Social Democratic Party when it finally unseated former Chancellor Helmut Kohl and the Christian Democrats in 1998 was to amend Germany's very old and widely condemned laws governing the naturalization of immigrants. Thus these two countries provide excellent arenas in which to think about the connection between immigration and national identity.

My goal here is not to offer specific policy proposals for how these two countries should handle immigration. Rather, I wish simply to offer illustrations of how debates over immigration are deeply bound up with considerations of national identity that vary from place to place. In doing so, I hope to indicate the kinds of issues that a people will consider in grappling with immigration. The point is less to offer advice than to illustrate the process that, I think, people actually engage in when they consider these issues. Since such an illustration shows the way in which questions of national identity help to shape immigration policy, it underlines the significance of the question that I discussed in chapter three: whether the kind of preference for our own way of life depicted in these examples is legitimate or not.

The United States

American immigration law is extremely complex—"Byzantine," in the words of one observer.[1] A full account of it is beyond the scope of this brief consideration, but a summary of its history and current provisions is desirable. It is common to divide the history of American immigration policy into several different periods, according to the country's changing attitudes towards immigration; precise divisions and the names given to different eras vary slightly, but the general outline is clear.[2] During the colonial period and well into the nineteenth century, immigration was regulated not by the federal government, but rather by the several states—often, in fact, private agencies handled the recruitment and settlement of immigrants. The states did little to restrict immigration and often actively recruited it as a way of providing cheap labor.

By the 1870s, however, so many immigrants were arriving that the federal government could no longer ignore the phenomenon, and in 1875 the Supreme Court ruled that the federal government had exclusive power to regulate immigration. In the late 1800s, the government gradually began to create a federal bureaucracy for controlling immigration. It doing so, it began to impose the first significant restrictions on immigration to America. Some of the first targets of restrictive legislation were Asians, especially the Chinese, against whom there was considerable agitation on the West Coast. But the Chinese were not the only group to arouse concern. As the nineteenth century drew to a close, the composition of the European immigrant stream had also changed considerably, with fewer immigrants now coming from the traditional countries of origin in northern and western Europe and more coming from southern and eastern Europe, regions whose peoples were generally considered inferior according to the popular, pseudo-scientific, racialist theories of the time. Concerns about the vast numbers of these "inferior" immigrants led to increasing attempts to restrict immigration.

Early attempts at restriction involved prohibiting certain classes of immigrants, such as those with contagious diseases, criminals, prostitutes, or those unlikely to be able to support themselves. Another frequently proposed restriction was a literacy requirement, which several Congresses attempted to pass just before and after the turn of the century, either failing or seeing the result struck down by presidential vetoes (such vetoes of restrictivist legislation, often on foreign policy grounds, were common in the first two decades of the 1900s). In 1907, Congress appointed the Dillingham Commission to study the effects of immigration and make policy recommendations. In 1910 the Commission published a massive, 42–volume report recommending various restrictions on immigration, among them a literacy requirement. Such a requirement finally became law in 1917.

The growing momentum for restriction that had been gathering steam for several decades finally culminated in the Quota Acts of 1921 and 1924. These acts limited the total number of immigrants who could be admitted to the United States annually at 150,000, as well as the number that could be admitted from any particular country. These limits for various countries were based upon the percentage of the American population belonging to the nationality in question. Thus the 1924 Act, for example, permitted immigration from a given nation equal to two percent of the number of Americans belonging to that nationality in the census of 1890.[3] These provisions, obviously, were designed to ensure that future immigration would reflect and maintain the ethnic composition of the American population at the time.

This national origins quota system remained in effect for roughly 40 years (though the number of would-be immigrants during the Depression and the beginnings of World War II was small anyhow). Following World War II, however, the system began to show signs of strain. For one thing, it proved too inflexible to deal adequately with the problems of refugees and displaced persons during and following the war, or with the foreign policy demands of the budding Cold War, which created a desire to provide refuge to those fleeing Communist oppression. Furthermore, as American racial attitudes became more liberal and tolerant, the national origins quotas came more and more to seem anachronistic, racially motivated elements from an antiquated and unjust past. Finally, in 1965, Congress abolished the national origins system and overhauled American immigration policy in the Hart-Celler Act of 1965. This act roughly doubled the number of immigrants who could be admitted annually, and it established a complex "preference" system for awarding visas, according to which approximately three-fourths of visas were to be allocated to various relatives of American citizens and of permanent residents, about 20 percent to people with particular skills needed by the American economy, and the remainder to refugees. Finally, because certain close relatives of American citizens were exempt from the overall limits and automatically entitled to admission, the limits could actually be (and routinely were) exceeded; thus, in practice, there was no fixed numerical limit to the number of immigrants who could enter the United States in any given year.

The effects of the 1965 legislation became apparent relatively quickly. Although its supporters had claimed that it would neither radically increase the amount nor alter the composition of American immigration, these predictions proved false. Beginning in the late 1960s, the number of immigrants to America grew rapidly, and by the late 1980s it had reached a level not seen since the turn of the century. Immigrants also began to arrive in large numbers from regions such as southeast Asia, India, central America, and the Caribbean, areas that had not previously generated many immigrants. The reason for the changes in overall numbers and in ethnic and geographical composition lay in the 1965 Act's provisions for family reunification, which led to a phenomenon known as "chain migration:" immigrants were able to bring in their relatives, who were in turn entitled to bring in *their* relatives, and so forth. Thus nationalities such as the Koreans, Vietnamese, or Mexicans—to name just a few of the groups that grew the fastest—were able, once they had gotten a foot in the door, to use the 1965 Act's preference scheme to continue increasing the number of immigrants from their respective countries.

The Hart-Celler Act continues to provide the basic framework for American immigration policy, though subsequent legislation has altered various aspects of it. The Refugee Act of 1980 removed refugees from the ordinary preference system and established separate regulations for their admission. The Immigration Reform and Control Act of 1986 sought (largely ineffectively) to reduce levels of illegal immigration, which had exploded following the imposition in 1976, for the first time, of a 20,000 per-country immigration limit within the Western hemisphere (the 1965 Act had established such a limit elsewhere) and which has garnered increasing public attention ever since. Finally, in 1990, Congress once again reformed immigration law by passing the most liberal law since the Quota Acts of the 1920s. The Immigration Act of 1990 raised the overall annual limit on immigration to 675,000, with the distribution of visas still determined largely according to the ideals embodied in the earlier 1965 Act. The percentage of skills-based visas was raised somewhat, and the different categories of family-reunification visas were slightly altered; in addition, a new category of "diversity" visas was created to award visas to countries (primarily Ireland) that had been squeezed out by the workings of the 1965 Act. As in the earlier act, the exemption of immediate relatives of American citizens from the numerical limits means that the number of legal immigrants in a given year can exceed 675,000, as, again, it routinely does. The 1990 Act continues to be America's governing immigration law.

It is difficult, for several reasons, to argue directly from this account of the law to a particular conception of American political community. For one thing, American immigration policy is extremely open and thus does not obviously reveal a particular American self-understanding. This is the result not so much of mere openness—after all, those whom we are willing to admit may reveal as much about us as those whom we desire to exclude—but rather of the numbers and diversity of the immigrants that America receives. Their abundance and variety make it hard to derive clear inferences about American identity—unless one concludes that there is no distinct American identity, or that it is sufficiently "thin" or abstract as to be in some sense universally accessible, a possibility we shall have to consider.

Other factors, besides the generosity of American policy, also make it difficult to see in it a clear reflection of our national identity. One important such factor is the sheer complexity of American immigration law, of which the foregoing account gives some indication. As we have seen, that law contains provisions regulating immigration for the purpose of family reunification (under which the vast majority of immigrants enter), which are themselves divided into different categories or "preferences" for nearer or more distant relatives, as well as into categories admitting various relatives of legal permanent residents; provisions admitting skilled workers, and others regulating temporary migration designed to meet particular labor needs, especially in the agricultural Southwest; and separate "diversity" provisions intended to increase the number of slots awarded to countries which had seen their numbers drastically decline following the immigration reforms of 1965. Other regulations govern refugees and asylees. And, of course, all of these provisions for legal immigration are intertwined with other provisions designed to combat illegal immigration. It can be hard to see how these disparate elements of our immigration policy fit together.

Indeed, they may not fit together in any coherent manner. For since about 1980, immigration policy has been driven by a peculiar and unexpected coalition of political allies. Higher immigration rates have been supported by free-market believers in the free movement of capital and labor, by ethnic groups seeking to preserve family reunification provisions that allow them to bring in more members of their nationalities, and by businesses eager for a supply of cheap labor. This peculiar coalition of the left and the right created a base of pro-immigration sentiment not only strong enough to derail attempts at restriction and maintain established levels of admissions, but also to raise those levels considerably in the Immigration Act of 1990. The existence of this unusual alliance, which has generated the core support for contemporary American policy but which is composed of different groups seeking distinct interests, is another element making it difficult to draw definite conclusions about a broader American identity from that policy.

A final factor complicating attempts to derive conclusions about national identity from American immigration policy is that policy's consistent divergence from public opinion in recent decades. Although the level of immigration to the United States has increased dramatically since the Hart-Celler Act of 1965, public opinion has remained consistently opposed to high levels of immigration—has become, in fact, somewhat more strongly anti-immigration. Rita J. Simon and Susan H. Alexander, in a study of American public opinion and media attitudes toward immigration, write,

> Between 1977 and 1990, six national polls asked "Should immigration be kept at its present level, increased, or decreased?" The percentage of respondents who favored increasing immigration levels ranged from 4 to 9 percent.

Thus, comparing the public's responses to this question over a 45–year time span, the data . . . show that only once, in 1953, did more than 10 percent favor increasing the number of immigrants permitted to enter this country and that, throughout this period, at least three times as many supported decreasing the number of people permitted to enter.[4]

Simon and Alexander summarize their study of polling data by writing, "The most consistent theme that emerges from all of the public opinion surveys is the essentially negative attitudes held by a majority of the U.S. public toward persons wishing to come to the United States."[5] And they conclude, "It is something of a miracle that so many immigrants gained entry to the United States between 1880 and 1990."[6] This does not necessarily mean, of course, that U.S. immigration policy in recent decades has simply been irrational or undemocratic; on the contrary, I shall suggest in a moment that this situation actually reflects an important feature of American politics. Still, however one seeks to explain this large gap between public opinion and the law, its existence surely complicates any attempts to derive general conclusions about American national identity from our current legislation.

Thus the openness of American immigration policy, its complexity, the unusual coalition of interests on the political left and right that has shaped it, and its divergence from public opinion all make it difficult to understand how that policy might reflect American national identity. This is not to say, of course, that we can say nothing about any parts of that policy. The emphasis on family reunification, for example, may reflect both humanitarian concerns as well as a sense that healthy, robust communal structures help to form the strong, risk-taking individuals who have loomed so large in the American self-image.[7] And the reservation of certain slots for people with valuable economic skills reflects a belief, going back at least to the restrictive quota acts of the early 1920s, that immigration could be used to benefit the American economy.[8]

One might further suggest that this description, in particular the gap between public opinion and public policy, reveals another important characteristic of the American political system. It does so by raising an obvious and puzzling question: How did immigration policy remain so generous, and even become more so, at a time when public opinion towards immigration was becoming increasingly negative? The answer lies in the pluralist nature of American democracy and has already been suggested by the description of the left-right coalition that coalesced in support of immigration. The American legislative process, with its complex system of congressional committees and legislators' susceptibility to pressure from interest groups able to contribute campaign funds, is open to considerable influence from an extraordinary array of special interest groups. In the case of immigration, a number of groups with interests in high levels of immigration joined forces, creating the coalition already described, to help maintain and expand immigrant admissions. On the right, businesses were eager for both skilled and unskilled immigrant workers, the former to fill important economic needs, the latter to provide a source of cheap labor. On the left, a wide array of ethnic groups pressed for higher immigration in order to increase their own numbers (and thereby their own legislative influence as well). Furthermore, powerful intellectual currents helped support the arguments these groups had at their disposal.

> Fortuitous historical changes ha[d] weakened the power of the restrictionist groups vis-à-vis the pro-immigration forces. First, the civil rights zeitgeist . . . empowered ethnic groups like the National Council on La Raza, which soon became major players in the Democratic Party. Secondly, the rise of conservative economics during the 1970s swayed many Republicans to support high levels of immigration as a way to keep America globally competitive. The power of [these] ideas should not be underestimated.[9]

At the same time that pro-immigration interest groups were invigorated by ideas such as these, traditional opponents of immigration were in various ways weakened. The very influence of the civil rights movement that helped strengthen ethnic interest groups also had the more general effect that most Americans came to consider illegitimate the straightforwardly ethnic arguments that had played a large role in previous immigration restrictions. The preferences in the immigration laws for relatives of American citizens and residents helped mute potential criticism from cultural conservatives, for whom "family values" had become an important concern. And labor unions, historically hostile to immigration, having fought hard for their primary goal of restricting illegal immigration—which they achieved in the IRCA of 1980—were less vocal in their opposition to legal immigration. Thus a number of groups with an interest in increased immigration, strengthened by prevailing intellectual trends, were able to join forces as their opponents' strength was diminishing.[10] This play of special interests visible in the immigration battles reveals an important characteristic of American democracy, namely, the way in which a majority popular will is filtered through a complex legislative process, sometimes producing surprising results, results that may not directly reflect public opinion or that may even seem to reflect a welter of conflicting opinions, as appears true of our complex immigration policies. Americans may at times complain about this system and the influence of special interests within it, but the blunting of majority will is surely a central element in our democracy, with roots reaching back to the Founding period.[11]

It is possible, then, to make sense of the preceding account of immigration policy and even to recognize in it some aspects of American identity. Nevertheless, observations such as these constitute at best partial, piecemeal suggestions about that identity, fragments of a larger whole. It is not clear what they tell us about "Americanness" in general; indeed, their fragmentary nature might even tempt us to conclude that American immigration policy—contrary to my hypothesis about immigration policies in general—does not reflect any broader, more fundamental understanding of national identity or political community, a possibility that only seems strengthened by the ad hoc coalition politics that helped produce that policy in the first place.

But such a conclusion would be premature. For if we take a step back from the complex picture presented by American immigration law and consider it from a wider perspective, we find, I think, that it does reflect some deeper questions about what it means to be an American. I want to draw attention in particular to two related questions about American identity. Both are suggested by the label that columnist Ben Wattenberg has given to the contemporary United States: "the first universal nation."[12] Wattenberg's phrase is intended to conjure up a whole range of optimistic facts about the United States' current position of dominance in the world (a position he expects it to maintain and even increase), but one of its meanings is a quite literal one, directly linked to immigration: "In America, we now come from everywhere, becoming one people, getting along pretty well with each other, and vastly enriched by our pluralism."[13] Wattenberg's claim calls up images of America as a "nation of immigrants," perhaps the description of America most likely to be encountered in discussions of immigration, one evoking deeply entrenched and emotionally powerful images of millions of immigrants arriving at Ellis Island under the shadow of the Statue of Liberty.

The suggestion implicit in this self-identification as a "nation of immigrants," of course, is that we should remain true to this identity. How can we deny to others the very opportunity that allowed our own ancestors to arrive and remain here? Such an impulse reflects the question which, I suggested in chapter three, a people first confronts when faced by the problem of immigration: Who are we, and who do we want to be? Answering this question involves the telling of a historical story, which in America includes successive chapters detailing the successes of a host of immigrant groups—Germans, Irish, Italians, more recently perhaps Chinese, Koreans, and Indians—who have struggled to achieve the American dream: arriving in poverty, working hard to climb the economic ladder and win a better life for their children and grandchildren, and ultimately successfully assimilating into mainstream American society. In recent decades we have come to recognize and emphasize other elements of the story as well: the difficulty and dislocation suffered by immigrants attempting to adapt to their new environment, or the changes they themselves have brought to mainstream America. But the essential outlines of the story have remained intact and extremely resilient, and it is surely plausible to suggest that the power and persistence of this self-image have been at least partly responsible for continued high levels of American immigration; or, to put it differently, that they have shaped a context in which continuing immigration appears as the normal or "default" state of affairs, occupying a kind of moral high ground in the debate. When an initially modestly restrictionist bill ultimately became the expansionist Immigration Act of 1990, for example, it may have been due in part to the efforts of an unusual and powerful left-right coalition;[14] but that coalition had the benefit of working in an atmosphere in which restrictions on immigration are inevitably seen as at best a kind of cowardice and stinginess and at worst an outright betrayal of America's noblest and most generous political traditions.

The force of this image of a "nation of immigrants" is also demonstrated by the efforts of immigration opponents to discredit it and show that it rests upon a partial reading of American history. Thus Peter Brimelow writes,

> No discussion of U.S. immigration policy gets far without someone making this helpful remark: *"We are a nation of immigrants."* . . . But [this] secretly amuses me. Do they really think other nations sprang up out of the ground? . . . The truth is that all nations are nations of immigrants. But the process is usually so slow and historic—extending over hundreds and even thousands of years—that people overlook it.[15]

He then emphasizes the significant ethnic and cultural homogeneity that existed in America at the time of the Revolution and even well into the twentieth century, and he argues that American history has been defined not only by considerable immigration, but also by the pauses in that pattern, the periods of restricted immigration that followed waves of high immigration and allowed America to "digest" them: "This pattern of pauses for digestion had recurred throughout American history. Waves of immigration have been followed by lulls right back into Colonial times."[16] Chilton Williamson, Jr., writes in the same vein, "Since the American people have historically opposed immigration, and since the Founding Fathers, as suggested by their more candid remarks on the subject, opposed it also, it seems fair to conclude that a split developed in American history—probably beginning after the Civil War—between the people themselves and their elected leaders," and then devotes roughly 50 pages to describing the forces in American life that have consistently been hostile towards immigration.[17] Similarly, Roy Beck writes that, following the "Great Wave" of immigration around the turn of the century, "'things turned out all right' only after Washington finally lowered immigration levels in 1924 and kept them down for forty years."[18] And he emphasizes that "mass immigration has always provoked wide-spread, deep-rooted objections from much of the public," arguing that "[p]artly because of the low immigration from 1925 to 1965, Americans developed a whole new attitude toward immigrants, becoming substantially positive about them for perhaps the first time since the country's birth."[19] Such efforts to rebut the claim that America is a "nation of immigrants" testify to that image's power, as well as to a belief that these historical facts about us are important for deciding how we ought to act in the present.

Nor are these critics incorrect about the history of American immigration. As I pointed out in my brief survey of that history, it has contained periods of restricted immigration as well as ones of extremely high immigration; and the most significant example of the former (following the Quota Acts of the 1920s) was triggered by the most significant example of the latter (the massive influx just before and after the turn of the century). Furthermore, as I have already noted, the survey data analyzed by Simon and Alexander confirm that the American public has consistently been broadly hostile towards immigration.[20] This suggests that one could appropriately call the idea of the United States as a "nation of immigrants" one of our most potent national myths: it tells a story of our own origins and thus helps us explain to ourselves who we are, but it does so by emphasizing certain features of our history while neglecting others. I have intentionally refrained, however, from referring to it as a myth, lest I suggest that the image of a "nation of immigrants" is simply a false one; despite the objections—even the correct objections—of restrictionists, it seems to me that no plausible account of American immigration can neglect what has been, by any reasonable historical standard, our extraordinary success in absorbing enormous numbers of people from various areas of the globe.

Thus when a scholar such as Reed Ueda begins his concise history of post-war immigration with these sentences—

> The United States became history's first 'worldwide' immigration country in the twentieth century. By the 1990's, the flow of newcomers swelled to include people from every region and culture of the globe. Forty million of the sixty million immigrants since the founding of the country—two out of three newcomers—arrived in the twentieth century, making it the greatest era of immigration in national and world history . . . . The United States had long been distinguished for the continuous and unique role that immigrants played in its population history—

he not only gives credence to images of a "nation of immigrants" and of the "first universal nation" but also illustrates that these images rest upon a genuine, if sometimes complicated, factual basis.[21]

This enduring and ambivalent posture—proud of our immigrant heritage yet wary of new arrivals—is, it seems to me, one of the most powerful dynamics in the politics of American immigration. It is attested to by additional evidence presented by Simon and Alexander, who note that "when the same public [that expresses general hostility towards immigration] is asked whether immigrants have been 'a good or a bad' thing for this country, a very interesting pattern emerges." Those ethnic groups that have been in this country the longest get consistently higher marks for having, on the whole, benefited the country, whereas more recent immigrant arrivals are judged much more harshly: "The responses show that immigrant groups who have been in the United States longer tend to receive more positive evaluations than do recent immigrant communities, even if the earlier ones had been feared, opposed, and disliked at the time of their arrival."[22] Similarly, a poll asking respondents to name countries from which the United States is receiving too many immigrants most frequently elicited as responses those countries with a briefer history of immigration here—the same countries that were more likely to receive negative evaluations in the previous poll.[23] This too indicates that Americans' negative attitude toward current immigration coexists with a more positive impression of the contributions of long-standing, and presumably more thoroughly assimilated, immigrant groups.

It also seems plausible to suggest that this dynamic helps explain the difference between American attitudes and responses to legal and illegal immigration. As I have pointed out, Congress increased levels of legal immigration in 1990, despite an unfavorable climate of public opinion. Just a few years earlier, however, Congress had passed the Immigration Reform and Control Act of 1986, a significant (though in the event largely unsuccessful) attempt to combat and reduce illegal immigration. This hostility to illegal immigration has remained strong—increased, even. This was evident in the deep public support for California's Proposition 187, which sought to deny various public services to illegal aliens.[24] And in 1996 Congress enacted the Illegal Immigration Reform and Immigrant Responsibility Act (IIRIRA), which made the treatment of illegal aliens much more severe:

> For example, it requires the INS to exclude aliens at the border summarily and without judicial review if they seem to lack proper documentation. The IIRIRA makes asylum claiming more difficult and bars the INS from granting discretionary relief from deportation to many aliens even for compelling humanitarian reasons as the previous law permitted. It mandates the detention of many removable aliens—perhaps forever if they come from a country like Vietnam that refuses to take them back. It equates the rights of aliens who entered illegally and live in the United States with those of aliens with no ties in the United States. It limits the rights of illegal aliens to reenter legally. It further expands the category of "aggravated felon" aliens, who can be deported summarily even if they have been long-term residents of the country. It bars judicial review of INS decisions to deport them.[25]

Being tough on illegal immigrants allows us to assuage public fears about immigration at the same time that admitting high numbers of immigrants lets us remain true to our sense of ourselves as a "nation of immigrants."[26]

Thus the debate over the extent to which the United States is a "nation of immigrants" and what the appropriate consequences of that are is one fundamental issue of American identity underlying the politics of immigration. Wattenberg's labeling of the United States as the "first universal nation" also suggests a second such issue: whether the principles upon which the American polity is based are themselves "universal," applying to all people in all times and places, and leaving no room for distinctions between members and strangers. When the Declaration of Independence opens with its ringing proclamation of self-evident truths—that "all men are created equal, that they are endowed by their Creator with certain unalienable rights, that among these are life, liberty, and the pursuit of happiness"—it does so in terms that apply to the entire human race, not simply the members of a single nation. The Declaration's emphasis on individual rights and consent seems to push beyond local boundaries. By the same token, freedom and equality, arguably the two central American political values, both potentially embrace the human community as a whole and thus seem to call for an extremely generous immigration policy: freedom because it suggests that all people ought to have control over their own lives, and equality because it discredits any distinctions we might make that would guarantee ourselves a special status at others' expense.

This apparent universality of fundamental American political beliefs is connected to the idea that we are a "nation of immigrants." This is not simply because of the pull these principles have exerted on so many people in other lands, but also because America's tradition of immigration has helped further solidify the centrality of these political ideals in the American imagination.[27] This is suggested by the common notion that the only thing holding together the extremely diverse members of the American polity is a shared commitment to the principles of the Declaration and Constitution. As Michael Walzer has written, for example, "Immigration turned the United States into a land of many different ancestors, languages, religions, manners and customs. Political principles, maxims of toleration: these constitute our only stable and common commitment."[28] On this view, American identity simply *is* a certain set of political principles. And because these principles are potentially embraceable by all people everywhere—since all are equal and enjoy the same natural rights—they appear to provide few grounds for excluding immigrants who are prepared to accept them.

Another way of putting this is to say that America is a liberal country, that liberal principles provide no firm basis for distinguishing between members and outsiders, and that a liberal country should therefore have a generous immigration policy. Peter Schuck, one of our foremost scholars of immigration law and policy, describes this view, which he suggests was more or less realized during the first century of the United States' existence, when borders were essentially open:

> Liberalism . . . regards any fixed or exclusive definition of community with profound suspicion. Indeed, in a truly liberal polity, it would be difficult to justify a restrictive immigration law or perhaps any immigration law at all. National barriers to movement would be anomalous. Criteria of inclusion and exclusion based upon accidents of birth, criteria that label some individuals as insiders and others as outsiders, would be odious. Wealth, security, and freedom would not be allocated on such grounds, especially in a world in which the initial distribution of those goods is so unequal. Instead, individuals would remain free to come and go, to form attachments, and to make choices according to their own aspirations, consistent with the equal right of others to do likewise.[29]

This is also the argument that Carens makes about American identity in response to Walzer's defense of the state's right to control admissions. Carens writes,

> Any approach like Walzer's that seeks its ground in the tradition and culture of *our* community must confront, as a methodological paradox, the fact that liberalism is a central part of our culture . . . . To take *our* community as a starting point is to take a community that expresses its moral views in terms of universal principles.[30]

Because America's fundamental political commitments have this universal reach, Carens argues, we ought to move our immigration policy in the direction of open borders.

Now, if this line of argument is true of any country, it seems to me, then it is true of America. Such language about the universality of American political principles is, to be sure, quite vague and in need of considerable spelling-out; still, it does seem to capture something important about America. There is no denying the centrality of the Declaration of Independence and the Constitution to the American political imagination and national identity, or the importance of abstract political ideals, theoretically applicable to all human beings, to those documents. Like the idea that America is a nation of immigrants, however, this image of America too is contestable— perhaps even more so. It is open to objection, I think, in at least two ways. First, it is not clear that American identity consists solely in allegiance to a certain set of abstract principles. Arguably, Americans share a common cultural core that extends beyond mere abstract principles. One might put this argument in historical terms, as Chilton Williamson, Jr., does:

> On the contrary, the United States *does* possess a fundamental character, which is that of a British culture modified to a truly unique culture by the frontier (a blend, essentially, of Russell Kirk's vision of America with Frederick Jackson Turner's), to which immigrants arriving after 1790 had at least in some degree to assimilate . . . . Will Herberg, writing in the 1950's, observed that "the American's image of himself is still the Anglo-American ideal it was at the beginning of our independent existence. The 'national type' as ideal has always been, and remains, pretty well fixed. It is the *Mayflower*, John Smith, Davy Crockett, George Washington, and Abraham Lincoln that define America's self-image, and this is true whether the American in question is a descendant of the Pilgrims or the grandson of an immigrant from southeastern Europe."[31]

Williamson's (and Herberg's) sweeping generalizations perhaps oversimplify a more complex reality, but surely they are right to point to the central influence of British culture in shaping the American character and to the stability and persistence of certain important American heroes and legends within our culture. Quite apart from such broad historical claims, though, there are more mundane ways of illustrating the existence of a more "concrete" American culture, extending beyond a handful of political ideals, as, for example, I sought to do through my anecdote (in chapter three) about the Chevrolet commercial from my childhood that portrayed Chevy vehicles as being "as American as baseball, hot dogs, and apple pie." The resonance of such an image suggests that American identity extends beyond mere allegiance to a set of universal political ideals.

More significant, perhaps, is the challenge that might be raised to the notion that liberalism's appeal to universal principles of equality or individual rights is irrevocably at odds with national boundaries or distinctions between members or outsiders. I raised this issue briefly in my discussion of Carens in chapter two. There I noted only that not all liberals agree with him about the implications of liberal principles; Rawls, for example, argues, contra Carens, that the original position should *not* be applied globally, which is the crucial move in Carens's use of the Rawlsian theory.[32] Other scholars, reacting against what might be called the cosmopolitan strain in some contemporary liberal thought,[33] have argued that national boundaries are not merely compatible with, but are even integral to liberal theory. Jeremy Rabkin, for example, has written that "at least in earlier times, nationalist concerns were intimately connected with regard for individual rights;" and referring specifically to Locke, he claims, "It is not a political constitution that makes a nation, in Locke's account, but the prior existence of a nation that makes it possible to have a liberal constitution . . . . A nation is a people willing to defend their independence in common."[34] Thomas West has made a similar argument, referring specifically to immigration, about the views of the American Founders.

> All human beings [in the view of the Founders] are equal in the sense of possessing the same natural rights to life, liberty, and the pursuit of happiness. But when men live outside of government (in a "state of nature," as Madison calls it in *Federalist* 51), "the weaker individual is not secured against the violence of the stronger." Therefore, says the Declaration, "to secure these rights, governments are instituted among men." That happens when one part of mankind, one people, separates itself from the rest and establishes a

political community. The government of that community secures the people's life, liberty, and property against those who might threaten them. It does not attempt to secure the inalienable rights of people outside of that community. In the sense of the Declaration, a people is any self-selected group which agrees to live together as a political community.[35]

In this view, a concern with human equality and individual rights points not to the abolition of distinct political groups, but rather to the establishment of a political organization capable of realizing such values for its members.

Furthermore, simple assertions about the abstractness of American political identity or the universal thrust of American liberalism do not seem to capture everything that is important in American politics. Some indication of this can be found in what is probably the most common label used to describe the kind of nation that America is: a liberal democracy. Even if we thought that scholars like Rabkin and West were wrong about the implications of liberalism, arguments about the "universality" of American values appeal to the liberal half of this formulation at the expense of its democratic component. But surely democracy is also an important American value and a major component of the American character, one which does not necessarily point towards a wide-open immigration policy. For one thing, the idea of democracy seems to involve a distinct, bounded, self-determining people: it requires the "independent existence of the . . . *demos,* people, community, that is . . . taking decisions on its own behalf."[36] For another, any attention to the democratic element of American identity, given the impressive survey data showing that Americans have historically been and still are skeptical about high levels of immigration, inevitably complicates attempts to claim that American ideals are straightforwardly on the side of high levels of immigration. Thus the existence of diverse American political principles counters claims that those principles point in a single direction.[37]

Obviously, a few brief comments like these cannot establish the nature of liberalism or the potential "universality" of American political ideals. But that is not my intention here. I wish merely to show that the debate is more complicated than is sometimes suggested by simplistic formulations about being "a nation of immigrants" or the "first universal nation." There are elements in American identity that buttress a generous immigration policy, such as our current one; but it is also possible to give other readings of that identity in support of a more restrictive policy. History or philosophy can show the importance of immigration in American society or the profound influence of a set of abstract political ideals, enunciated at our

Founding, on subsequent American thought and action. In doing so, they can help delineate the limits within which Americans can regulate immigration while remaining true to their own heritage. But no reading of history or philosophical discussion can fully reveal the "correct" implications of American identity.[38]

What then is the purpose of asserting, and examining, this complexity? Doing so accomplishes three valuable ends. First, it serves as a defense of sorts for the American people. As we have seen, broad American majorities have repeatedly professed hostility to high levels of immigration. If one were simply to concede, without question or elaboration, that the United States is a "nation of immigrants;" that it is committed to certain universal political principles which admit no distinctions among human beings, all of whom are equal and possessed of identical individual rights; and that these facts ought to generate our support for a generous immigration policy, then one could hardly avoid forming an extremely unfavorable impression of the American citizenry. One would have to conclude that they must be either ignorant of their own traditions and values, too stupid to understand the implications of their own beliefs, or perhaps simply irrational or even mean-spirited. But an appreciation of the complexity of American identity permits a more charitable evaluation. There are arguments available, even within the American tradition, for a more restrictive approach to immigration; citizens wishing to reduce current levels can justify their views without being merely "un-American."[39] Our quite different contemporary responses to legal and illegal immigration, for example, rather than being incoherent, might reflect instead a genuine attempt to harmonize diverse strands within American identity.

Furthermore, exploring the complex connections between American identity and our immigration policy points beyond the question of immigration itself toward a whole set of issues that are at the heart of current debates about American political life and the proper course for the nation to chart. Questions about the sense in which America is or is not a "universal" nation underlie the cluster of problems that are often collectively referred to as the "culture wars." Ranging from bilingual education to affirmative action, from the content of the liberal arts to the place of religion in our public life, from government funding of controversial works of art to a perceived decline of general civility within American society, these issues all raise questions about the content of our cultural heritage, that heritage's relation to the political principles underlying our republic, and the extent to which that heritage can or should provide guidance for shaping our future.[40] They point towards the tension between the apparently universal claims of abstract liberalism and the distinctive (and perhaps threatened) American culture in which they are historically embedded.[41] Immigration is only one issue within this debate, but by directly raising questions about the meaning of vital American experiences and ideals, and about whether these ideals can or should be extended to ever more people, it focuses our attention on the currently divisive questions of identity that drive many of our fiercest political disagreements.

Finally, emphasizing the complexity of the American case—which might at first glance appear, as it is sometimes taken to be, a fairly straightforward one—also serves the salutary purpose of forcing us back to the theoretical issues discussed in the previous chapter. There I suggested that the first thing a people does when confronted by the problem of immigration is to reflect on its own identity and consider what kinds of immigration policies would accord with and sustain it; and I claimed that the results of their consideration—different immigration policies for different peoples, matching their different and particular identities—are presumptively legitimate. Pointing out both the room that exists to maneuver within the American tradition, as well as the limits to that room, invites us to ask how we should respond to this indeterminacy and, in particular, how it should practically be resolved. As the argument from chapter three suggests, I believe that the proper response is to let Americans argue about it. This does not mean that they can give any answer they please. America's history of immigration and commitment to the ideals of the Declaration have shaped and ought to shape its immigration policy in ways that will be unique to America and that will differentiate that policy from those of other countries. It is undeniable, I think, that our heritage, both historical and philosophical, entails a certain openness towards immigration, to a degree unusual (though not entirely unique) among the countries of the world.[42] But that openness surely leaves some room for maneuver, room to consider how traditions can be applied in a way appropriate to changing contemporary circumstances.[43] In particular, one could hardly argue that the American heritage of immigration precludes debating questions that, as the brief survey with which I began this discussion showed, have always been a part of that tradition—questions about the number, diversity, or assimilability of immigrants. In an important sense, then, the "correct" implications of American traditions and beliefs depend upon how Americans themselves continue to interpret them.

Ironically, the importance within American identity of abstract political principles, potentially applicable to all of humanity—principles which are sometimes taken to undermine the legitimacy of national boundaries—

actually strengthens this line of argument. For if I was correct to suggest in the last chapter that the central question raised by immigration policy is whether we may legitimately prefer ourselves and our own way of life to others, then for Americans to argue about their own identity—precisely to the extent that universal ideals inform that identity—*is* for Americans to argue about the right answer to this question. Addressing these particular questions of American identity necessarily involves a confrontation with some of the deeper theoretical puzzles I explore in this work. All the more important, then, to let Americans debate them, lest we prejudge the answers to such fundamental questions.

I have sought here simply to illustrate how some abiding issues of national identity underlie and are deeply entangled in the American immigration debate. I have not made specific proposals of my own, mainly because I do not think such an exploration by itself determines a particular outcome. It sets limits to what might be a recognizably "American" immigration policy, but the important questions at stake permit of different answers, some more and some less open to immigration. In such a situation, I have suggested, the appropriate response is to let the American people argue about which aspects of their identity they find most important and compelling. Sometimes, though, examining the relationship between national identity and immigration policy, in addition to revealing what is at stake in a country's debates over immigration, can itself indicate problems that demand some resolution, problems for which old conceptions of identity appear inadequate. Such has been the dilemma faced by Germany in recent years, and it is to that case that I now turn.

Germany

On May 21, 1999, the German parliament approved a groundbreaking reform of the country's citizenship laws. The reform, which took effect on January 1, 2000, departed from previous German practice in two fundamental ways. For the first time, it attributed German citizenship at birth to children of permanently resident non-citizens based solely upon their birth in German territory (thus introducing the principle of *jus soli,* the attribution of citizenship according to place of birth, into German law). And by doing so, it created a potentially sizable class of dual citizens, since many of these children would also inherit a foreign citizenship from their alien parents (through the principle of *jus sanguinis,* the attribution of citizenship according to descent). Although this dual citizenship is only intended to be a temporary status—the children in question are expected to choose one of their citizenships upon reaching maturity (and will automatically lose the German one should they fail to do so)—it nevertheless represents a significant departure from the extremely hostile view of dual citizenship traditionally embodied in German law and policy. These reforms were passed in response to growing unease over the substantial number of aliens, often second- and third-generation immigrants, who were permanently settled within Germany but had not acquired citizenship, either because they had been legally excluded from it or because a combination of social and political factors (especially the prohibition of dual citizenship) had made it difficult or undesirable to obtain, even for those who were legally entitled to it.[44]

The history of German citizenship law and policy and the story of these recent reforms provide a superb example of how national identity shapes a country's approach to immigration, and also of how a focus on national identity can help identify and resolve certain problems in that approach. In what follows, I first describe how German immigration and citizenship law has traditionally reflected a particular understanding of national identity; I then explain how various political events of recent decades made that legal structure problematic; and, finally, I suggest that the struggle over the recent reforms provides an object lesson in how a country can attempt to right wrongs in immigration policy while being guided by its particular understanding of political community. As in the American case, the discussion of Germany will show how deeply embedded in particular visions of national identity immigration policy is.

Rogers Brubaker, in his classic comparison of immigration and citizenship policy in France and Germany, has pointed out that German self-understanding rests upon a sense of shared cultural identity with deep historical roots in the late consolidation of the German state:

> Since national feeling developed before the nation-state, the German idea of the nation was not originally political, nor was it linked to the abstract idea of citizenship. This prepolitical German nation, this nation in search of a state, was conceived not as the bearer of universal political values, but as an organic cultural, linguistic, or racial community—as an irreducibly particular *Volksgemeinschaft*. On this understanding, nationhood is an ethnocultural, not a political fact.[45]

This is the identity of a *Kulturnation,* to use one term of Friedrich Meinecke's famous general distinction between *Kulturnationen* and *Staatsnationen. Kulturnationen,* writes Meinecke, "rest primarily upon the possession of a certain commonly experienced culture . . . . A common language, common literature, and common religion are the most important and effective cultural possessions that create and maintain a *Kulturnation*."[46]

I wish to focus on a crucial word from Brubaker's description of German identity: "ethnocultural." There is, of course, as Brubaker himself notes, "an important difference between ethnic and cultural definitions of nationhood" (210, n. 48). Although the sense of German identity probably rests more on cultural than on explicitly ethnic elements (even if the ethnic elements have at times, needless to say, assumed a distressing prominence), ethnic elements attain a certain official significance through the legal institution of *jus sanguinis*. As Brubaker points out, the close practical connection between these theoretically distinct elements is, due to the pervasive influence of the family, not surprising:

> Common culture may be independent, in the long run, of common descent. But the family plays a crucial part in the transmission of national culture— including not only language but cultural markers such as mores, gestures, and modes of thinking and feeling that are more resistant than language to formalized, organized transmission. Consequently, there is an elective affinity between the familial transmission of citizenship (*jus sanguinis*) and cultural— as well as explicitly ethnic—conceptions of nationhood. (210, n. 48)

Because of the way these elements have traditionally been combined in German citizenship law, Brubaker appropriately refers to the German self-understanding as "ethnocultural." But the potential cleavage within this description is important for our story.

This ethnocultural identity, which arose prior to the creation of a German state, was strengthened by the Prussian failure in the late nineteenth and early twentieth centuries to assimilate its vocal Polish minority, a defining experience for the initial codification of German citizenship law (Brubaker, ch. 6, esp. 125–37). And ironically, just when the horror of National Socialism might have discredited it, "the peculiar circumstances of the immediate postwar period—the total collapse of the state, the massive expulsion of ethnic Germans from Eastern Europe and the Soviet Union, and the imposed division of Germany—reinforced and powerfully relegitimated that self-understanding" (Brubaker, 168). The considerable immigration of postwar decades, however, brought this ethnocultural understanding of German identity under increasing attack.

German citizenship and immigration law—or rather, since Germany has no specific immigration law as such, the provisions of its citizenship law regulating naturalization—traditionally reflected this understanding of Germany as an ethnocultural community quite closely. Unlike that of almost all other Western countries, which typically involve some mixture of *jus sanguinis* and *jus soli,* German citizenship law (prior to the recent reforms) was based entirely upon *jus sanguinis,* ascribing citizenship solely upon descent from citizen parents. This statement requires some qualification: there were, for example, provisions easing the naturalization requirements for spouses of German citizens or for young foreigners who had spent most of their lives and undergone much of their schooling in Germany. It nevertheless remained true that the *ascription* of German citizenship was based exclusively upon *jus sanguinis,* and that attempts to introduce forms of *jus soli* into German law met consistently with suspicion and hostility.

German citizenship has been governed by the *Reichs- und Staatsangehörigkeitsgesetz* (law of citizenship in the empire and state) of 1913.[47] The conditions outlined in this law for the naturalization of foreigners do not, at first glance, sound terribly restrictive; they require, for instance, residence in Germany, the ability to support one's self and one's dependents, and the lack of any criminal record providing legal grounds for expulsion. Yet these conditions do not tell the full story. For they represent only the minimal necessary preconditions for naturalization, without being, by themselves, sufficient to secure that naturalization. Instead, having set a baseline, they leave the actual decision about a prospective naturalization to the relevant administrative authorities, whose decision is guided by the official "Guidelines for Naturalization" (*Einbürgerungsrichtlinien*), a set of administrative regulations agreed upon by the Ministry of the Interior and the various German *Länder.*

These guidelines indicate the genuine difficulty of naturalizing in Germany. Among the "general principles for naturalization" they state clearly,

> The legal prerequisites [for naturalization] in paragraphs 8, 9, and 13 of the *Reichs- und Staatsangehörigkeitsgesetz* (RuStAG) . . . are minimal prerequisites, without which a naturalization cannot be carried out. Their existence alone does not yet justify the naturalization. The conferring of German citizenship can only be considered when a public interest in the naturalization exists. A "public interest" is here a political interest or a social interest of the same rank; the personal wishes and economic interests of the applicant for naturalization can not be decisive, especially because the foreigners resident

here enjoy extensive rights and freedoms according to the German legal order.

The guidelines go on to clarify the content of the required public interest. "The naturalization requires a voluntary and lasting orientation to Germany, fundamental knowledge of our political order, and loyalty to the free, democratic constitutional order." This presumes the mastery of the German language "in speech and writing." Furthermore, naturalization presumes a "fitting-into the German conditions of life; this presupposes as a rule a long-term settlement in the German environment."

Naturalization, then, has been subject to the discretionary judgement of state officials entitled to reject an applicant whom they do not deem thoroughly assimilated into German culture and a valuable addition to the German people. The legal scholar Reinhard Marx has described this administrative discretion in the following terms:

> According to the standing jurisprudence of the *Bundesverwaltungsgericht* [federal administrative court], the regulation of paragraph 8 of the *Reichs- und Staatsangehörigkeitsgesetz* places the naturalization of a foreigner who fulfills the minimal prerequisites cited in this regulation in the dutiful discretion of the relevant authorities. In the exercise of this discretion, the only thing which needs to be taken account of is whether a public interest in the requested naturalization exists. Accordingly, the authority needs to examine not only whether the applicant for naturalization, in light of his personal circumstances, represents a valuable addition to the population, but also whether his naturalization is desirable according to general political, economic, and cultural points of view. In this regard, it is not a matter of balancing the personal interests of the applicant and the interests of the state.[48]

The difficulty of naturalization under this system is neatly summed up by the fundamental "maxim of national policy for German immigration law" (Marx, 153), found among the "general principles for naturalization" in the guidelines: *Die Bundesrepublik Deutschland ist kein Einwanderungsland,* "The Federal Republic of Germany is not a country of immigration"—a sentence often repeated by supporters of the law and as often criticized by its opponents.

The ascription of German citizenship through descent and the difficulty of naturalization for foreigners indicate the strong ethnocultural emphasis that shaped German citizenship and immigration law. But the extent of that emphasis only becomes clear when we contrast the difficulty of naturalization for foreigners with the automatic claim to citizenship that has been extended to ethnic German immigrants. The German constitution speaks primarily not of German citizens, but rather simply of Germans. Article 116 clarifies the meaning of this usage: "A 'German' in the meaning of this Basic Law, subject to other regulation, is a person who possesses German citizenship or who, as a refugee or expellee of German ethnic origin or as the spouse or descendant of such a person, has been admitted into the area of the German Empire according to its state on December 31, 1937." The members of this group of "Germans without German citizenship" were extended a right to naturalization by the first Law for the Regulation of Questions of Citizenship (*Gesetz zur Regelung von Fragen der Staatsangehörigkeit*) of 1955. The relevant section of this law provides, "Whoever is, on the basis of Article 116, section 1, of the Basic Law, a German without possession of German citizenship must be naturalized upon application, unless circumstances justify the assumption that he would endanger the internal or external security of the Federal Republic or of a German province [*Land*]."

These legal provisions were originally intended to help regulate the status of the millions of ethnic Germans who were persecuted in and expelled from eastern Europe following World War II. But they became a tool of Cold War policy following the consolidation of the East German state and the Soviet bloc, when the status of "Germans without German citizenship" continued to be attributed to ethnic Germans fleeing from the East, thus making them eligible for naturalization upon application. This sharp contrast between ethnic Germans and other foreigners was, as Brubaker observed, the most telling indication of the ethnocultural character of German citizenship law: "[W]hile German citizenship is closed to non-German immigrants, it is remarkably open to ethnic German immigrants from Eastern Europe and the Soviet Union" (84).[49]

The combined effects of post-war German immigration and of the Soviet Union's collapse, however, raised a challenge to this legal framework. As scholars have noted, Germany has always been the site of considerable migration: it has witnessed internal labor migration, has served as a way-station for those passing through on their way to the great ports of northern Germany for the journey to more distant destinations, and has produced massive emigration. And during the economic expansion following the war, Germany was finally transformed from a net exporter to a net importer of people, creating what Klaus Bade, a leading German scholar of migration issues and a vocal critic of German immigration policy, has called "a new kind of country of immigration."[50] The new German situation, he says, has been characterized by five main factors or problems:[51] (1) First is the very large group of former guest-workers (*Gastarbeiter*) and their descendants, of whom the greatest number are Turkish. This group now extends sometimes into the third generation on German soil, and thus includes large numbers of young adults and children who have been born and raised in Germany but are not German citizens and who might, theoretically, one day return to their "real" homeland. Bade refers to these people as "einheimische Ausländer," that is, "native foreigners," and sums up their situation thus: "Einheimische gibt es auch mit fremdem Paß" (There are also natives with a foreign passport). (2) In addition to these are large numbers of *Aussiedler*, ethnic Germans from the regions of Eastern Europe that were once either German possessions or heavily settled by German migrants, who have been automatically entitled to German citizenship upon their "return" to Germany, although many of them have little understanding of contemporary German culture and may not even speak the language. In contrast to the *einheimische Ausländer*, Bade names this group "fremde Deutsche," foreign Germans, and he sums up their situation with the words: "Fremde gibt es auch mit deutschem Paß" (There are also aliens with a German passport). (3) A third large group of immigrants is composed of asylees and asylum seekers. These became a source of special concern during the '80s (and have remained such), as Germany's especially inviting asylum laws attracted ever greater numbers of refugees. Significant restrictions of those laws in 1993 led to a decrease of applications, but also to an increase in illegal immigration.

The remaining two elements of Germany's new immigration situation that Bade describes refer to internal German processes of integration: (4) One of them he labels "Menschen über Grenzen," people across borders. This refers to the refugees and others (known as *Übersiedler*) who fled from East Germany to West Germany. Many of these people, Bade notes, experienced "a kind of German-German culture shock" as they discovered "how great the distance between West and East had become, not only in material culture and forms of life, but also in mentalities." (5) Finally, there are "Grenzen über Menschen," borders moving across people, or what occurred with the reunification of Germany. Because this event was shaped and dominated by the West, many of those in the East found themselves in "a kind of imported immigration situation," even though they had never left home. Thus they became "Fremde im eigenen Land," strangers in their own land.

These are the factors that, in Bade's account, constituted Germany's new immigration situation. Perhaps one could add to the list—the movement toward European union and the accompanying internal continental mobility are surely relevant—but Bade's description gives a sense of the complexity and difficulty of the German problem. It has been the first two groups in particular, I want to argue, the *einheimische Ausländer* and the *fremde Deutsche,* that together have raised the most difficult questions about German national identity. Their juxtaposition posed the clearest challenge to the ethnocultural understanding of identity and its consequences for immigration and citizenship, a challenge that led finally to the recent reform legislation.[52]

When the German economy began to recover following World War II, the country faced a severe labor shortage.[53] To fill this need, the government signed agreements with a number of other countries allowing for the recruitment of *Gastarbeiter,* "guest workers." As the name implies, these workers were only supposed to stay temporarily, working for a certain period and then returning home. The agreements were intended to benefit both parties: Germany would meet its need for labor, while the *Gastarbeiter* would find work for themselves and return wealth to their home countries. The first agreement was with Italy in 1955; then came agreements with Spain and Greece in 1960; and others followed. Turkey would ultimately produce both the largest migrant population—there were more than two million Turkish citizens living legally in Germany at the end of 1995[54]—as well as the most visible and obviously different one, so that the Turkish minority in Germany has in some ways come to stand for the whole set of problems associated with the former *Gastarbeiter.*

The number of foreign workers rose steadily until the oil crisis of 1973, when the government ended the policy. This caused a temporary decline in the number of foreign workers in the country, but it then had the unexpected effect of actually increasing the total number of foreigners present: with the prospect of a return to Germany officially foreclosed, people became more reluctant to leave in the first place, and the process of family reunification then swelled their ranks. The foreign population, enjoying relatively high birthrates compared to Germans, continued to grow, and it became more and more obvious that the vast majority of foreigners would remain residents of Germany. In the mid-1980s the German government sought to encourage many of them to return to their countries of origin by offering large sums of money to those who would do so, but even this did not substantially alter the situation.

By now, of course, many of the former *Gastarbeiter* have had children in Germany; indeed, many of those children are now, in turn, raising children of their own. We are thus into the third generation of migrants in Germany, the last two born and raised on German soil. They are no longer temporary sojourners, but permanent immigrants. Many of them know no country other than Germany; they speak the German language; and their culture is much more German than it is anything resembling that of their countries of origin—or, rather, of their parents' and grandparents' countries of origin. As Bade writes,

> People of foreign citizenship, who have lived continuously in the Federal Republic for decades, as well as their children and now even grandchildren, who have been born and raised here, are in a legal sense, to be sure, still mostly foreigners. But for a long time they have been no longer aliens with a German residence permit, but rather natives with a foreign passport. In-between and transitional forms dominate their forms of life, mentalities, and self-understandings. In the discussion about multicultural, every-day life, they are paradoxically described—in a way corresponding to the paradoxical immigration situation in Germany—as 'native foreigners,' 'foreign domestics,' 'domestic foreigners,' and as 'foreign, hyphenated Germans' in a 'non-country of immigration with immigrants.'[55]

But German citizenship law, which continued to be based on *jus sanguinis,* did not change to accomodate this situation. To be sure, changes in the law in 1993 granted a right to naturalization to young foreigners who had regularly resided in Germany for at least eight years and had attended a German school for six years, and also to other foreigners who had regularly resided in Germany for at least 15 years and could provide for themselves and their dependents. But the law, reflecting the German hostility toward multiple citizenship (a hostility not surprising in a country with a traditionally ethnocultural identity) retained the crucial requirement that one give up one's previous citizenship, something many foreign residents have been reluctant to do, often because it would create political or economic hardships for them in their home countries. They have, of course, been all the more reluctant to do so, because, as the immigration guidelines indicate, "becoming German" is thought to involve a far-reaching process of assimilation into the German way of life. Even those with a right to naturalization, then, such as thoroughly acculturated youths who have grown up in the country, are in a sense invited to give up the last formal tie to their heritage in exchange for reluctant acceptance into a community that regards them as something less than fully "German." Thus it is not surprising that these changes in the laws have produced relatively small increases in naturalizations. As Brubaker writes, "Without a changed understanding of what it is to be—or to become—German, the liberalization of naturalization policy will not produce a dramatic surge in naturalization" (79).[56]

The *Aussiedler* present exactly the opposite phenomenon. Germany had historically sent out large numbers of emigrants into Russia and Eastern Europe. After World War II, more than 12 million of these ethnic Germans were persecuted and either fled or were expelled and sent back to Germany.[57] Still, roughly four million remained in areas throughout the East, where they often faced diverse forms of persecution and discrimination, including forced resettlement.[58] Despite their long residence abroad, many of these groups had maintained a strong sense of their German identity and culture, which now made them obvious targets in countries that had suffered so heavily from the Nazi attackers and occupiers. The difficult position of these ethnic Germans fostered a strong desire to return to their ancestral homeland and live once again as "Germans among Germans."[59] Those who eventually succeeded in returning, as we have seen, possessed, by virtue of their German ethnicity, an automatic right to naturalization under the provisions of the constitution and citizenship laws which were originally intended to regulate the status of the expellees following the war.

Unfortunately, the idea of living as "Germans among Germans" that many of these *Aussiedler* cherish often has only the most tenuous connection to contemporary reality. As Bade writes,

> The 'Germanness' of the *Aussiedler* should not be confused with what is happily discussed in the Federal Republic as 'German identity' and is often even held, in the Western world, to be itself a kind of identity-shaping mental fad of the Germans. 'Germanness' [for the *Aussiedler*] meant the long-lived cultural and mental bonds of integration that were passed on from generation to generation, which today are still partly visible only in dialect and custom. In the apparently so enlightened Federal Republic, on the other hand, talk about 'Germanness' reminds many precisely of that ethnonationalist error of German history that culminated ultimately in National Socialism—the consequences of which were so disastrous for the fate of the *Aussiedler* in particular. The *Aussiedler* thus came under suspicion, at their longed-for destination, as supposed harbingers of a dark past—precisely because of their orientation towards that 'Germanness' that had been grounds for persecution, expulsion, and oppression in the regions from which they came.[60]

These "Germans" had lived elsewhere for so long that the Germany they remembered (or that had been described to them) bore little resemblance to its present version. Accustomed to authoritarian polities and controlled economies, they suddenly found themselves in a pluralistic democracy and free-market economy. Both the diversity and vitality of liberal democracy as well as the ways of "thinking and acting in the cold elbow-society of the 'wild West'" were strange to them.[61] Many of them could not even speak German, and those who could had often had to learn it as a foreign language.[62] Despite their claim to naturalization, the *Aussiedler* were genuinely foreign. In Bade's words, "At their longed-for destination, the 'new citizens' will long remain alien—as 'Germans among Germans,' possessing all the rights of citizenship, but nevertheless in a real and in many respects even especially complicated immigration situation."[63]

The pairing of these two groups, the former *Gastarbeiter* and the *Aussiedler,* has directly challenged the ethnocultural understanding of German national identity. They are, in a sense, that understanding's embodied contradiction. As Bade puts it, their combined presence creates "an experience that irritate[s] those who [are] accustomed to thinking in the conceptual pairs 'German/native' and 'foreign/alien:' alongside long resident native foreigners appeared newly immigrated alien Germans . . . ."[64] The second- and third-generation descendants of the former *Gastarbeiter,* born and raised in Germany, are culturally German—what else could they be?— but ethnically foreign. The *Aussiedler,* after sometimes several generations in a foreign country, are ethnically German but culturally foreign. The striking contrast between these groups inevitably drives a wedge into the ethnocultural understanding of identity and pries apart its two halves. If it was once possible for Germans to overlook the distinction between membership based on ethnicity and membership based on a shared culture, because the two usually went together in practice, it is possible no longer. The ethnocultural understanding has become untenable.

Some may initially resist this conclusion. After all, the German government's repeated claim, *Deutschland ist kein Einwanderungsland*—Germany is not a country of immigration—does not merely seek to represent a set of empirical facts. As Brubaker has cogently observed,

> Since the mid-1970s critics have challenged this formulation, marshaling impressive evidence that temporary labor migrants had become permanent settlers. Yet in a sense the critics have missed the point. For the *kein Einwanderungsland* claim articulates not a social or demographic fact but a political-cultural norm, an element of national self-understanding. (174)

Yet even if that claim does not simply express a social or demographic fact, it is nonetheless surely dependent upon such facts. And the gap between the social facts of contemporary Germany and the idea expressed in the *kein Einwanderungsland* statement has simply become too wide to remain plausible. Insofar as that statement is intended to express an idea of Germany as an ethnocultural community, it can no longer be maintained—not when the acculturated children of undisputed immigrants are held at arm's length while culturally foreign immigrants are simultaneously granted full membership solely on the basis of ethnicity.

The recent reforms in the citizenship laws are Germany's response to the rift created between ethnicity and citizenship by contemporary events. In the abstract, one can imagine a country responding to the collapse of its ethnocultural self-image in three ways: by focusing on the ethnic aspect of its identity; by abandoning the identity altogether and starting new with something else; or by emphasizing the cultural elements of its identity. I want to suggest that the German reforms represent a partial move in the third direction, and that this is both a reasonable and a defensible choice for contemporary Germany to make. First, though, it may be worth briefly commenting on the other two possibilities.

Omitting considerations of culture and focusing exclusively on ethnicity would have had the advantage of requiring little change in the laws—on such a view, there would be no reason to make immigration or naturalization easier for ethnic foreigners, and every reason to maintain an open door towards whatever *Aussiedler* continued to come. But for other reasons it would have been undesirable and surprising. Certainly, the world would hardly have welcomed a renewed emphasis upon ethnicity as a criterion for inclusion and exclusion in a united Germany. And despite the worries occasionally raised by new outbreaks of right-wing violence, a sense of responsibility for and guilt about the Nazi past seems strong enough in the minds of Germans at large to have precluded such a move. Furthermore, it is doubtful that such a reconceptualization of German identity would have actually satisfied many people. Take away the cultural bonds that traditionally accompanied ethnicity, and there is little reason to think that a community formed around the latter alone would serve the same ends that the combination of ethnicity with culture served.

A second possibility would have been to reject both elements of the ethnocultural combination. One might have then sought to build a new German identity around, for example, allegiance to a particular set of constitutional principles. This might have resembled the sort of "constitutional patriotism" that Jürgen Habermas, for instance, has proposed. Habermas argues that because the diverse citizens of contemporary multicultural societies do not share any single "ethical-cultural" understanding of human life, any polity that seeks to embody such an understanding fails to treat them as equals and cannot serve as the focus of their loyalty. In such circumstances, he suggests, the appropriate object of citizens' loyalty is rather the set of liberal, democratic, and constitutional principles—and the procedures embodying them—that constitute the political culture and that recognize the equal autonomy of all individual citizens.

> The neutrality of the law vis-à-vis internal ethical differentiation stems from the fact that in complex societies the citizenry as a whole can no longer be held together by a substantive consensus on values but only by a consensus on the procedures for the legitimate enactment of laws and the legitimate exercise of power. Citizens who are politically integrated in this way share the rationally based conviction that unrestrained freedom of communication in the political public sphere, a democratic process for settling conflicts, and the constitutional channeling of political power together provide a basis for checking illegitimate power and ensuring that administrative power is used in the equal interest of all. The universalism of legal principles is reflected in a procedural consensus, which must be embedded in the context of a historically specific political culture through a kind of constitutional patriotism.[65]

Such a view would point towards a more generous immigration policy and, with respect to naturalization, would require of applicants that they "become German" only in the limited sense of agreeing to the liberal, democratic principles of the German constitution rather than adopting some broader vision of "Germanness": "the identity of the political community . . . is founded on the constitutional principles anchored in the political culture and not on the basic ethical orientations of the cultural form of life predominant in that country."[66]

Furthermore, it might be suggested, such a position has roots in postwar German identity. I have already alluded to Germany's extremely—even uniquely—generous asylum policy, which despite some restrictions in recent years continues to be quite generous.[67] This policy, one might claim, reflects Germany's commitment to liberalism and its recognition of universal human rights that transcend national boundaries and depend upon neither ethnic nor cultural affiliation. A Germany committed to these ideals might regard all potential immigrants and citizens impartially, necessarily putting the "native foreigners" and the "foreign Germans" on an even footing.

Though preferable to the previous alternative, this approach would not, I think, have been the best solution. The attempt to connect this proposal with German identity relies heavily upon the appeal to asylum policy, although it is not clear that asylum policy, which of its nature seeks to address exceptional circumstances, is the most appropriate basis for drawing general conclusions about national identity—to say nothing of the fact that, when the number of asylum-seekers began to cause problems in the late '80s and early '90s, it was asylum policy that was restricted and not naturalization policy that was liberalized, suggesting that, in the eyes of most Germans at least, the latter was more central to German identity than the former. Furthermore, even if we accept the weight given to asylum policy, this proposal still raises difficult questions about the implications of liberalism and its compatibility (or incompatibility) with various forms of ethnic or cultural preference.[68]

More troubling, however, is the radicality of this proposal and of the corresponding changes it would have required both in law and in national identity. Indeed, the history of the recent reform legislation strikingly illustrates the distance separating this view from any understanding of German identity widely shared among the German people. In September of 1998, Gerhard Schröder and the Social Democrats (SPD) ended the decades-long government of Helmut Kohl and the Christian Democratic Union (CDU). One of the SPD's prominent campaign promises was to reform Germany's citizenship laws and facilitate the naturalization of the country's large foreign resident population. In January of 1999, the government presented proposals to accomplish this, of which perhaps the most significant was to permit for the first time large numbers of people to acquire German citizenship without renouncing their previous citizenship, and thus to acquire dual citizenship, of which German law—as one would expect of law based on an ethnocultural perspective—has traditionally taken an extremely dim view. The government's conservative opponents, the CDU and its Bavarian sister party, the Christian Social Union (CSU), immediately launched a nation-wide petition drive against the proposed reforms.[69] They quickly gathered millions of signatures, and in February their drive met with greater success than even they had probably dreamed of: In state elections in Hessen, one of the German *Länder*, after a campaign in which the CDU had made opposition to the proposed introduction of dual citizenship its primary issue, the governing SPD-Green coalition was soundly defeated and replaced by a coalition of the CDU and the Free Democrats (FDP). Not only did the CDU's victory appear to reflect a striking renunciation—all the more striking for having been unexpected—of the proposed citizenship reforms, it also had profound practical consequences for Schröder's government, which as a result lost its majority in the Bundesrat, the house of the German federal parliament representing the individual

Länder (analogous to the U.S. Senate). Because the Bundesrat's approval is necessary for changes in Germany's citizenship law, this meant that the government could no longer expect to pass its desired reforms.[70]

These events suggest powerfully that Germany does not view itself as an association of people joined simply by their shared commitment to certain constitutional and democratic ideals, open in principle to anyone willing to assent to them, regardless of ethnocultural status. On the contrary, they demonstrate the radical and unrealistic change entailed by any proposal to abandon the ethnocultural vision of German identity entirely. It is one thing to ask a people to modify its self-understanding, another to jettison that self-understanding altogether, and the remarkable resistance inspired by these initially proposed reforms show clearly that such a jettisoning—even if we were prepared to accept it on its merits, which I do not claim to do here—is simply not in the cards for Germany. If there had been no way of adapting conventional notions of German identity to address contemporary difficulties, then this initial reform proposal might have been the best to be hoped for. But subsequent events demonstrated that a less radical alternative was available.

Following its rout in Hessen and the loss of its majority in the *Bundesrat,* the government—visibly chastened by its setback—proposed a new compromise plan, which, with the support of the FDP, ultimately passed and became the new law. Under the compromise plan, children born in Germany to foreign parents, at least one of whom has resided in Germany for eight years, automatically receive German citizenship, even if they simultaneously acquire the citizenship(s) of their parents by descent. If they thus acquire multiple citizenships, however, they must choose, between the ages of 18 and 23, which citizenship they wish to maintain, and the failure to choose (apart from certain exceptional cases in which special hardships prevent their release from a foreign citizenship) will result in the loss of their German citizenship.[71] The new law thus introduces *jus soli* into German citizenship law, and it does so in a way that will inevitably create a substantial number of dual citizens. At the same time, this newly permitted form of dual citizenship is only intended to be a temporary phenomenon, since its possessors are ultimately required to opt for one citizenship or the other (hence the German name for the plan, *Optionsmodell*).

These reforms, I suggest, are closest to the third type of possible response to the fragmentation of ethnocultural identity mentioned earlier, namely, a shift away from the ethnic elements in favor of the simply cultural elements within it. The introduction of *jus soli* weakens the ethnic character of German citizenship law in a crucial way: one can now become a German citizen, regardless of one's ethnicity or the nationality of one's parents, simply by virtue of birth on German soil. Indeed, the new provisions for *jus soli* are in some respects even more far-reaching than they might have been, since many west European countries automatically attribute citizenship to a child born of foreign parents only if one of those parents was also born within the country, whereas the German reforms require only eight years' residence.[72] At the same time, the *Optionsmodell* that the government was compelled to accept, requiring children who acquire dual citizenship at birth to choose upon maturity which citizenship they wish to maintain, reflects a continuing understanding of German citizenship as embodying an extremely close relationship between the individual citizen and the people as a whole, a relationship that is ultimately incompatible with similar, competing loyalties.

The German reforms do not, of course, perfectly correspond to any of the three possible responses considered in the abstract. One additional element of the changes, for example, might be taken as a move towards a kind of Habermasian constitutional patriotism. Under the new laws, foreigners legally residing in Germany are now entitled to citizenship after only eight years, instead of the previous fifteen.[73] In order to gain that citizenship, the applicant must express his commitment to Germany's free, democratic, constitutional order. This reduced waiting period, combined with the emphasis on a kind of constitutional loyalty, might appear to be a form of the second possibility considered, a move away from the ethnocultural identity towards a simple union around shared political values. It would, however, be a mistake to make too much of this. For one thing, the required expression of commitment to the constitutional order is paired with a second requirement for receiving citizenship, mastery of the German language. Furthermore, it is important to emphasize that both of these are requirements for claiming entitlement to German citizenship. The mere fact of eight years' residence, in other words, does not by itself guarantee one's right to citizenship; rather, the right to naturalization only exists if an applicant makes the required declaration of loyalty and demonstrates mastery of German. And adult applicants for naturalization, unlike the children who may acquire dual citizenship at birth, are still required to give up any other citizenships they may have when acquiring the German one.

It is also worth emphasizing that the limited introduction of *jus soli* is itself a recognition of the cultural elements of national identity, as I understand it. The granting of citizenship to adults who have resided in the country for eight years, speak the language fluently, and profess loyalty to the regime, like its attribution to children whose parents reside in the country and who are likely to grow up there themselves, indicates a recognition that citizenship should rightly reflect certain facts about cultural membership. Though a country can certainly take steps (like immigration regulations) to nourish or preserve elements of its culture, culture is not something set in stone or that can be frozen over time in the face of changing circumstances. A concern with culture broadly, with national identity as I have discussed it, though it may contain aspects that are in some sense mythical, cannot be purely a myth: it must be concerned with who "the people" really are. It must, that is to say, be concerned with certain actual facts. Insofar as much of the German dilemma arose because people who had spent their entire lives within the German culture, and whose parents may have done the same, faced deep obstacles to full acceptance through citizenship as a member of the German people, the introduction of *jus soli* and the easing of naturalization indicate a recognition that, as a people becomes ethnically less homogeneous, a genuine concern for its culture must also reach beyond ethnic bounds to embrace those who actually participate in it.[74]

Finally, the new German laws may even be a more satisfactory compromise than other, more abstractly pure attempts to focus on (traditional German) culture might have been. For example, if all that were desired were to eliminate the discrepancy between excluding the children and grandchildren of long-resident aliens and automatically including ethnic Germans whose ancestors had lived elsewhere for generations, it would have sufficed to become more restrictive towards the latter, eliminating all preferences for the *Aussiedler* without becoming any more lenient towards the *Gastarbeiter* and their descendants. If both groups were viewed as culturally foreign, then immigration and naturalization policies reoriented towards culture, even without any reference to ethnicity, could have become simply more restrictive, rather than less. But this would surely not have been a preferable solution. Not only would it have neglected the facts described in the previous paragraph—the way culture changes as the people themselves change, and the varieties of assimilation, integration, and adaptation that inevitably occur when an immigrant group settles somewhere permanently—it would also have arguably done the *Aussiedler* an injustice, since their original emigration had often been encouraged by the German government and since that government's imperial ambitions (assisted, often enough, by persecution in the emigrants' new countries) helped to keep alive over time their sense of themselves as German. The more cautious reforms actually embraced by Germany, by contrast, show nicely how a people can adjust its sense of national identity in light of changes in the nation, while still holding to important aspects of its self-understanding, seeking in the process to recognize a variety of conflicting moral claims. Indeed, simply by showing how complex the web of such conflicting claims can be, the German case provides a salutary reminder against simple solutions or the careless application of noble principles, even in the name of justice.

The German reforms are not, of course, perfect. Indeed, their very caution predictably provoked criticism from those who thought they had not gone far enough, and who would have preferred, for example, a more unambiguous embrace of dual citizenship. On the other hand, the equally forceful criticisms from the other side, those who thought the new reforms already departed too radically from German norms, may indicate that the compromise was a reasonable accommodation of conflicting points of view. But they do leave important questions unanswered. The most important of these, perhaps, relates to the *Optionsmodell:* If a child who now acquires German and another citizenship at birth refuses to choose one or the other by his 23rd birthday, does the German constitution permit him to be deprived of his citizenship against his will?[75] Thus we should not expect to have heard the last of the debates over the meaning of German citizenship.[76] Nevertheless, Germany's struggle to adapt to changing circumstances and do justice to a complex moral and political situation while still remaining true to its own vision of political community provides an excellent illustration of how a people, by reflecting upon its own national identity, might try to meet, in a fair and reasonable way, the challenges posed by contemporary immigration dilemmas.

In closing, I want to say a brief word about the reflections on America and Germany presented here. First, I wish to comment on what might be perceived as a discrepancy between the two treatments: my discussion of the United States is quite neutral and noncommittal, whereas that of Germany, by contrast, claims to identify an important shortcoming in policy that needed to be rectified by some such changes as the recent reforms. Why the different assessments? The first thing to be said is that the degree of criticism implied by the discussion of Germany should not be exaggerated. Indeed, if it is properly understood, the apparent discrepancy more or less vanishes. For the claim about German policy advanced here is no more than this: that policy, even on its own terms, no longer made sense, perhaps by the mid-eighties, certainly by the mid-nineties. I have not argued that German policy failed to live up to some abstract standard or universal principle; I have not argued that it was necessarily or inherently unjust, regardless of circumstances. I have claimed only that in the particular circumstances that had developed in Germany by the end of the century, old citizenship policies had become incoherent. Developed to reflect and preserve an ethnocultural understanding of German identity, they were being applied in a setting where ethnicity and culture no longer went together. Far from being a strong claim or bold criticism, I consider this a fairly cautious and uncontroversial description; after all, the laws' incoherence was sufficiently evident to enough Germans that it sparked the extraordinary recent debate over reforming the laws. I make no similar criticisms of America simply because I do not currently see the same kind of dilemma within American policy.

Incoherence is not the whole of injustice, of course, and perhaps some readers will be disappointed by such a tame assessment. It is therefore worth emphasizing that this kind of criticism is especially appropriate here, given the nature of my larger approach, for two reasons. First, it is precisely the burden of my argument that countries are entitled to considerable discretion in crafting immigration policies reflecting their particular identities and visions of political community. From this perspective, the kind of criticism directed here at German policies, careful though it is, is quite valuable, for it serves, as it were, as an invitation to the German people to reflect upon their identity and their dilemmas, to ponder the questions of who they are and who they wish to be. If my arguments have merit, theory can sketch the outlines or limits of a country's reasonable discretion—as my discussion of America also, if less obviously, seeks to do, by drawing attention to the competing universalist and particularist understandings of American identity—but then, having sketched those limits, it should leave a people broad scope to make its own decisions.[77]

The second reason why this kind of criticism is appropriate here is simply that my purpose is not primarily to criticize at all—less, as I suggested at the outset, to offer advice than to illustrate a process. The discussions of America and Germany are intended to flesh out the claim that immigration policies are, inevitably, deeply connected to particular visions of political community—to drive us back, in other words, to the argument of chapter three. Understanding the complexity and particularity of the relationship between identity and immigration should, I hope, make us respectful of the delicate judgements, fraught with rich historical meaning, that countries make in these areas. To condemn a country's decisions about how it will be shaped by immigration—assuming that its policy represents some plausible interpretation of that country's history and identity—is inevitably to condemn the way of life that its policy is designed to nurture and sustain. In such circumstances, a degree of humility and circumspection is appropriate, and theory should press its claims with caution.

Chapter 5

IMMIGRATION AND POLITICAL COMMUNITY:
TWO CASE STUDIES IN THEORY

In chapter two I discussed at length Joseph Carens's argument in favor of open borders, claiming that it rests upon an allegiance to liberalism (or even a certain variety of liberalism). In chapter three I broadened that argument, suggesting that any position on immigration is inevitably linked to a larger understanding of the nature and purposes of politics, an understanding which, among other things, will include some view of the extent to which culture and politics may appropriately be intertwined. In the last chapter I sought to illustrate this intertwining at the level of practice by examining the immigration policies of the United States and Germany. Now I want to ascend once more to the level of theory and illustrate it there by thinking about the close relationship between immigration and conceptions of political community in the work of two highly regarded contemporary theorists, Will Kymlicka and Michael Walzer.

In the case of Kymlicka, I shall be working from the ground up, as it were. Kymlicka has not, to the best of my knowledge, taken an explicit position on what norms a country might be subject to in setting immigration policy.[1] But in the course of writing on multiculturalism and minority rights he has commented upon immigrants and their relation to the society around them. Furthermore, because Kymlicka is the thinker who has done the most in recent years to argue that culture should play an important role in liberal theory, he addresses many of the issues that I raised in chapter three. So I ask what type of immigration policy might naturally arise from his general arguments about the place of culture in liberal polities. Finally, although I discussed the implications of postmodernism for immigration in chapter two, considering Kymlicka also gives us the opportunity to think about what kind of immigration policy a non-postmodern multiculturalist might be inclined to support.

The discussion of Walzer will work in the opposite direction, much as did my earlier discussion of Carens. Walzer's account—which, it will become clear, resembles my own—is the most sophisticated scholarly defense of a state's right to determine its own immigration policy. So in his case I will be reflecting upon the theoretical foundations that support his argument in favor of such a right.

The main purpose of these discussions, then, is further to illustrate the claim already made in chapter three: that the position one takes (or would be likely to take) on immigration is connected to one's broader under-standing of political life. In discussing these thinkers, I shall also try to address some of the problems raised by their arguments, and I shall disagree with them at points. For the sake of clarity, I should state here at the outset that I do not imagine these disagreements to be decisive objections to either of the authors under consideration, both of whose arguments I find sophisticated and stimulating. Rather, the cautions I raise represent simply my own attempt to explore more deeply the issues of politics and culture that lie just beneath the surface of any discussion of immigration. In any case, the reader should remember that the point of these discussions and disagreements is to illustrate the connections between theories of politics and immigration policies and to suggest how changes in emphasis at the theoretical level might also shape policy decisions.

Kymlicka

Will Kymlicka is the foremost contemporary defender of group rights for minorities. He bases his defense upon an argument about the relation between individual autonomy and culture, an argument first made in *Liberalism, Community, and Culture* and repeated more recently in *Multicultural Citizenship.*[2] This argument constitutes a response to the debate of the last few decades between liberals and communitarians. Specifically, Kymlicka seeks to counter charges that liberals view human beings as isolated, atomistic individuals without any important ties to the surrounding culture. Kymlicka's response has two parts: first, an argument that the central value of liberalism is individual autonomy, and second, an argument that such autonomy is only possible within a culture that functions as a "context of choice" (MC, 82). Because liberals value individual autonomy, Kymlicka reasons, they must also value the cultural context that makes the exercise of autonomy possible.

This argument is worth spelling out in more detail. Kymlicka argues that from a liberal point of view, the primary interest that individuals have is in leading a good life, and this interest produces a number of important freedoms.

> The defining feature of liberalism is it that [*sic*] ascribes certain fundamental freedoms to each individual. In particular, it grants people a very wide freedom of choice in terms of how they lead their lives. It allows people to reconsider that decision, and adopt a new and hopefully better plan of life. (MC, 80)

This definition contains two elements, choice and revisability. First, people must be permitted to choose their own plans of life, rather than have those plans dictated to them. Kymlicka offers several reasons for this, but the most important is that "paternalistic restrictions on liberty often simply do not work—lives do not go better by being led from the outside, in accordance with values the person does not endorse" (MC, 81). The second element of the definition, that people be free to reconsider their decisions, is also important. In the course of the quest to lead a good life, we may decide that we were mistaken—that the beliefs or actions we thought would produce that life in fact do not, and that some other set of beliefs or actions would be better. And when this happens, we should be free to change course and act on our new beliefs. "Since we can be wrong about the worth or value of what we are currently doing, and since no one wants to lead a life based on false beliefs about its worth, it is of fundamental importance that we be able rationally to assess our conceptions of the good in the light of new information or experiences, and to revise them if they are not worthy of our continued allegiance" (MC, 81). Thus Kymlicka offers "two preconditions for leading a good life:" first, "that we lead our life from the inside, in accordance with our beliefs about what gives value to life;" and second, "that we be free to question those beliefs, to examine them in light of whatever information, examples, and arguments our culture can provide" (81). In other words, Kymlicka offers an account of liberalism in which the fundamental value is individual autonomy.[3]

This may not sound like a position especially open to a defense of culture. Yet Kymlicka's argument then takes an interesting turn. For the individual autonomy that liberalism values, he suggests, does not exist in a vacuum. Rather it has certain prerequisites. In particular, the free individual must have various possibilities from which to choose and the ability to understand what those choices would entail. It is one's culture that provides these options and clarifies their practical meaning. "[F]reedom involves making choices amongst various options, and our societal culture not only provides these options, but also makes them meaningful to us" (MC, 83). Kymlicka envisions this in a fairly concrete way, I think. He writes,

> The decision about how to lead our lives must ultimately be ours alone, but this decision is always a matter of selecting what we believe to be most valuable from the various options available, selecting from a context of choice which provides us with different ways of life. This is important because the range of options is determined by our cultural heritage. Different ways of life are not simply different patterns of physical movements. The physical movements only have meaning to us because they are identified as having significance by our *culture,* because they fit into some pattern of activities which is culturally recognized as a way of leading one's life. (LCC, 164–5; italics in original; paragraph division omitted)

The exercise of individual freedom, on this view, is not some abstract enterprise, but rather involves concrete decisions about actual choices that affect the course of one's life: whether to attend a given school, take a certain job, marry a particular person. But the specific content of these choices—what it will really be like to pursue a particular occupation, for example—varies from place to place, depending upon the standards, values, and expectations of the local culture. Thus to become a Catholic priest, for instance, is surely a very different sort of thing in Italy than in China. The choices available to an individual, in other words, are the products of the surrounding culture, and that culture, through its traditions, customs, and institutions, provides its members with concrete examples of what it means for someone living in it to make a particular choice. As Kymlicka puts it, "The freedom which liberals demand for individuals is not primarily the freedom to go beyond one's language and history, but rather the freedom to move around within one's societal culture, to distance oneself from particular cultural roles, to choose which features of the culture are most worth developing, and which are without value" (MC, 90–1).

It is on the basis of this account of culture as a "context of choice," the necessary prerequisite for the individual autonomy that liberalism values, that Kymlicka develops his defense of group rights for minorities. He distinguishes between two different kinds of groups and their corresponding rights. The first type of group he calls "national minorities," that is, "historical communit[ies], more or less institutionally complete, occupying a given territory or homeland, sharing a distinct language and culture," which form minorities within a larger such nation in which they are located (MC, 11). Such groups, Kymlicka argues, are typically entitled to various rights of self-government. The second type of group includes ethnic communities formed within a country through immigration. Unlike national minorities, immigrant groups do not possess what Kymlicka calls a "societal culture—that is, a culture which provides its members with meaningful ways of life across the full range of human activities, including social, educational, religious, recreational, and economic life, encompassing both public and private spheres. These [societal] cultures tend to be territorially concentrated, and based on a shared language" (MC, 76).[4] Immigrants (with some exceptions, such as refugees) have voluntarily left their own societal cultures and homelands behind in order to start a new life in a new nation, and they do not expect to recreate their former society in their new country. Thus they are not entitled to the same rights of self-government as national minorities are. What they are entitled to, Kymlicka suggests, are "polyethnic rights," which are "intended to help ethnic groups and religious minorities express their cultural particularity and pride without it hampering their success in the economic and political institutions of the dominant society" (MC, 31).

This argument looks as though it might very well provide support for a government's right to regulate immigration. For the members of a majority culture—or of the only culture, in states with only one—appear to have exactly the same interest in their culture as a "context of choice" as do the members of minority cultures. Kymlicka focuses on the rights of minority cultures because they, unlike majority ones, face the serious threat of extinction. But his argument rests upon the idea that every individual, regardless of the culture to which she belongs, has the same interest in that culture's preservation. And, in fact, he has explicitly recognized that a "minority which seeks to sustain a distinct societal culture must . . . have some control over immigration policies," because of the dangers that unrestricted immigration (or immigration regulated by someone else with other interests in mind) could pose for the minority culture's continued existence.[5] Presumably, on this argument, whatever rights a minority culture possesses in this regard, a majority culture—so long as it respects the rights of any minority cultures within it—should also possess, for exactly the same reasons.

This train of thought is supported by two other features of Kymlicka's argument. First is his discussion of the rights to which immigrants are entitled. As I have mentioned, Kymlicka, though he thinks that immigrants are entitled to "polyethnic rights" as a way of helping them adjust to the conditions of their new society without undue suffering, does not think them entitled to the rights of self-government that are due a national minority. Thus, a country which receives immigrants is not obligated to help them recreate their original societal culture in their new homeland; on the contrary, it can justifiably expect them to assimilate to its own culture. "After all," Kymlicka says,

> most immigrants (as distinct from refugees) choose to leave their own culture. They have uprooted themselves, and they know when they come that their success, and that of their children, depends on integrating into the institutions [in the case of America] of English-speaking society . . . . In deciding to uproot themselves, immigrants voluntarily relinquish some of the rights that go along with their original national membership. (MC, 95–6)

If culture has the importance attached to it in Kymlicka's theory, and if a country is justified in expecting immigrants to assimilate, then it seems reasonable to conclude that that country is justified in regulating immigration in the first place, restricting it, for example, when it has reason to fear that the requisite degree of assimilation is unlikely to occur.

A second factor in support of this reading is that Kymlicka explicitly raises the analogy between minority nationalities and states with regard to regulating immigration. He writes,

> The existence of states, and the right of governments to control entry across state borders, raises a deep paradox for liberals. Most liberal theorists defend their theories in terms of 'equal respect for persons', and the 'equal rights of individuals'. This suggests that all 'persons' or 'individuals' have an equal right to enter a state, participate in its political life, and share in its natural resources. (MC, 124)

In fact, though, few people are willing to endorse such a position.[6] On the contrary, it is generally accepted that states are entitled to reserve the rights of entry and participation to citizens, and the prosperous liberal countries of the West routinely refuse to admit large numbers of people who simply had the bad fortune to have been born elsewhere. But, Kymlicka continues, the apparent paradox dissolves when we realize that even liberals ought to regard cultural membership as an important good: "[S]ome limits on immigration can be justified if we recognize that liberal states exist, not only to protect standard rights and opportunities of individuals, but also to protect people's cultural membership" (MC, 125). Kymlicka's point, of course, is that accepting this notion also requires one to accept the legitimacy of various group rights: "I believe that the orthodox liberal view about the right of states to determine who has citizenship rests on the same principles which justify group-differentiated citizenship within states, and that accepting the former leads logically to the latter" (MC, 124). Obviously, though, this argumentative move is nonsense unless one is prepared to accept the view that states do have the right to regulate admissions on the grounds stated.[7]

These considerations strongly suggest that Kymlicka's theory might support the view that states are entitled to control immigration in light of their particular identities. There are, however, other elements of Kymlicka's argument that point in a different direction and stand in considerable tension with this interpretation. We can best see this by considering a specific problem that Kymlicka addresses: What should we do about nonliberal minorities? Protecting their societal cultures obstructs, rather than promotes, individual autonomy and thus undermines the very reason we have for valuing culture in the first place. Perhaps such cultures do not deserve protection. In terms of immigration, then, one could envision Kymlicka's adopting a variation of one of the possibilities suggested in my examination of Carens: immigration restrictions are only acceptable on the part of those states that already embody Kymlicka's preferred form of liberalism; other states, which do not protect individual autonomy, are not entitled to protect their cultures in this way.

Kymlicka does not take this position, however. Rather, he adopts a more conventional view of how a liberal state ought to respond to a non-liberal one: by tolerating it, protesting its injustices and offering it various incentives to change but not actively seeking its destruction or dissolution. Thus he writes, "The aim of liberals should not be to dissolve non-liberal nations, but rather to seek to liberalize them" (MC, 94). In making this argument, Kymlicka distinguishes between "*identifying* a defensible liberal theory of minority rights" and "*imposing* that liberal theory" (MC, 164; his italics). "Liberals have a right, and a responsibility, to speak out against such [illiberal] injustice. Hence liberal reformers inside the culture should seek to promote their liberal principles, through reason or example, and liberals outside should lend their support to any efforts the group makes to liberalize their culture" (MC, 168). What remains unclear, though, is who actually has the authority to right the wrongs in question, who is entitled to compel obedience to principles of justice (MC, 165). For this reason, we should normally refrain, in disputes between national majorities and minorities just as in the affairs of another state, from seeking to impose liberal principles through the use of outright coercion.[8] Note, though, that on this view nonliberal groups, though tolerated, clearly do not enjoy the same standing as liberal ones. Unlike liberal groups, one would not want to say that non-liberal groups are really *justified* in seeking to preserve their cultures; on the contrary, they *ought* to change them and make them more liberal. This produces an ironic tension in Kymlicka's argument: a theory motivated by the desire to respect diverse cultures ends up merely tolerating many that it does not truly respect.

This irony arises, I think, from a deeper tension at the heart of Kymlicka's project: the difficulty of trying to base a defense of culture upon the primary value of individual autonomy. The resulting defense is inevitably purely instrumental and quite limited. Kymlicka himself is perfectly clear about this. "Cultures are valuable, not in and of themselves," he writes, "but because it is only through having access to a societal culture that people have access to a range of meaningful options" (MC, 83).[9] Exploring such a view's consequences for immigration policy nicely illuminates this tension in Kymlicka's argument. If individual autonomy is our primary concern—and assuming that, other things being equal, increased freedom of mobility obviously increases the scope for autonomy—then presumably a country would only be justified in enacting limitations on immigration to the effect necessary to prevent the dissolution of its societal culture. Thus, for example, a country might conclude that there was a limit to the number of immigrants it could successfully assimilate in a given year. More extensive restrictions, however, would appear as superfluous protections of culture for its own sake, at the expense of individual autonomy. This defense of a state's right to regulate immigration looks much more qualified than what we might have expected after our initial reflections on Kymlicka's theory. Indeed, it pushes us back in the direction of Carens's "public order restriction," the view that immigration may only be restricted when it poses a real threat (a "clear and present danger," to adapt language from another context) to public order.[10]

The instability of trying to defend culture on the basis of individual autonomy manifests itself in a distinction Kymlicka makes between culture as a "context of choice" and the particular "character" of that culture at any given time. He writes,

> It is of sovereign importance to this argument that the cultural structure is being recognized *as a context of choice* . . . . In one common usage, culture refers to the *character* of a historical community. On this view, changes in the norms, values, and their attendant institutions in one's community (e.g.

> membership in churches, political parties, etc.) would amount to loss of one's culture. However, I use culture in a very different sense, to refer to the cultural community, or cultural structure, itself. On this view, the cultural community continues to exist even when its members are free to modify the character of the culture, should they find its traditional ways of life no longer worth while. (LCC, 166–7; italics in original)

This distinction is important because it shows how it is possible to defend both culture and individual autonomy:

> Protecting people from changes in the character of the culture can't be viewed as protecting their ability to choose. On the contrary, it would be a limitation on their ability to choose. Concern for the cultural structure as a context of choice, on the other hand, accords with, rather than conflicts with, the liberal concern for our ability and freedom to judge the value of our life-plans. (LCC, 167)

But this distinction, so important to Kymlicka's argument, raises two difficult problems for him.

First, some such distinction is necessary for the argument; it is the only way to mediate the tension produced by the attempt to ground a defense of cultural membership in the value of autonomy. But it ultimately isn't clear that such a distinction can be made. I, at least, have difficulty imagining exactly what a culture as a "context of choice," entirely abstracted from its actual character, would *be*. Recall that Kymlicka's argument about culture's serving as the necessary background for individual choice makes most sense when that context of choice is understood in a fairly concrete way: one's culture provides one with a finite range of specific options that carry certain meanings within it. Thus, for example, one might choose to become a lawyer; but one could not determine what it will mean to be a lawyer in a particular society, how the practice of law will operate there, what the general societal attitude towards lawyers will be. It is hard to know what a context of choice could *mean* other than the particular set of options available to a person, the conditions within which one is free to choose. To alter these options or conditions is necessarily to alter the context of choice itself.[11]

This doesn't mean, of course, that one must accept without question every aspect of that cultural context. One could, for example, try to change the meaning of being a lawyer or alter the practice of law. If one succeeded, though, one would have changed the options available to others—that is to say, one would have altered their context of choice. Thus it seems preferable simply to say that the culture has changed in some respect, that cultures are constantly evolving, that they change in some ways while remaining the same in others. This change can occur slowly or quickly, but when it happens, it is the culture itself that is changing, not simply the content of some larger, stable framework.

Indeed, Kymlicka's own favorite example of how the character of a culture can change radically while its fundamental context of choice remains stable—Quebec before and after the "Quiet Revolution"—lends credence to this criticism.[12] Prior to the Quiet Revolution, Kymlicka says, Quebec was "conservative and patriarchal."[13] During and following the Revolution, however, it was greatly liberalized, so that "Québécois society now exhibits all the diversity that any modern society contains."[14] Now clearly, from the perspective of a Quebecer living through this change, his or her "context of choice" has been drastically altered. What exactly has remained the same?

One obvious answer is the French language. And, indeed, language plays an important role in Kymlicka's account of societal cultures—he stresses perhaps no other element as strongly. This is not surprising, because language can provide an example of continuity even in situations of rapid and far-reaching change. But the kind of influence exerted by language hardly seems sufficient to justify speaking of some constant "context of choice." Through the way it shapes ideas, language can affect our lives by making certain ways of thought and expression more or less accessible to us. But these effects are immensely subtle and hard to define. Surely they are not sufficient to constitute a stable cultural context of choice.

Perhaps such a context can be found in certain social institutions? This, however, seems equally problematic. For one thing, clearly not all institutions can be included. We have already seen, for example, that a change in the practice of law—certainly an important social institution—ought to count as changing people's "context of choice." Furthermore, in the case of Quebec, as Kymlicka himself points out, one of the most important results of the Quiet Revolution was vastly to reduce the influence of what had been a dominant institution in Quebec's culture, the Catholic church.[15] So, whatever exactly the cultural "context of choice" in Quebec encompassed, it clearly did not include at least one very important social institution. (Recall, too, that, in the passage cited earlier, Kymlicka explicitly relegates "membership in churches" to those items constituting the *character* of a culture.)

One might try to restrict the institutions in question to purely political ones. Thus it would be possible to claim that a very abstract cultural context of choice remained stable in the sense that, say, Quebec maintained a representative legislature. But not only does this kind of claim move away from the concreteness that gave Kymlicka's argument its original appeal and plausibility, it also overlooks the ways in which changes in the character of a culture can affect how institutions, though remaining formally the same, operate—in other words, how they serve as (part of) a context of choice. To continue the lawyer example, consider the argument that Edmund Burke makes about the French legislature following the French Revolution. Burke writes that he saw the course the Revolution would take as soon as he learned the composition of the new legislature.

> Judge, Sir, of my surprise when I found that a very great proportion of the assembly (a majority, I believe, of the members who attended) was composed of practitioners in the law. It was composed, not of distinguished magistrates, who had given pledges to their country of their science, prudence, and integrity; not of leading advocates, the glory of the bar; not of renowned professors in universities;—but for the far greater part, as it must in such a number, of the inferior, unlearned, mechanical, merely instrumental members of the profession . . . . [T]he general composition was of obscure provincial advocates, of stewards of petty local jurisdictions, country attorneys, notaries, and the whole train of the ministers of municipal litigation, the fomenters and conductors of the petty war of village vexation . . . . The degree of estimation in which any profession is held becomes the standard of the estimation in which the professors hold themselves. Whatever the personal merits of many individual lawyers might have been, and in many it was undoubtedly very considerable, in that military kingdom no part of the profession had been much regarded except the highest of all . . . . The next rank was not much esteemed; the mechanical part was in a very low degree of repute. Whenever the supreme authority is vested in a body so composed, it must evidently produce the consequences of supreme authority placed in the hands of men not taught habitually to respect themselves, who had no previous fortune in character at stake, who could not be expected to bear with moderation, or to conduct with discretion, a power which they themselves, more than any others, must be surprised to find in their hands.[16]

Burke suggests that the more distinguished members of the French legal profession possessed the virtues, reputation, and sense of their own worth that would have made them capable of legislating responsibly. But the ordinary provincial lawyers—those who actually comprised the assembly—did not. And one of the important reasons for their defects, he suggests, was that French society's generally low opinion of the legal profession inevitably affected the way in which its ordinary practitioners viewed and conducted themselves, producing undesirable results when they came to enjoy unexpected power in the legislature. Quite apart from any questions of the accuracy of Burke's overall analysis of the French Revolution and legislature, his argument here provides a nice example of how cultural elements may affect the operation of political institutions, in subtle ways that a merely formal analysis of the institution's abstract constitution could not predict. The point is thus similar to one made in chapter three: that one cannot draw a clear line separating political culture from culture in general. Insofar as this is true, this possible strategy for describing a cultural context of choice apart from that culture's character is also problematic.

The only remaining way of trying to salvage the distinction between a culture's character and the culture as a context of choice, it seems, is to say something like this: a stable cultural context of choice exists whenever it is possible to identify a distinct cultural group existing over time, regardless of specific changes occurring in the life of that group. In other words, the cultural context of choice just *is* the group, and it exists as long as the group exists.[17] Thus one could say in the case of Quebec, as Kymlicka does, that, despite the profound cultural changes taking place during the Quiet Revolution, "the existence of a French-Canadian cultural community itself was never in question . . . . There was no danger to cultural membership in the sense I am concerned with—i.e. no danger to the existence of people's context of choice, no danger to their ability to examine the options that their cultural structure had made meaningful to them" (LCC, 167). The character of that community was very different after the Quiet Revolution from what it had been before, but there was never a moment at which one could doubt that *a* French-Canadian, Québécois culture existed. Indeed, this seems to be the idea that Kymlicka suggests by writing, "I use culture in a very different sense, to refer to the cultural community . . . itself" (LCC, 166–7). But this is also unsatisfactory. For this approach—which, instead of attempting to abstract from elements of the culture's character in order to find a broader, stable, context of choice, simply leaps to the opposite extreme by designating the community *itself* as the context of choice— provides absolutely no way of generating or maintaining the distinction between the context of choice and a culture's character. If the context of choice just *is* "the cultural community . . . itself," how could we possibly decide which features of that community are to count as part of its character and which belong instead to the larger "cultural structure" (which is of course precisely the sort of thing that members of the culture will argue about)? The equation of culture as a context of choice with the mere existence of an identifiable group over time offers no guidance in determining which elements of the group's identity are definitive and which belong to its mutable "character," perpetually open to challenge and redefinition.

Thus there seems to be no entirely satisfactory way of making this distinction, so vital to Kymlicka's argument. His attempt to do so, I think, relies upon a subtle ambiguity in the meaning of culture as a "context of choice." In explaining how culture supports and is necessary for individual autonomy, Kymlicka describes the cultural context of choice in fairly concrete terms, as providing people with various limitations that make the exercise of choice possible in the first place, as offering them a finite range of options within which they are free to choose but which are not simply of their own creation (though they may be always potentially open to challenge). But in trying to show that this cultural context of choice does not curtail individual freedom, he must either drain it of all the content that made his earlier argument plausible, removing from it any number of things that would certainly appear to count as changes in people's "context of choice" on any ordinary understanding of that phrase; or, alternatively, he must collapse the context of choice into the simple existence of an identifiable group, thus rendering it impossible to determine what elements of that group's culture might actually be definitive, part of the stable "context of choice" that represents its continued existence, as opposed to the elements that are merely part of its temporary and contingent character at any given point in time.

The attempt to defend culture on the basis of individual autonomy also raises a second problem, one created by the instrumental nature of that defense. Kymlicka argues that people are entitled to preserve their societal culture because that culture makes possible the individual autonomy that gives them the opportunity to pursue the richest, fullest, best life they can envision for themselves. In other words, he offers a universalistic justification for particular preference. Now, there is nothing inherently contradictory about such an argument. We could, for example, make an analogous sort of argument to justify parents' preference for their own children over other children (assuming that such a justification is possible). We might say that, in general, children will be better raised if they are in the care of people who have a special attachment to them. So the whole world will be better if we make room for this special attachment. Thus, parental preference is justified on universal grounds.

But this kind of argument, though logically possible, is troubling for two reasons. First, it seems descriptively false: that is, it isn't clear that this actually captures the reason why anyone is attached to her own children. By the same token, Kymlicka's argument about culture as a context of choice enabling individual freedom, though it may describe one element that we (at least those of us living in relatively free societies) value about our culture, does not seem to be a sufficient description of our attachment to our own way of life. Second, such an argument might actually undermine the particular preferences it purports to defend. To the extent that people accepted such an argument, they would feel forced to justify their particular attachments, be they to family, country, or some other group, on universal terms, which might or might not prove convincing. Moreover, the attempt to do so would permit them to retain their particular loyalties only if they could justify them from an impersonal and unattached standpoint. Thus they would be required to justify their national loyalty in terms that might actually threaten to undermine it.

Neither of these problems—the difficulty of distinguishing between a culture's character and that culture as a context of choice, or the potentially self-defeating nature of universalistic arguments for particular preferences—is a decisive, knock-down criticism of Kymlicka, the complexities of whose argument, rich and sophisticated as it is, I have not exhausted here. I do hope to have shown, though, that there is a deep tension at the heart of his theory, produced by the attempt to justify cultural preference on the basis of individual autonomy. And this tension raises questions about the kind of support that such a theory—first impressions notwithstanding—might provide for a state's right to regulate immigration. The precise way in which one chooses to navigate the dilemmas I have described here—between, for example, the value of individual autonomy and that of one's cultural context—affects whether and to what extent one is likely to accept immigration regulation by particular communities. Kymlicka's theory thus nicely illustrates the way in which positions on immigration are influenced by deeper assumptions about such weighty theoretical considerations as the relation between the individual and the community or the acceptability of political preference for one's own people and culture.

Walzer

Michael Walzer's defense of a state's right to restrict immigration, which comes in the second chapter ("Membership") of his book *Spheres of Justice,* is part of a larger argument about distributive justice, so it is necessary to start with a brief discussion of that broader argument. It begins with the claim, "People conceive and create goods, which they then distribute among themselves."[18] People are, that is, "culture-producing creatures" (314), who collectively create meanings for the vast array of things—food, health, religion, money, love—that together constitute the complex worlds of their social relationships. Different things are important to different groups of people; even things which are important to all people, such as food (to use an example of Walzer's), are understood differently in different times and places. "Bread is the staff of life, the body of Christ, the symbol of the Sabbath, the means of hospitality, and so on" (8). The meanings of more complex goods, such as office, honor, or love, are even more clearly socially constructed and vary more widely among different peoples.

On the basis of these plural worlds of human meaning, Walzer proposes the following principle of justice: "All distributions are just or unjust relative to the social meanings of the goods at stake" (9). This means that a good is justly distributed when its distribution accords with the meaning it has for members of the society in question. Thus, for example, we might think that certain goods—blenders, say, or red balloons—are justly distributed to those who have the wealth (and the desire) to buy them. Nothing about the way in which we understand blenders renders this unjust. (Though it could, of course, be otherwise—in a society where the members' religion held that certain rituals required the eating of only puréed foods, the just distribution of blenders, or their functional equivalent, might require that everybody had one.) But we might understand other goods, such as love or education, differently, so that simply distributing them through the market, to those with the necessary resources to purchase them, would appear unjust. Thus, in Walzer's view, "[T]he principles of justice are themselves pluralistic in form" (6). No single distributive principle can apply to all social goods, because we understand them and their purposes in different ways; furthermore, the principle by which we justly distribute a given good might prove to be unjust if used to govern the distribution of the same good elsewhere (though this way of putting it really misses the point—if goods are socially created, the same good elsewhere isn't really "the same good" at all).

Obviously, the operation of this theory requires that there be a sphere in which people share roughly the same understandings of social goods—otherwise there would be no distributive principles to apply. Walzer suggests that "the political community" is such a sphere, or our best approximation of it. "[T]he political community is probably the closest we can come to a world of common meanings. Language, history, and culture come together (come more closely together here than anywhere else) to produce a collective consciousness" (28). We could imagine doing away with such communities and attempting a global distribution of goods. But, Walzer plausibly suggests, a global community of shared meanings does not (not yet, at any rate) exist; and therefore any global distribution of a particular good would seriously violate various sub-groups' understandings of what a just distribution of that good would look like.

If we accept local political communities, with their particular and different sets of shared meanings, as the appropriate loci for applying principles of justice, the first distributive problem comes into view: How are those communities themselves constituted? As Walzer puts it, "The primary good that we distribute to one another is membership in some human community" (31). Most people, of course, are simply born into a particular community, a distributive method which, as Walzer notes, can be regulated only to a degree through policies designed to increase or decrease the size of the population.[19] But, he suggests, "The larger and philosophically more interesting questions—To what sorts of people [do we grant membership]?, And To what particular people?—are most clearly confronted when we turn to the problems involved in admitting or excluding strangers" (35)—when, that is, we take up the question of immigration.

Walzer explores these questions by comparing countries to three other kinds of association, neighborhoods, clubs, and families. The comparison to clubs is designed to suggest that a country's admissions decisions, like those of a club, are made by the group's current members, based upon their collective understanding of the group's nature and purposes. The comparison with the family illuminates what Walzer calls the "kinship principle" (41), the recognition that a country, despite its general entitlement to choose among potential new members, may feel certain obligations to admit relatives of citizens or members of its extended "national 'family'" (42), such as when the two Germanies after World War II accepted millions of ethnic Germans who had been expelled from the countries of eastern Europe.

Most important for our purposes, however, is the comparison Walzer draws between countries and neighborhoods, for here he most clearly suggests his reasons for thinking that countries may determine their own admissions policies. The crucial feature of the neighborhood, Walzer writes, is that it is "an association without an organized or legally enforceable admissions policy. Strangers can be welcomed or not welcomed; they cannot be admitted or excluded" (36). One could imagine nations following the same policy of unrestricted immigration, allowing people to move freely around the globe. But, says Walzer, this vision of perfect mobility is probably just a "mirage" (38). Most people, "inclined to stay where they are unless their life is very difficult there" (38), prefer not to move. They are attached to the familiar surroundings of their homes and will try to defend and preserve them against threats to their existence, such as large influxes of outsiders. Thus, Walzer writes suggestively, "if states ever become large neighborhoods, it is likely that neighborhoods will become little states . . . . Neighborhoods can be open only if countries are at least potentially closed" (38). Unrestricted migration threatens the continued existence of communities by exposing them to external forces, in neighboring countries and around the world, beyond their control. Face-to-face with large numbers of others who could transform their common life, members will tighten ranks, as it were, and seek to protect themselves against the outsiders. "To tear down the walls of the state is not, as Sidgwick worriedly suggested, to create a world without walls, but rather to create a thousand petty fortresses" (39).

If we find the prospect of "a thousand petty fortresses" undesirable, then we must allow control over admissions at some other level. Walzer suggests that the state, arguably the most plausible location for "political community" in our age, is appropriate: "The politics and the culture of a modern democracy probably require the kind of largeness, and also the kind of boundedness, that states provide" (39). Such control is necessary at some point, because the survival of distinct communities with their distinct sets of social understandings depends upon boundaries.

> The distinctiveness of cultures and groups depends upon closure and, without it, cannot be conceived as a stable feature of human life. If this distinctiveness is a value, as most people (though some of them are global pluralists, and others only local loyalists) seem to believe, then closure must be permitted somewhere. At some level of political organization, something like the sovereign state must take shape and claim the authority to make its own admissions policy, to control and sometimes restrain the flow of immigrants. (39)

If we think, then, that it is good for people to belong to thick cultures with richly developed understandings of the world, and if we think that no such culture exists (or will soon exist) at the global level, then we must accept the plurality of local communities that does exist. And these communities can maintain their identity and distinctiveness only when they have the ability to determine (on the whole) their own membership. Without such power, "there could not be *communities of character*, historically stable, ongoing associations of men and women with some special commitment to one another and some special sense of their common life" (62).[20]

Indeed, this plurality of local memberships is a necessary consequence of Walzer's broader theory of distributive justice, according to which goods should be distributed according to the meanings they possess for a given group of people. If membership is a good, and if it is understood by different groups of people to entail different things, then such a theory requires that these different groups be able to distribute membership according to their particular understandings of it—requires, that is, that distinct groups be able to determine their own admissions policies. This is not to say (and Walzer does not say) that their discretion is unlimited. But it does mean that they must possess considerable control over their own membership. Thus a community's control over immigration flows naturally from Walzer's broader understanding of distributive justice. That broader view rests upon a deep respect for the particular social worlds that people create through interaction with the fellow members of their "political communities;" and this respect, in turn, arises from people's profound attachment to those communities. This, I take it, is the fundamental message of the analogy with neighborhoods and its suggestion that "if states ever become large neighborhoods, it is likely that neighborhoods will become little states" (38).

But even if we concede all this to Walzer—that the world is divided into groups of people who have constructed their own particular sets of social meanings, that justice requires the distribution of social goods according to particular groups' understandings of them, that one consequence of this is that these groups are entitled to determine their own standards for membership—it doesn't necessarily follow that the *state* ought to control immigration. Walzer speaks of human communities and the meanings they construct, but without some further argument establishing the coincidence of those communities with actual states, he does not seem justified in attributing a right possessed by a certain kind of community to a state which may or may not be such a community. Carens raises precisely this point in response to Walzer:

> No liberal state restricts internal mobility. Those states that do restrict internal mobility are criticized for denying basic human freedoms. If freedom of movement within the state is so important that it overrides the claims of local political communities, on what grounds can we restrict freedom of movement across states? This requires a stronger case for the *moral* distinctiveness of the nation-state as a form of community than Walzer's discussion of neighborhoods provides.[21]

In other words, Walzer's argument, if correct, establishes that those communities that create their own worlds of shared meanings ought to control membership, but not that the state is (or consistently is) such a community.

On what grounds, then, might Walzer grant *states* the right to control immigration?

As it happens, though, Walzer does not actually insist that his argument establishes the rights of *states*. This may sometimes be unclear in *Spheres of Justice*, but it is clear enough in other statements Walzer has made on the subject. Thus, for example, in an article entitled "The Moral Standing of States," a defense of arguments made in his book on just war, Walzer writes, "The real subject of my argument is not the state at all but the political community that (usually) underlies it."[22] As the "usually" indicates, Walzer does go on to argue that most of the time this political community coincides with a state, and that as outsiders we should generally presume this to be true of a given country.[23] In any particular case, though, it might turn out to be false. When it is, Walzer is prepared to permit the break-up of the state into smaller ones designed to coincide with the actually existing political communities: "Rather than supporting the old unions, I would be inclined to support separation whenever separation is demanded by a political movement that, so far as we can tell, represents the popular will. Let the people go who want to go."[24] Similarly, in his lecture "Nation and Universe" Walzer recognizes that the nation-state is just one example of the kind of community he is describing:

> The nation is by no means the most important of the collectivities within which moral ideas and ways of life have been elaborated . . . . Even with reference to self-determination, the national entity, itself differently constituted and understood in different historical periods, could as easily be replaced by the clan or the tribe or the city-state or the community of faith. The argument, for better and worse, would be the same. Any collectivity can provide the institutional structures and the patterns of agency necessary for working out a version of the good life.[25]

Walzer is thus aware that his argument does not establish a single form of association as the correct or privileged form of human community, the single location in which shared social worlds are created.

Nevertheless, he does conclude from his argument about membership that, in general (and subject to some restrictions), states should have the right to regulate immigration. Why is this? Some possible reasons have already been suggested. As a rule, he thinks, we ought to presume that a government does in some way represent "its" people.[26] And he suggests, as we have seen, that the contemporary state, insofar as it provides both a meaningful area of internal mobility and a realm in which our common life is secure, is an appropriate institution for protecting these needs in the modern world.[27] Furthermore, Walzer's theory of distributive justice operates within "political communities" of shared meanings, and, as we have seen, he views the state as the broadest such community in the world today. There will of course be special cases, instances in which an actually existing state does not really coincide with a given community—perhaps it contains two clearly distinct communities, perhaps it represents a community part of which has been cut off and included in a neighboring state, perhaps it is not obvious that it contains any clear community at all. There may also be cases in which it is hard to identify the broadest community of shared meanings—the European Union is a good example.[28] These are practical problems calling for solutions attentive to the particular circumstances of the individual case.[29] But the existence of difficult cases does not undermine Walzer's general claim that our most relevant community of shared meanings is usually the state. Finally, I suspect that there is another reason for Walzer's willingness to concede general control over membership to the state, having to do with the special role of politics in his theory and the fact that the state is arguably the primary locus of political activity in the contemporary world, a possibility I shall elaborate in the following discussion.

These, then, are the essential elements of Walzer's argument that states are entitled to control immigration and membership. Human beings are creatures who together, through their social interactions, create a common world of meanings explaining the nature and purposes of the goods that they share; or rather, they create many different common worlds, since every set of shared meanings is local, particular to the group that created it, and not capable of simply being transported into other social settings.[30] One of the goods that will be understood differently in different communities is membership itself—what does it mean to be one of *us*, what does membership in *this* community entail? Indeed, membership is a crucial, even fundamental, good—the "primary good that we distribute to one another" (31)—because it shapes the very community within which all other goods are understood and shared. Only if communities have control over their own membership—control over immigration, for example—can they preserve their distinctive conceptions of membership, of the meaning and purpose of their particular association.[31] And in our world, the most relevant communities, the widest ones in which meanings still seem to be generally shared, are most often states. So if we think that the "distinctiveness of cultures," with their different conceptions of membership and political community, is valuable, "as most people (though some of them are global pluralists, and others only local loyalists) seem to believe" (SOJ, 39), then we should grant states, as a general rule, control over immigration.

But why *should* we believe this? Why should we value this diversity and distinctiveness of cultures? Why not determine which cultures are better than others, or even which one is best of all, and then seek to install it or them everywhere? Ultimately, this appears to be the question upon which the argument will turn; its answer is not apparent from what has been said thus far. Does Walzer give an answer? Why does *he* think that a plurality of diverse cultures is something we should preserve and protect?

The answer—foreshadowed, in a way, by Walzer's recognition that his theory could apply to any genuine "political community," whether it constitutes an existing state or not—can be summed up in a single word: self-determination. Walzer states this very clearly in his discussion of international relations in *Thick and Thin,* the sequel to *Spheres of Justice.* There, in discussing how to handle situations in which two distinct peoples are unwilling to live together in a single state, he writes

> I doubt that we can find a single rule or set of rules that will determine the form of the separation and the necessary constraints. But there is a general principle, which we can think of as the expression of moral minimalism in international politics. The principle is "self-determination."[32]

He describes self-determination in the familiar terms of self-government, writing that the members of a community "have the basic right that goes with membership. *They ought to be allowed to govern themselves* (in accordance with their own political ideas) . . . ."[33] This self-determination is the proper response to a defining characteristic of humanity, our division into and attachment to distinct groups.

> Tribalism names the commitment of individuals and groups to their own history, culture, and identity, and this commitment (though not any particular version of it) is a permanent feature of human social life. The parochialism, the moral thickness, that it breeds is similarly permanent. It can't be overcome; it has to be accommodated, and therefore the crucial minimalist principle is that it must always be accommodated: not only my parochialism but yours as well, and his and hers in their turn.[34]

This parochialism—a word Walzer uses here without any negative connotation—is, he suggests, an abiding feature of human life, something we should not expect to change: "our common humanity will never make us members of a single universal tribe. The crucial commonality of the human race is particularism: we participate, all of us, in thick cultures that are our own."[35] Walzer describes the foundation of his approach in similar terms when he asks, in *Spheres of Justice,* "By virtue of what characteristics are we one another's equals?" His answer: "One characteristic above all is central to my argument. We are (all of us) culture-producing creatures; we make and inhabit meaningful worlds. Since there is no way to rank and order these worlds with regard to their understanding of social goods, we do justice to actual men and women by respecting their particular creations" (314).

This line of argument is similar to the one I laid out in the third chapter. There I suggested that human beings naturally form groups and are attached to them, wanting to preserve them in existence over time. I further argued that, lacking widely persuasive answers to a number of difficult questions about whether we may prefer our own way of life to others, we ought to work from the presumption that the vast majority of these distinct communities are legitimate and entitled to maintain their ways of life as best they can. Thus I think that Walzer's argument about the rights of human communities is essentially correct.[36] In closing, though, I want to point toward an ambiguity in his understanding of self-determination and to offer a caution about the meaning that term should have in discussions of the independence of different cultural communities.

One can think of self-determination in two different ways. The first—of which the passages cited from Walzer thus far provide examples—might be called "passive participation." Human beings create cultural worlds simply by being what they are: the natural course of their ordinary, daily interaction with one another produces a shared life-world of mutual understandings. Self-determination, in this sense, requires no special effort or activity of its own; rather, it is something people do even without especially trying to, the inevitable product of their association with other people. To be a human being is to be born into a given cultural community and into its ongoing process of cultural creation. But it is also possible to understand this process in a much more "active" manner; indeed, the words "self-determination" or "culture-producing creatures" may even seem to suggest this. They call to mind some kind of activity that people could intentionally engage in together, and in more than a temporary fashion. They suggest not simply, for example, that groups of people could engage in deliberate actions aimed at changing particular features of a culture's identity, which seems undeniable, but rather something more: that a self-determining culture as a whole engages consciously and continuously in activity of this sort and is self-determining insofar as it does so.

These different meanings arise out of a tension within the idea of self-determination itself. Patrick Thornberry has suggested that self-determination "has more than one dimension or aspect."[37] He describes it as having an "external" and an "internal" dimension. The external dimension, which "defines the status of a people in relation to another people," is perhaps the more conventional; it is the familiar idea that a people is entitled to run its own affairs, in the sense of not having them run by someone else against its will—"continuous defence against external subversion or intervention," as Thornberry puts it.[38] The internal dimension, by contrast—which Thornberry also calls the "democratic" dimension—concerns the "relationship between a people and 'its own' State or government."[39] Its purpose is to "translate the achievement of freedom by a people into a continuing process of authentic self-rule, to anchor their liberation in the culture of democracy."[40] There is, however, a potential incompatibility between these two dimensions. The point of the external dimension, one might say, is to protect a people's common life (for the sake of which the right of self-determination in this sense exists), whatever it may be, as it is has been (and is being) created in the "passive" ways described above. And there is, of course, no guarantee that this common life will be or become a democratic, self-governing one; a given people might understand itself and its way of life very differently, as subject to the sustaining power of God, for example, or shaped by creative forces in the cosmos beyond human control. In such cases, the effect of external self-determination, in protecting a people's way of life, will be directly contrary to the goal of internal self-determination, which is precisely to encourage the kind of democratic self-government that I earlier described as self-determination in the "active" sense.

Since the language of "self-determination" or "culture-creation" is ambiguous in this respect, it can be difficult to tell exactly what an author has in mind on the basis of selected quotations. Where, for example, does the emphasis lie when Walzer writes, "A nation is a historic community, connected to a meaningful place, enacting and revising a way of life, aiming at political or cultural self-determination"?[41] He might, after all, have written "possessing a way of life," rather than "enacting and revising" one (not to mention the implication of "aiming at . . . self-determination"). Or what is the force of "participation" or the nature of the "development" referred to when he says that people have a right to "their participation in the 'development' that goes on and can only go on within the enclosure" of their political community?[42] Untangling this ambiguity is important in a discussion of immigration. For if we are to defend, as I have done, the right of different peoples to preserve their own, distinct ways of life; and if we are to do so, as Walzer does, on the basis of a principle of self-determination; then we want to avoid smuggling into the meaning of "self-determination" a content that would in fact restrict the kinds of cultures worthy of protection to only familiar, Western-style, liberal democracies. But here I want to suggest—with a caution appropriate to the limited space available to me but also a degree of confidence that will, I think, be shared by those familiar with his work[43]—that Walzer does this; that, at least sometimes, he intends something closer to the second, more active understanding of self-determination.

Some hint of this can be found in Walzer's writings on war, in which the principle of self-determination, not surprisingly, plays a significant role. In the course of discussing foreign interventions in the affairs of other countries, for example, Walzer, referring approvingly to an essay of Mill's on self-determination, writes, "A state is self-determining even if its citizens struggle and fail to establish free institutions, but it has been deprived of self-determination if such institutions are established by an intrusive neighbor. The members of a political community must seek their own freedom, just as the individual must cultivate his own virtue."[44] Here self-determination appears as a kind of activity, a "struggle" even. Again, Walzer writes (still referring, approvingly, to Mill), "Self-determination, then, is the right of a people 'to become free by their own efforts' if they can, and nonintervention is the principle guaranteeing that their success will not be impeded or their failure prevented by the intrusions of an alien power."[45] Here too the emphasis is on a people's "efforts." A similar perspective finds slightly different expression in the statement, "It is not true, then, that intervention is justified whenever revolution is; for revolutionary activity is an exercise in self-determination, while foreign interference denies to a people those political capacities that only such exercise can bring."[46] Walzer does not, of course, say that self-determining activity is always revolutionary; but in offering revolution as an example of it (and not suggesting that it is in any way an unusual or atypical example), he seems once again to emphasize its active nature.

This last passage in particular raises an important consideration.[47] For its association of self-determination with the acquisition of "political capacities" draws our attention to Walzer's conception of politics, and here, I think, we find something of interest for our purposes. Within Walzer's theory of different "spheres of justices," different facets of human life in which particular goods are distributed on the basis of the principles that correspond to their own, socially constructed meanings, the sphere of politics has a special place. As Walzer notes in *Thick and Thin,* in a passing, parenthetical remark, "the sphere of politics has a specially extended form."[48] And in

Spheres of Justice he notes that political power "is not simply one among the goods that men and women pursue; as *state power*, it is also the means by which all the different pursuits, including that of power itself, are regulated. It is the crucial agency of distributive justice; it guards the boundaries within which every social good is distributed and deployed" (281; emphasis in original). Politics has a certain pride of place because it is the means through which people ensure that the other various goods are properly distributed according to their shared social meanings.

But there is more to it than this. For Walzer's descriptions of political activity sound very similar to the process of self-determination (in the active, democratic sense) itself. Perhaps the most illuminating passage in this regard is the following, worth quoting at length, in which Walzer describes his vision of democratic citizenship:

> Once we have located ownership, expertise, religious knowledge, and so on in their proper places and established their autonomy, there is no alternative to democracy in the political sphere . . . . The citizens must govern themselves. "Democracy" is the name of this government, but the word doesn't describe anything like a simple system; nor is democracy the same thing as simple equality. Indeed, government can never be simply egalitarian; for at any given moment, someone or some group must decide this or that issue and then enforce the decision, and someone else or some other group must accept the decision and endure the enforcement. Democracy is a way of allocating power and legitimating its use—or better, it is *the political way* of allocating power. Every extrinsic reason is ruled out. What counts is argument among the citizens. Democracy puts a premium on speech, persuasion, rhetorical skill. Ideally, the citizen who makes the most persuasive argument—that is, the argument that actually persuades the largest number of citizens—gets his way. But he can't use force, or pull rank, or distribute money; he must talk about the issues at hand. And all the other citizens must talk, too, or at least have a chance to talk. It is not only the inclusiveness, however, that makes for democratic government. Equally important is what we might call the rule of reasons. Citizens come into the forum with nothing but their arguments. All non-political goods have to be deposited outside: weapons and wallets, titles and degrees. (SOJ, 304; emphasis in original)

Walzer also notes that this political process is ongoing and open-ended: "Political rights are permanent guarantees; they underpin a process that has no endpoint, an argument that has no definitive conclusion. In democratic politics, all destinations are temporary. No citizen can ever claim to have persuaded his fellows once and for all" (SOJ, 310).

Now something like this, I believe, is also what Walzer has in mind by self-determination. Not that this passage perfectly describes the actual process by which cultures come into being in the world. Certainly, they are shaped by various factors ranging from the wealth or prestige of individuals to brute force (though this alone is surely insufficient to negate a culture's claim to be self-determining). But, of course, the same is true of politics in the real world. By the same token, the process of cultural self-determination is not really one to which all individuals contribute equally; again, though, the same is true of politics, even in Walzer's description, for political equality gives an advantage to those who can make "the most persuasive argument"—"A perfectly democratic decision is likely to come closest to the wishes of those citizens who are politically most skillful" (SOJ, 304). But just as the passage describes an ideal form of democratic politics, so too might it offer an ideal description of cultural self-determination: a process in which all citizens come together on an (at least initially or presumptively) equal basis and have an equal chance to shape the emerging culture as best they can through their free interactions with their fellows. Such an account has a powerful attraction—indeed, I suspect that we generally take it more or less for granted (even if it is, for the reasons already stated, an only partially adequate account) that the self-determination of *a people,* considered as a unit, is legitimate precisely insofar as it emanates from a kind of fundamental internal democracy, in which all members interact with one another on a free and equal basis.[49]

The plausibility of reading Walzer in this way is strengthened, again, by his arguments about war, specifically about those circumstances in which foreign intervention in another country's internal affairs is justified (as it normally is not). One of these occasions, Walzer suggests, is "whenever a government is engaged in the massacre or enslavement of its own citizens or subjects"—whenever, that is, "we must doubt the very existence of a political community to which the idea of self-determination might apply."[50] Why is it impossible in such circumstances for us to think of the community in question any longer as self-determining? Precisely because some of its members—those in power—have used the resources at their disposal (in this case, force) illegitimately to stop the processes of conversation and interaction from which one might reasonably imagine a culture freely arising through the combined actions of its members. One group has pre-empted the process, stopped it cold. Thus the kinds of actions that Walzer rules out from his ideal description of politics are, it seems, the same kinds of actions that make it impossible to talk of a community's being self-determining.

Walzer's article on "The Moral Standing of States," a response to criticisms of his book *Just and Unjust Wars,* also reveals him blurring the distinction between self-determination and political action. Speaking there of the Algerian revolution, for example, and of various democratic movements that could conceivably have arisen from it (though they did not), he writes, "All that is Algerian self-determination, a political process that also has value, even if it isn't always pretty, and even if its outcome doesn't conform to philosophical standards of political and social justice."[51] Here he explicitly calls self-determination "a political process." Even more significant is the conclusion of the article, which provides the clearest indication that Walzer consciously thinks of self-determination as an active, political process. There he summarizes his argument—that the right to self-determination entitles states to freedom from foreign interference—in precisely these terms: "My own argument is perhaps best understood as a defense of politics, while that of my critics reiterates what I take to be the traditional philosophical dislike for politics."[52] He describes that dispute as follows: "It has to do with the respect we are prepared to accord and the room we are prepared to yield to the political process itself, with all its messiness and uncertainty, its inevitable compromises, and its frequent brutality. It has to do with the range of outcomes we are prepared to tolerate, to accept as presumptively legitimate, though not necessarily to endorse."[53] So self-determination—the process that creates a right against external interference and that, we have seen, is ultimately the foundation for the state's control over its own membership—turns out to be a "political process," a form of what I have called self-determination in the "active" sense.

Thus, although Walzer's precise views may not be fully explicit, I believe that this reading conveys something of his deeper understanding—perhaps we should say his mixed understanding—of the process of communal self-determination. But I think we would be well-advised to resist any blurring of the distinct senses of self-determination.[54] This is not to deny Walzer's claims that communities can be politically self-determining in the more active sense, that the results will reflect their own internal cultural understandings, and that these results are worthy of respect and protection. I argued as much in chapter three when I suggested that there is no easy way to draw a line between culture at large and political culture specifically, that the culture at large will reveal itself politically in a variety of ways, and that the majority of these are, in Walzer's phrase, "presumptively legitimate." But this does not mean that the production of social meanings, the creation of a shared cultural world, is itself a political process. The lines are no doubt as difficult to draw in this direction as in the other—just as culture infiltrates politics in various ways, so too does politics infiltrate culture. But the distinction, however hazy or hard to delineate, is worth preserving, for it is not only the "active" manifestations of self-determination that are significant. Self-determination in the passive sense is equally—I am inclined to say, even more—important, precisely because it arises from ordinary human interaction that is not in any obvious way political. "What actually happens is harder to describe. Over a long period of time, shared experiences and cooperative activity of many different kinds shape a common life."[55] Our shared worlds of cultural meaning, the "communities of character" that Walzer's arguments, whether about membership or war, are intended to nourish and protect, are largely the product of what we do and say in our private, non-political lives, in backyard conversations between neighbors, in little league baseball games, at church picnics. Much of the force of Walzer's argument derives, I think, precisely from our sense that politics ought to protect these non-political aspects of our lives and the bonds we create through them. Thus it is worth remembering that the most valuable processes of cultural self-determination are often what I have called its more "passive" forms.[56]

In fairness to Walzer, this is a point to which he is sometimes sensitive. Indeed, his brief but superb essay "A Day in the Life of a Socialist Citizen"—which he himself characterizes as a defense of "the rights of the ardent non-citizen"[57]—is an extraordinarily fine appreciation of the values of private life, coming from a philosopher who is in general so attached to participatory citizenship. Here Walzer expands on Oscar Wilde's famous quip about socialism:

> Oscar Wilde is supposed to have said that socialism would take too many evenings. This is, it seems to me, one of the most significant criticisms of socialist theory that has ever been made . . . . Socialism's great appeal is the prospect it holds out for the development of human capacities: An enormous growth of creative talent, a new and unprecedented variety of expression, a wild proliferation of sects, associations, schools, parties: this will be the flowering of the future society . . . . [But a] powerful figure looms behind Marx's hunter, fisherman, shepherd, and critic: the busy citizen attending his endless meetings.[58]

But, of course, many people do not want to attend the citizen's endless meetings; they have other things in mind.

> [S]ocialism and participatory democracy will depend upon, and hence require, an extraordinary willingness to attend meetings, and a public spirit and sense of responsibility that will make attendance dependable and activity consistent and sustained. None of this can rest for any long period of time or

among any substantial group of men upon spontaneous interest . . . . When will there be time for the cultivation of personal creativity or the free association of like-minded friends? In the world of the meeting, when will there be time for the tête-à-tête?[59]

Walzer recognizes that the demands of political participation, of "active" self-determination, are potentially terribly oppressive.

[W]hat a suffocating sense of responsibility, what a plethora of virtue would be necessary to sustain the participation of everybody all the time! How exhausting it would be! Surely there is something to be said for the irresponsible nonparticipant and something also for the part-time activist, the half-virtuous man (and the most scorned among the militants), who appears and disappears, thinking of Marx and then of his dinner?[60]

There is, I submit, a great deal to be said for the "half-virtuous man," thinking of his dinner. Most of us, after all, are that man, and he, whether consciously or not, represents an important truth: that much of what we value most in life is not and should not become the stuff of politics. As Walzer concedes, "Radical politics radically increases the amount and intensity of political participation, but it does not (and probably should not) break through the limits imposed on republican virtue by the inevitable pluralism of commitments, the terrible shortage of time, and the day-to-day hedonism of ordinary men and women."[61]

That "probably," it seems to me, is an unnecessary qualification. The inevitable pluralism of commitments, the day-to-day hedonism of ordinary men and women—these are important things indeed, and we rightly expect politics to protect, not invade, them. It is for this reason that we should remember the distinction between the more passive and more active varieties of self-determination. Walzer's account is immensely valuable both for its understanding that the line between these can be difficult to draw and for its firm and consistent defense of the results of communal self-determination, however exactly those results are produced. But it is also worth insisting upon what he remembers, we might say, only half the time: that the more active sense of self-determination is valuable and to be defended precisely because it rests upon the more passive varieties. "The moral standing of any particular state depends upon the reality of the common life it protects . . . ."[62] If we value and respect the political self-determination of a group of people, as I think we should, we do so because it reflects the prior existence of a shared way of life among them, a way of life which is not, in the first instance, political.

★ ★ ★ ★ ★

In the last chapter I tried to show how different conceptions of national identity lead to different immigration policies, and in this chapter I have attempted a parallel illustration in the realm of theory. By considering the arguments of Walzer and Kymlicka, we can see how different conceptions of political community influence one's approach to a question such as immigration. Kymlicka's theory, with its defense of the right to a stable cultural context of choice, seems to offer some support for thinking that a country is entitled to restrict immigration. Nevertheless, we have seen that his argument's foundation in the value of individual autonomy calls the extent of that support into question. The tensions inherent in defending community and culture on the basis of individual autonomy are particularly apparent in Kymlicka's attempted distinction between the character and structure of a culture, and the way one navigates these tensions affects whether such a theory is ultimately more likely to buttress or to undermine a community's attempts to preserve itself by regulating immigration. In the case of Walzer, we have seen that his defense of a people's right to control admissions rests upon the principle of self-determination. But we have also seen that—not always, but sometimes—his vision of a democratic, participatory politics colors the concept of self-determination, giving it an "active," democratic cast that might ultimately threaten to restrict the variety of lives that people could actually adopt, which would undermine the general purpose of his theory. Both examples thus help to reveal the way in which fundamental conceptions of political life—in particular, conceptions of the relation between the individual and the community—shape the views we hold about immigration.

Chapter 6

THE BOUNDARIES
OF THE POLITICAL

The last two chapters have sought to illustrate, in different ways, the close connection that exists between visions of political community and responses to immigration. In doing so, they should help us appreciate how deeply intertwined control over membership is with particular national identities. People do not wish to look on passively and helplessly as their way of life is transformed into something different and unfamiliar. And so they seek to regulate immigration, which affects the very constitution of their political community. The particular shape that those regulations take will depend upon the community in question and its own conception of itself. Imposing immigration restrictions does not, of course, guarantee a community against involuntary change. No doubt there are numerous forces in the world, not all of them within our control, that affect us in various ways. But lack of total control is not the same as complete political incapacity. Immigration regulation is one way in which people can seek to preserve the distinctive elements of their past and to exert some influence over the shape of their future.

Allowing peoples this degree of self-determination, to use Walzer's language, is—or so I have argued in this work—the appropriate consequence of a genuine respect for the diverse ways of life developed by different groups of people. If we recognize different cultures with their corresponding ways of organizing political life as legitimate—if we see in them different expressions of the latent potentialities within humanity—then, unless we are either able to persuade people to change their way of life or willing to force them to do so, we should grant them the right to nurture and mold their collective life as they see best. To make this case has been the burden of my first five chapters.

I should not stop here, though. For one thing, to do so might give the mistaken impression that I consider states entitled to complete discretion in controlling immigration, justified in admitting or excluding whomever they choose, subject to no restrictions. More importantly, I have argued through- out this work that different approaches to immigration are entangled with larger understandings of politics, and it would be anomalous to suggest that my own suggested policy of deference to different national approaches is otherwise. Like Carens's argument for open borders or Walzer's for (quali- fied) state sovereignty, my own view surely involves assumptions of its own—views about the proper place of community in human life, for exam- ple, or the importance of values such as stability or comfort. So here at the end, and indirectly, I want to challenge these assumptions, to construct a (partial) defense of immigration. Is there nothing to be said for open, or at least permeable, borders—for some real "right" to migrate not based on any particular country's self-understanding?

In this chapter I shall briefly consider a few exceptions to what I have claimed thus far, lines of argument which, I think, suggest that, although immigration debates may be fueled by visions of national identity and we should therefore be reluctant to declare particular nations' resolutions of those debates illegitimate, immigration may nevertheless not simply be a matter that each nation is entirely free to determine for itself. Perhaps there are limits within which debate should take place, or exceptions about which we can reach agreement. I should emphasize that the suggestions I make here are not intended as absolute principles, exceptionless rules which utterly confine states' freedom of action. Thus, although I shall argue that states have an obligation to help desperate outsiders facing death, this does not mean that any given state is obliged to accept every such outsider at any given moment. Perhaps the state is small, crowded, or poor; perhaps the desperate outsiders are extremely numerous. In such circumstances, I am not prepared to say that a state is required to let itself be simply over- whelmed, to risk its own existence (though I am also not sure that it could never have such an obligation)—as Walzer has put it in his own attempt to balance competing interests, the restrictions on state discretion "can only modify and not transform admissions policies rooted in a particular com- munity's understanding of itself."[1] Rather, the suggestions contained here are offered in the same spirit as the argument which has preceded them: just as a people's right to preserve its way of life and shape its own future is a weighty value, worthy of respect and deference, so too are the interests described below. We can say, I think, that states must make a serious, good faith effort to recognize them. But what exactly that will or should look like in any particular circumstances will call for the exercise of judgement. What follows, then, is simply my attempt to describe some values that circumscribe states' freedom of action.

The Truly Desperate

It is perhaps good to begin with an area of agreement, and international law presents us with one group of people who, it is widely agreed, have a right to be admitted to the territory of a foreign country: refugees. Guy S. Goodwin-Gill, a leading scholar of international law regarding the movement of people, writes in a recent treatise, *The Refugee in International Law,*

> The legal framework within which the refugee is located remains characterized, on the one hand, by the principle of state sovereignty and the related principles of territorial supremacy and self-preservation; and, on the other hand, by competing humanitarian principles deriving from general international law (including the purposes and principles of the United Nations) and from treaty. The sum of developments over the last half-century, and particularly since 1945, is that significant limitations now confine and structure states' apparently absolute or near absolute discretion . . . over the entry of foreign nationals . . . .[2]

The situation of refugees thus reflects both the general right of states under international law to control their borders, as well as the limits to that power. Goodwin-Gill notes the general agreement that, "for states at large, refugees are a class known to general international law and, as a matter of law, entitled to a somewhat better and higher standard of treatment [than many other classes of migrants]."[3]

If, then, there is widespread agreement that refugees constitute a special class of migrants entitled to special treatment, who counts as a refugee? The most widely accepted definition is that from the United Nations' 1951 Convention relating to the Status of Refugees, which defines as a refugee any person who, "owing to well-founded fear of being persecuted for reasons of race, religion, nationality, membership of a particular social group or political opinion, is outside the country of his nationality and is unable or, owing to such fear, is unwilling to avail himself of the protection of that country; or who, not having a nationality and being outside the country of his habitual residence . . . is unable or, owing to such fear, is unwilling to return to it."[4] In addition to its role in guiding activities of the United Nations, this definition has been adopted by many countries and incorporated into their own immigration or refugee laws. The United States, for example, incorporated this definition of refugees into its Refugee Act of 1980.[5] Goodwin-Gill notes that this definition establishes four basic characteristics of refugees:

> (1) they are outside their country of origin; (2) they are unable or unwilling to avail themselves of the protection of that country, or to return there; (3) such inability or unwillingness is attributable to a well-founded fear of being persecuted; and (4) the persecution feared is based on reasons of race, religion, nationality, membership of a particular social group, or political opinion.[6]

This definition of refugees is as important for what it does not say as for what it does. Under it, the class of refugees is carefully limited. It does not, for example, include victims of natural disasters or those fleeing severe economic disruptions. Rather, it embraces a particular group of people who suffer, one might say, from a certain kind of political hardship, the deliberate refusal by their government to offer them basic protection of life and liberty. Refugees are people who, because they possess particular disfavored characteristics (race, religion, nationality) or hold certain disfavored political opinions, cannot enjoy the normal expectation of every individual, the protection of his own government. As Atle Grahl-Madsen has explained, the definition of refugee presumes that there normally exists a "mutual bond of trust, loyalty, protection, and assistance between an individual and the government of his home country."[7] In the case of the refugee, as envisioned by the standard U.N. definition, this bond has been broken by some deliberate policy of the refugee's home government.

The narrow political emphasis of this definition has, predictably, engendered criticism. It permits governments to distinguish between "real," or "political," refugees—those fleeing persecution on the grounds stated—and so-called "economic" refugees—those who may be simply fleeing poverty in search of a better life—and to grant the legal status of refugee, with all the benefits it confers, to only the former.[8] Some have argued, therefore, that the definition of refugee should be broadened to include those whom we might normally, in our everyday usage, think of as refugees: "A refugee, we might say, is a person fleeing life-threatening conditions."[9] Andrew Shacknove, for example, has argued powerfully that there is no logical reason for restricting the definition of refugee to include only those driven from their country by political persecution or the well-grounded fear of it, while excluding victims of civil war, foreign invasion, natural disasters, or poverty (when the last is due at least in part to state neglect). This is because these classes of people all suffer from the same fundamental problem: they lack the basic political protection that we associate with the usual bond between state and citizen, the bond of "trust, loyalty, protection, and assistance" noted above. As Shacknove writes, "the normal bond between the citizen and the state can be severed in diverse ways, persecution being but one. Societies periodically disintegrate because of their fraility [sic] rather than because of their ferocity, victims of domestic division or foreign intervention."[10] The lack of the most ordinary sorts of state protection, however it comes about, establishes the core meaning of refugee. "Persecution is but one manifestation of a broader phenomenon: the absence of state protection of the citizen's basic needs. It is this absence of state protection which constitutes the full and complete negation of society and the basis of refugeehood."[11]

It is not my intention here to debate the technical legal meaning of "refugee." There may well be good reasons, overlooked by Shacknove, for applying the term only to a narrower class of "political" refugees. It is not necessarily the purpose of refugee law, after all, to right all wrongs or correct all misfortunes that people may endure. It may be valuable to single out a particular, narrow class of persons, about whom widespread agreement is possible, and who suffer from a particular kind of harm that other states can most obviously and appropriately rectify through the offer of immigration and territorial asylum (whereas other remedies might be available for other problems). As Walzer has written, "There is . . . one group of needy outsiders whose claims cannot be met by yielding territory or exporting wealth; they can be met only by taking people in. This is the group of refugees whose need is for membership itself, a non-exportable good."[12] It is possible to send humanitarian and technical assistance to victims of natural disasters; it is possible to prop up unstable governments. But people who cannot return to their country for fear of their lives need someplace to live. Furthermore, refugee law also functions as a way of assigning blame—people become refugees because they are targets of deliberate policies on the part of their governments. To declare someone a refugee is thus, in effect, to criticize his government for violating humanitarian norms. But a government some of whose citizens are displaced by a natural disaster, for example, may not deserve the kind of blame that refugee status implies.[13] For reasons such as these, it may be sensible and useful to define refugees narrowly by focusing on a particular dilemma requiring a certain kind of solution.

Nevertheless, Shacknove's underlying point seems well-taken: that what ultimately concerns us about all of these people, whether they fit the conventional definition of "refugee" or not, and what grounds their claim on our assistance, is the same, "the absence of state protection of the citizen's basic needs." Surely there is something to this argument. I suggest, therefore, that we can identify a group of people whom we might call the "truly desperate" who make a powerful claim on other countries to grant them residence.[14] This is vague language, of course, but by the "truly desperate" I mean to indicate people whose need is immediate and dire; those, we might say, who literally face death if they do not find somewhere else to live. It seems hard to justify insisting that they remain where they are and passively accept their doom. Hobbes suggested that those who are unable to support themselves are entitled to move to "countries not sufficiently inhabited: where nevertheless they are not to exterminate those they find there, but constrain them to inhabit closer together and not range a great deal of ground to snatch what they find."[15] Hobbes's claim (in effect a defense of colonization), since it presumably includes not only those facing imminent death but also those simply struggling through poverty, is stronger than what I mean to suggest here with my notion of the truly desperate. But it points toward the fundamental idea that those who cannot provide for their own lives where they are have an especially strong claim on a residence someplace else, where they can do so.[16] This group of the "truly desperate" will overlap but not be identical with those who fall under the standard definition of refugee. Some of those who fall under the standard definition, after all, may face torture or persecution but not actual death. I should emphasize, therefore, that the point of identifying the "truly desperate" is not to deny these others the right to refugee status that they currently enjoy. The idea of the "truly desperate," in other words, is intended not as a replacement for the current definition of refugees, but rather as an (only partially overlapping) additional principle, one that attempts to describe a human value that might also limit states' sovereign control over immigration.[17]

A historical example may help flesh out what I mean by the "truly desperate." Consider the Great Famine that occurred in Ireland from 1845–1849.[18] As the nineteenth century progressed, the lower classes in Ireland had become more and more dependent upon the potato. By the middle of the century, it constituted the essential—sometimes the entire—diet for roughly one-third of the population; adult men are estimated to have eaten between 10 and 15 pounds of potatoes per day. In 1845 a potato fungus, transported from North America via the Low Countries to Ireland, first struck the potato crop. The damage in this first year of the blight was limited but considerable, resulting in the loss of about one-third of the crop. The disaster became vastly more severe in 1846, when three-fourths of the crop were lost. The blight receded in 1847, allowing for normal yields, but because few seed potatoes had been available for planting, the harvest was still small—whereas 2 million acres had been planted with potatoes before the famine, this number had fallen to only around a quarter of a million acres in 1847. And in 1848 the potato blight struck again, destroying almost half of the crop. After 1848, conditions gradually began to improve, though smaller potato failures in 1849 and 1850 caused continued hardships.

Many died of starvation. Disease took even more. Large numbers of laborers—perhaps 100,000—were evicted from their small plots of land as Irish landlords found themselves trapped between, on the one hand, the increasing taxes imposed by the English government to help fund its limited relief efforts and, on the other, their inability to collect rents from poverty-stricken tenants. The evicted only increased the flood of weakened and destitute people into already overcrowded workhouses, where illness spread quickly. Outbreaks of diseases such as typhus, relapsing ("yellow") fever, and cholera killed many, especially the very young and old. Contemporary accounts testify to the devastation and horror of what occurred. W. Steuart Trench, an Irish land agent and farmer, wrote,

> [M]y own losses and disappointments, deeply as I felt them, were soon merged in the general desolation, misery, and starvation which now rapidly affected the poorer classes around me and throughout Ireland. It is true that in the more cultivated districts of the Queen's County and the midland counties generally, not many deaths occurred from actual starvation. I mean, that people were not found dead on the roads or in the fields from sudden deprivation of food; but they sank gradually from impure and insufficient diet; and fever, dysentery, the crowding in the workhouse or hardship on the relief works, carried thousands to a premature grave. The crop of all crops, on which they depended for food, had suddenly melted away, and no adequate arrangements had been made to meet this calamity,—the extent of which was so sudden and so terrible that no one had appreciated it in time—and thus thousands perished almost without an effort to save themselves.[19]

Similarly, William Russell, who was sent to report on the famine and would go on to become a famous war correspondent, later wrote about the "agony of suffering and death" that he had witnessed in Ireland: "[I]n all my subsequent career . . . breakfasting, dining, and supping full of horrors in the tide of war I never beheld sights so shocking as those which met my eyes in that famine tour of mine in the West."[20] Census figures give some sense of the extent of the catastrophe. In 1841 the population of Ireland was roughly 8,175,000; by 1851 it had fallen to almost 6,550,000. Of those lost, almost one million are estimated to have died; the remainder emigrated.

It is people like the Famine victims, whose lives are immediately at stake, whom I mean to designate the "truly desperate." With their survival dependent upon escaping the dangers threatening them at home, they seem to present an especially strong claim for admission as immigrants. This does not, of course, solve various practical problems. It does not, for instance, tell us exactly what our obligations are in terms of removing the desperate from their current situations. Should we enter a suffering country and transport out whoever wants to leave? Or should we simply refrain from sending back those who manage to escape their plight? Or something in between? Nor does it tell us how the truly desperate should be distributed among countries that can accept them. Need we accept everyone who shows up at our borders? What if the country next door suffers a famine like the Irish one? Or should the desperate be distributed equally among more prosperous countries? Or in proportion to a country's wealth, or population density? It does not offer a country any procedure to follow if the number of the truly desperate is very large and it becomes necessary to pick and choose among them. Do we hold a lottery, drawing names from a hat? Is there a way of distinguishing degrees of desperation ("the truly, *truly* desperate")? Can we select those with whom we already have certain bonds?[21] These are all difficult questions, and I know no easy answers to them. Finally, focusing on the truly desperate, as I have done here, will leave many in the world whose poverty and need is real, but who do not seem to fit this more restricted category. This result is, of course, deliberate; if the argument of my first five chapters—that different states are entitled to preserve their legitimate ways of life—carries weight, then we will be cautious about identifying people whose claims override the ability of established national groups to preserve their pasts and shape their futures. Identifying the restricted but important group of the "truly desperate" is thus an attempt to strike a balance; in them, the limits of state discretion begin to become visible.[22]

The Littlest Platoon

E.M. Forster famously wrote, "[I]f I had to choose between betraying my country and betraying my friend, I hope I should have the guts to betray my country."[23] While I certainly don't intend to suggest that any friend of a citizen is entitled to immigrate, Forster's stark challenge to the state does raise the question of whether we possess any bonds that might be sufficiently important to ground such a claim. The most obvious candidate for such a bond is clearly that of the family, especially the immediate family. Richard Plender has written, "The strongest claim to enter a State's territory can often be advanced by members of the immediate family of a national of that State; for if they are denied admission, the national is confronted with a choice between expatriation and disruption of the unity of the family."[24] In putting it this way, Plender nicely emphasizes the direct challenge to a citizen's political loyalty that occurs if his country prevents his nearest relatives from joining him. Can we, or should we, expect people to remain loyal subjects of states that enforce such deep disruptions of their most profound personal relationships?

Although not as firmly entrenched as the claims of refugees, the value of family unity has also received increasing support as a principle of international law over past decades. Plender observes, "Several of the multilateral legal instruments governing the protection of human rights place emphasis on the sanctity and unity of the family."[25] He notes in particular the statement in Article 12 of the Universal Declaration of Human Rights that "no-one shall be subjected to arbitrary interference with his . . . family." The importance of the family is asserted again in Article 16 of the Declaration ("the family is the natural and fundamental group unit of society and is entitled to protection by society and the State"), as well as in the International Covenant on Economic, Social and Cultural Rights and in the International Covenant on Civil and Political Rights.[26] Various regional agreements contain similar provisions.[27] As we have already seen, family reunification is an overriding interest of American immigration law, and family members of nationals (and often of legally resident aliens) also receive preference in the immigration procedures of numerous other countries.[28] Plender also notes that "[f]or two categories of migrants"—migrant workers and refugees—"there exist networks of treaties and other arrangements designed to ensure reunification of the family."[29] On the basis of this assorted evidence, he concludes,

> [T]hese international and regional provisions do not amount to evidence of a right to family reunification in general international law. They do, however, establish the widespread acceptance of the moral or political proposition that States should facilitate the admission to their territories of members of the families of their own citizens or residents, at least when it would be unreasonable to expect the family to be reunited elsewhere.[30]

A study group formed by the American Society of International Law to determine the established and emerging principles of international law regulating the movement of persons across borders came to a slightly more emphatic conclusion, stating that one of these principles is the following: "In the formulation and administration of its immigration laws, and of its laws and regulations relating to admission of aliens into its territory, a State shall respect the unity of the family."[31]

I suggest that this special status given to very close family members is desirable and ought to give them a presumptive claim to override the state's discretionary control over immigration. Some indication of why this should be the case is given by the expression of support for family unity already quoted from Article 16(3) of the Universal Declaration of Human Rights: "the family is the natural and fundamental group unit of society and is entitled to protection by society and the State." What does it mean to call the family the "natural and fundamental group unit of society?" Consider the following passage by Edmund Burke, which expresses a similar sentiment:

> We begin our public affections in our families. No cold relation is a zealous citizen. We pass on to our neighborhoods and our habitual provincial connections. These are inns and resting places. Such divisions of our country as have been formed by habit . . . were so many little images of the great country in which the heart found something which it could fill. The love to the whole is not extinguished by this subordinate partiality. Perhaps it is a sort of elemental training to those higher and more large regards by which alone men come to be affected, as with their own concern, in the prosperity of a kingdom so extensive . . . .[32]

This suggests at least two reasons why we might think that family bonds could overrule state regulation of immigration. The first has to do with how political loyalty develops. As Burke suggests—and as is, I think, implicit in the Universal Declaration's description of the family as the "natural and fundamental group unit in society"—the family is the first sphere of social interaction in which we begin to learn to direct our affections and loyalties outward from the self to encompass others. From the original, intimate bonds of the family, we proceed gradually to extend our sentiments through the increasingly distant social bonds of neighborhood, region, country—and presumably, more tenuously still, to humanity as a whole (which might help explain our sympathy with refugees). As Burke put it in another of his famous descriptions, "To be attached to the subdivision, to love the little platoon we belong to in society, is the first principle (the germ as it were) of public affections. It is the first link in the series by which we proceed toward a love to our country and to mankind."[33] Thus to reject the bonds of family affection and unity is ultimately to cut at the very root of a process that helps us develop broader bonds of political loyalty in the first place, to challenge the basis of the individual's commitment to the polity as a whole. When this happens, affection for the state no longer appears as a natural outcome or logical extension of our feelings for those around us, but rather as the enemy of that group in which we experience these feelings most immediately.

The family might thus be called the "fundamental group unit in society" in the sense of being the first, or original, source of our broader public affections. But it is the first of those affections in another sense as well: it is the location of our deepest and most important experience of social bonds. Most people, presumably, love their spouses and children more than they do other random countrymen (to say nothing of strangers elsewhere throughout the world). And it seems both natural and appropriate that they do so. We are bound to our family members through a more richly complex web of relationships, a mixture of love and dependence, than we share with any other people. These relationships give rise to especially intense feelings of mutual affection and concern. To deprive someone of these relationships is to deprive him of his richest and most significant bonds with other human beings. That is something we should do only in rare circumstances indeed.

Because the family bond is of such vital importance, it is not something governments should ask residents to relinquish. The familiar terms of social contract theory can help illustrate for us why this might be so. Social contract thought asks what ends people want government to serve, and how much authority they are willing to grant it to accomplish those ends. My suggestion here is that one cannot imagine people—certainly not under ordinary circumstances—wanting to give government the authority to break apart their family bonds; or, to put it differently, that the preservation of the family ought to be thought of as included among the ends which government is intended to protect. Locke writes at one point that among the ends for which people form political societies is "their comfortable, safe, and peacable living one amongst another."[34] Surely "comfortable, safe, and peacable living one amongst another" includes the preservation of the family and precludes its destruction.[35]

Just as establishing the presumptive claim of refugees leaves practical problems to be resolved, so does establishing that of family members. The most obvious problem, of course, is the question of how to define the family and determine which of its members might be entitled to admission.[36] Clearly, the nearest relatives, such as spouses, minor children, and perhaps aged, dependent parents, have the strongest claims, and they are most likely to be recognized by current state practice. As was noted by the previously mentioned study group of the American Society of International Law, "States usually do not deny admission to an alien who is the spouse of a citizen resident in the country, if he or she seeks entry for the purpose of taking up residence and setting up a matrimonial home."[37] They also wrote, "A State normally permits minor dependent children of a citizen resident in the country to enter and reside in its territory, and often allows also persons who are close relatives of a citizen and solely dependent upon the citizen to enter the country for the purpose of settlement."[38] Beyond this, as we move out towards more distant relatives, or towards the complications raised by divorces or remarriages and their associated offspring, it becomes more difficult to specify in advance exactly who should be admitted and who not. Probably some latitude is due states in working out reasonable solutions. At least in the very closest family members, though, spouses and minor children, I think we can identify a group of people whose extremely close relationships to current residents support a powerful argument that they ought not be denied entry. In the deepest relationships of the family bond, we again see the contours of the limits to state power.

The Politics of Humility

In the plight of the truly desperate, then, as well as in the close bonds of the family, we confront powerful challenges to state sovereignty over immigration. Now, in closing, I want to say something—even if only briefly and indirectly—about why this should be so. In some ways, of course, I have already hinted at reasons. The consensus in international law—established in the case of refugees, rapidly developing in that of family unity—that these groups present states with particularly compelling claims to immigrate indicates a wide recognition that there is something special about these cases. Yet that consensus is not itself the reason for their special claim; rather, it reflects a deeper truth about them. We have approached that truth in thinking about the importance of the familial bond. There I suggested that the ties we experience in our families are our first social relationships in two senses: they are first in time, forming the foundation for broader, more extensive bonds, and first in importance, experienced by us with special depth and intimacy. Perhaps we ought to say simply that in the family—and the same can be said of the truly desperate—we find an end which politics should not violate. In protecting the truly desperate we seek to protect life itself, and in protecting families we seek to preserve the most fundamental form of human community, one which nourishes and reproduces life. We engage in political action for the sake of ends such as these; they are purposes which politics exists to serve.

When we deny the claims of families or the truly desperate, we push politics, in a sense, too hard, asking it to accomplish more than it ought. This is due to the element of force in all political action. We desire to regulate immigration in order to protect our own way of life. But in doing so we necessarily call upon the power of the state. Thus our attempt to protect our own way of life relies upon the exercise of coercion, at a cost to others. Carens is surely correct to point to this fact in making his argument for open borders:

> Borders have guards and the guards have guns. This is an obvious fact of political life but one that is easily hidden from view . . . . To Haitians in small, leaky boats confronted by armed Coast Guard cutters, to Salvadorans dying from heat and lack of air after being smuggled into the Arizona desert, to Guatemalans crawling through rat-infested sewer pipes from Mexico to California—to these people the borders, guards and guns are all too apparent. What justifies the use of force against such people?[39]

I have already argued that the conclusions Carens draws from this fact are too strong; politics serves a variety of ends, among them ones that particular groups of people share in their particular ways of life. The costs that a group's exercise of political force in pursuit of those ends may impose on outsiders is not always unacceptably high. But we should ask ourselves when it might be, and I believe—and the general agreement displayed in international practice suggests that the view is more widely shared—that attempts to exclude the truly desperate or a citizen's immediate family members introduce costs that we generally do better not to impose. The element of force inherent in all political activity ought to inspire caution and lends a note of ambiguity to even well-intended communal actions. Even if one of the goals of politics is to let a people develop a common life, perhaps we should not always insist on pursuing that goal.

This is a point perhaps more easily evoked than explained, and it is evoked especially well by Vergil's *Aeneid,* one of the profoundest reflections we possess on the promise and the danger of political action in history.[40] The *Aeneid* tells the story of the Trojan hero Aeneas, "a man," as we learn in the poem's opening lines, "remarkable for goodness" (I.15–16).[41] Together with a band of followers, Aeneas escapes the sack of Troy and journeys to Italy, where he is destined to found what will ultimately become the city of Rome. The first half of the poem describes Aeneas' travels as he attempts to reach Italy, the second the war he must fight against the native Italians and their leader Turnus in order to settle there and found his kingdom. The poem is thus, in a sense, one of our great tales of migration, and as such it may appear to teach a very simple and obvious lesson to those interested in thinking about immigration: if people show up, don't let them in, because they'll steal your women, kill your men, and take your land. The *Aeneid* thus lets us see how large-scale immigration can become, from the perspective of a land's native inhabitants, no different from a foreign invasion.

The poem's deeper themes reveal a more ambiguous message, however, one apparent in the two conflicting interpretations that have contended for preeminence in the extensive literature on the *Aeneid*.[42] The first and more common view holds that the poem is essentially a glorious propaganda-piece for the Roman Empire. Vergil uses the ancient legend of Aeneas and the founding of Rome in order to foreshadow the great achievements of Rome and especially of Augustus.[43] Several prominent passages in the poem support such a reading, among them Jupiter's opening prophecy of Roman "empire without end" (I.390); the description of Aeneas' shield, forged by Vulcan, upon which are portrayed scenes from (future) Roman history culminating in Augustus' victory at Actium; and especially the famous scene in which Aeneas visits his father in the underworld and witnesses a great pageant of Roman heroes, his future descendants, with Augustus in the center. Addressed here for the first time as "Roman," Aeneas hears a ringing declaration of what will be the particular, political virtue of the Romans:

> . . . [Y]ours will be the rulership of nations,
> remember, Roman, these will be your arts:
> to teach the ways of peace to those you conquer,
> to spare defeated peoples, tame the proud. (VI.1134–7)

This reading of the *Aeneid* offers us an optimistic picture of the political order and of our loyalty or devotion to it. The poem serves as a justification for Augustus and the Roman Empire, and also for whatever losses Aeneas suffers or actions he takes in pursuing his political mission. Its portrayal of the specifically Roman greatness—"to teach the ways of peace to those you conquer, / to spare defeated peoples, tame the proud"—offers a vision of the good that politics can accomplish in the world and thus teaches that political order is a valuable human end, one to which human beings might rightfully devote their lives. Indeed, such devotion, on this view, is the very essence of Aeneas' greatest virtue, *pietas.*

The second interpretation, by contrast, is much darker, paying special attention to Vergil's famous pathos. On this view, a sense of melancholy gathers over the poem and creates a mood ill-suited to any supposed glorification of Rome. Prominent instead are Aeneas' intense suffering and loss, beginning with his persecution by Juno and extending through the destruction of Troy, the death of Aeneas' wife and father, and the divine insistence that Aeneas, when he seems for a brief moment content during his budding love affair with Dido, queen of Carthage, depart and sail on to Italy, an act that leads to Dido's suicide. These losses, far from being merely accidental, are part and parcel of Aeneas' willingness to devote himself to the political mission of founding Rome, and they thus practically compel the reader to ask whether this accomplishment is, for Aeneas himself, worth the cost. The poem's conclusion raises this question with special force. There Aeneas, after days of fierce battle with the native Italians, finally comes face-to-face with their leader, Turnus, in decisive single combat. Turnus falls, but begs for mercy, and Aeneas, moved by his plea, hesitates; but then, catching sight of Turnus' armor, stripped from one of Aeneas' fallen comrades, Aeneas slays his foe:

> . . . Aeneas,
> aflame with rage—his wrath was terrible—
> cried: "How can you who wear the spoils of my
> dear comrade now escape me? . . .
> Relentless,
> he sinks his sword into the chest of Turnus.
> His limbs fell slack with chill; and with a moan
> his life, resentful, fled to Shades below. (XII.1263–6, 1268–71)

These final, breathtakingly abrupt lines of the poem do not display the goodness for which Aeneas is renowned; on the contrary, we see him mad with anger, driven by the very forces of rage and fury which he has combated throughout the poem and from which he has suffered so greatly. Especially worthy of comment is his failure to exhibit those qualities that his father had declared the special political virtues of the Romans: "to teach the ways of peace to those you conquer, / to spare defeated peoples, tame the proud."

This darker reading carries correspondingly more pessimistic implications for political action. Whatever Augustus may accomplish, the poem's ending suggests that no more than Aeneas will he be able to conquer the forces of rage and madness, to suppress permanently strife and civil war. At their best, his achievements will remain precarious, vulnerable to the destructive forces that pervade human life. Even more troubling, perhaps, is what this reading suggests about the relation of the individual to politics. For on this view the poem reveals the terrible cost that devotion to a political cause can impose, a cost exacted most vividly and disturbingly within Aeneas himself, when, in his attempt to fulfill his destiny and found Rome, he ultimately finds himself unable to live up to his own finest virtues, the qualities for which he is known and admired. We need not conclude from this, as some have, that Aeneas ceases to be a hero altogether, or that the poem's ending utterly undermines the more positive reading of the poem.[44] Neither interpretation of the poem is entirely false; rather, the epic's greatness lies precisely in its ability to hold these two very different aspects of human life together, to praise the important accomplishments that politics can offer while also gazing steadily upon the dangers that political dedication can pose. As Wendell Clausen has put it, "It is the paradox of the *Aeneid,* the surprise of its greatness, that a poem which celebrates the achievement of an exemplary hero and the founding of Rome itself should be a long history of defeat and loss."[45] The good that politics can achieve, and the sacrifices that can sometimes be its price, with neither predominant over the other: in its ability to maintain this tension lies the *Aeneid*'s fascination.

But what can this suggest to us about immigration? In terms of specific details, probably very little; in terms of a general attitude, possibly a great deal. I have suggested that peoples attempt to regulate immigration in order to preserve their particular ways of life. In doing so, however, they call upon the coercive power that the state makes available. And this raises a tension similar to the one portrayed in the *Aeneid:* immigration policies are one tool people use in their pursuit of their various political goals, goals which may be quite valuable and praiseworthy; yet the pursuit of those goals, involving as it does the use of state power, can carry costs of its own. The *Aeneid* at least suggests that we should be cautious about pushing the claims of state power too far and that whether its associated costs are worth paying is always an open question. In the first sections of this chapter I have suggested two kinds of cases in which the costs seem to me, as a general rule, too high. This is at least in part because the ends which we pursue together, as a political community and using the force of the collectivity, are only some of the ends which human beings have, and these ends can some-times conflict with each other. Thus if we recognize the importance of, for example, preserving human life or sustaining the family unit, we may occa-sionally find ourselves called upon to temper other ends we may have. This, at least, is how the situation that a country faces when confronted by the claims of refugees or separated family members appears to me.

Such a situation calls for a careful balancing of the different claims at stake. I have no simple formula for carrying out this balancing act, no equation with which one could solve the difficult cases. I doubt that any exists. What I can recommend, though, is an attitude, an attitude which the *Aeneid* helps to illustrate: an attitude of sensitivity, of caution and even humility, towards the variety of genuine and worthy ends that human beings pursue, the ways in which they pursue them, and the conclusions they reach about these ends' relative value or their proper ordering in dif-ferent circumstances. Such an attitude alerts us to both the possibilities as well as the limits of political action. It is not simply an uncritical attitude. On the contrary, I hope I have said enough here to suggest that we can, in my view, reach some conclusions about what some of these important ends are and how they may be related and that we can argue reasonably about how best to realize them in practice. Even to say, though, that we can argue reasonably about such things is itself to concede that people will have dif-ferent plausible arguments to make, different plausible answers to give. In my first chapter I sought to describe some of the huge variety of motives we encounter in thinking about human migration—different motives for moving, different motives for accepting or not accepting strangers. And all these motives occur in a world of different human communities, with dif-ferent ways of life, pursuing various goals, and calling upon political power in a complex variety of ways to do so. We can hardly expect to come up with some simple way of resolving the tremendous variety of situations that result. But we can seek to approach the problem in a manner appro-priate to its complexity, sensitive to both the enduring needs of human beings—the demands of life itself, for example, or the deep needs satisfied in the family—as well as the rich, variegated creativity of people in meet-ing these needs.

Because immigration policies are closely related to different conceptions of political community, as I have shown in the previous chapters, easy answers to the problems posed by immigration would be possible only if we could show that there is a single form of political community that all human beings ought to share. But, as I suggested in chapter three, that argument has not been made; or, more precisely and cautiously, even if it has been made, there are many people who have not yet been persuaded of it and who, moreover, can offer plausible arguments to the contrary. In such circumstances, the appropriate response is, I think, the one I have sketched here: to concede to different communities considerable discretion in shaping and preserving their particular ways of life, while also trying to be attentive to what the limits of that discretion might be. This, I admit, is a view of politics that seeks to establish only certain baseline requirements—a floor of legitimacy, one might say—and leaves the rest up to people's inevitably diverse attempts—political and non-political, individual and collective—to respond to changing circumstances as they deem best. But it is justified, I would submit, by the difficulty of establishing—or of establishing in a way sufficient to persuade many (most?) people—that the baseline requirements, the minimal standards of legitimacy, are more far-reaching and restrictive than suggested here. The distance between what is legitimate and what is required leaves considerable scope for diversity and experimentation. This does not mean, of course, that no response to a given problem is better than any other. There may be good reasons for preferring one legitimate course of action to another—but that is always a matter for argument among the people whose decision it is to make.

I have argued in this chapter that we ought not to push the claims of political power too far, that we instead ought to recognize other important claims before which politics should bow. This may at first glance appear to be a rather different argument from the one made in chapter three, where I sought to carve out as wide a sphere as possible for political action and to acknowledge that politics and national identity may merge in a wide variety of acceptable ways. I therefore want to emphasize here that the two parts of the argument, in my view, are very much in harmony with one another, and that they are derived from a common impulse. In both cases, the purpose of the argument is to protect people's ordinary, everyday lives, whatever those may be like. Politics can threaten this end in two ways. It can seek to swallow up the whole of life, to deny that there might be any other moral claims that exceed its grasp or transcend it in importance. It is against that danger that I have cautioned here in seeking to explore the limits of the political. But it also threatens the normal texture of everyday life when it seeks—often, ironically, in the very name of limited, liberal, neutral government—to stifle expressions of that life, when, for example, it imagines that its task is to thwart the various ways in which a people's culture, ideals, principles, or traditions—its identity—inevitably bubble over into the public, political sphere. It is against this danger that the earlier argument in chapter three sought to guard, by warning against unduly restricting the range of forms that political life, under the influence of particular customs, circumstances, and desires, can take. In both its parts, then, the argument is intended to ensure that politics remains our servant instead of becoming our master, an endeavor that requires vigilance against both kinds of threat.[46]

I end this reflection on the limits of state discretion in the realm of immigration with one final example, again a literary one—and again more evocative than directly explanatory—of why we ought not close our countries entirely to strangers. I take this example from the life of Robert Louis Stevenson. Stevenson was a Scot, and proud of his native country, which was always very dear to him. Yet he suffered from poor health his entire life and consequently spent much of it traveling in search of relief from his afflictions. These travels eventually took him to the South Seas and ultimately to the island of Samoa, where he settled and spent the last years of his life.[47] There—in so many ways as far as it was possible to get from his native Scotland—he found a second home, building himself a great house, inhabited by his family and a number of devoted Samoan servants. He became deeply involved in the life of the natives, often defending their interests in print against the ambitions of competing European colonial powers, and the natives in turn came to love him deeply, referring to him in their own language as *Tusitala,* teller of tales. Stevenson died in Samoa and was buried, as he had instructed, on top of a high mountain there, where he had inscribed upon his tombstone his own poem "Requiem:"

> Under the wide and starry sky,
> Dig the grave and let me lie.
> Glad did I live and gladly die,
>   And I laid me down with a will.
>
> This be the verse you grave for me:
> *Here he lies where he longed to be;*
> *Home is the sailor, home from sea,*
>   *And the hunter home from the hill.*[48]

The ultimate point of Stevenson's poem, of course, is that the final home for human beings lies on the other side of the grave. But it is also striking that he was willing to have this particular poem posted over a grave in Samoa, so far from his native land. That he did so may suggest to us something about the ability of human beings to find "home" in surprising places. This is not to say that Stevenson ever forgot or abandoned his love for Scotland; indeed, there are two plaques over his tomb, and one of them bears the thistle, emblem of Scotland. But Samoa had truly become a second home for Stevenson; and the second of the plaques bears the hibiscus flower, emblem of Samoa.[49] As Stevenson wrote in a letter to his friend Sidney Colvin,

> Fanny [Stevenson's wife] and I rode home [from a Samoan celebration], and I moralised by the way. Could we ever stand Europe again? did she appreciate that if we were in London, we should be *actually jostled* on the street? and there was nobody in the whole of Britain who knew how to take *ava* [a native Samoan drink, important in rituals] like a gentleman? 'Tis funny to be thus of two civilisations—or, if you like, of one civilisation and one barbarism. And as usual the barbarism is the more engaging.[50]

Stevenson's discovery that he could be "of two civilisations," as well as the placement of his haunting "Requiem" over a tomb in a far-away land, can remind us that "home" may not always be where we expect it. For some people, perhaps, "home" may be someplace other than where they now live—may even be among us. And the more literal meaning of Stevenson's poem, of course, reminds us that our own current home is at most a temporary one. As Augustine wrote of the Christian, we live "like a pilgrim in a foreign land."[51]

The possibility that home may be someplace else—the human ability to discover and build a new home—may make us at least hesitant about shutting our doors to outsiders completely. The national bond is an important one, but it is not our only important bond, nor need it be immutable or unbreakable. To recognize this is to recognize something about the fragility of even the best states and of the political power that helps preserve them. This fragility has multiple implications, indicating both their need for support as well as the evanescence of the claims they make. Gesturing towards this fragility may not be the worst way to end a book about immigration.

Notes

Introduction

1. For what follows, see, for example, Stephen Castles and Mark J. Miller, *The Age of Migration: International Population Movements in the Modern World,* 2nd. ed. (London: Macmillan Press, 1998); William Rogers Brubaker (ed.), *Immigration and the Politics of Citizenship in Europe and North America* (Lanham, New York, and London: University Press of America, with the German Marshall Fund of the United States, 1989); and David Jacobson, *Rights Across Borders: Immigration and the Decline of Citizenship* (Baltimore: The Johns Hopkins University Press, 1996).

2. For Carens's argument, see "Aliens and Citizens: The Case for Open Borders," *The Review of Politics* 49.2 (Spring 1987), pp. 251–73. See also Bruce Ackerman, *Social Justice in the Liberal State* (New Haven: Yale University Press, 1980), ch. 3, "Citizenship"; Veit Bader, "Citizenship and Exclusion: Radical Democracy, Community, and Justice. Or, What Is Wrong with Communitarianism?", *Political Theory* 23.2 (May 1995), pp. 211–46; and Roger Nett, "The Civil Right We Are Not Ready For: The Right of Free Movement of People on the Face of the Earth," *Ethics* 81.3 (April 1971), pp. 212–27. The balance of essays in Warren F. Schwartz (ed.), *Justice in immigration* (Cambridge: Cambridge University Press, 1995), a valuable collection, is also instructive; of the five essays in the volume which Joseph Carens, in his introductory essay, identifies as employing a "discourse of justice," four argue that justice would require significantly more open borders than currently exist. Similarly, Brian Barry, in his concluding essay in Brian Barry and Robert E. Goodin (eds.), *Free Movement: Ethical issues in the transnational migration of people and money* (University Park, PA: Pennsylvania State University Press, 1992), refers to "the consensus among the contributors that morality ideally mandates open borders" (p. 283), even though some of them might accept limited restrictions as concessions to practical necessities. Another body of literature attempts to assess the role of receiving states in producing immigrant flows in the first place. Authors such as Saskia Sassen, Alejandro Portes, Frank Bonilla, and Douglas Massey have examined how states' policies regarding (for example) foreign investment, free trade, or war help

create conditions that in various ways lead to the migratory flows which are then portrayed, often negatively, as "immigration." A full treatment of this complex and growing literature would require a separate book; it is one of the numerous avenues I have left unexplored in my attempt to focus my arguments here on the ethical permissibility of preference for one's own people and way of life. Including it would not, I think, fundamentally alter the theoretical landscape described here in the introduction, since attempts to show greater receiving state responsibility for immigrant flows would presumably reinforce the political and intellectual trends restricting the state's sovereignty and questioning its traditional authority to control its borders. Nevertheless, this perspective deserves greater attention than space considerations here permit.

3. Cf. Plato, *The Republic*, bk. III; Aristotle, *Nicomachean Ethics*, bks. VIII and IX; St. Augustine, *The City of God*, bk. XIX.

4. Cf. Hobbes, *Leviathan*, bk. II, ch. xxviii; Locke, *Second Treatise of Government*, chs. 6 and 8; and Rousseau, *The Social Contract*, bk. I, chs. 6 and 7.

5. Cf. Rawls, *A Theory of Justice*, ch. 1. Among the most important communitarian responses are Michael Sandel, *Liberalism and the Limits of Justice* (Cambridge: Cambridge University Press, 1982), and Michael Walzer, *Spheres of Justice* (New York: Basic Books, 1983).

6. The quoted passage is Harry Clor's partial list of the various principles and purposes "of our complex liberal [American] polity;" see Clor, "Constitutional Interpretation and Regime Principles," in Robert A. Goldwin and William A. Schambra (eds.), *The Constitution, the Courts, and the Quest for Justice* (Washington, D.C.: American Enterprise Institute, 1989), p. 131. Clor also usefully draws attention to the similar emphasis in *Federalist* 37 on "combining the requisite stability and energy in government with the inviolable attention due to liberty, and to the republican form" and "mingling them together in their due proportions" (cited at Clor, p. 131).

7. Some scholars have recently attempted, largely in response to communitarian criticisms of Rawls, to justify allowing cultural concerns a place in liberal politics. Will Kymlicka's *Liberalism, Community, and Culture* (Oxford: Oxford University Press, 1989) and *Multicultural Citizenship* (Oxford: Clarendon Press, 1995) are the foremost examples of this argument. It is telling that such attempts typically focus, as Kymlicka does, on problems of minority cultures or group rights. Simple fairness, however, would suggest that if culture is valuable and politically relevant, this is as true of majorities as it is of minorities. Though it is hardly my main emphasis, one might think of my approach as an attempt to redress this imbalance. At any rate, my approach certainly implies a far more robust defense of culture, even within liberal democracy, than someone like Kymlicka contemplates.

8. The view outlined here has certain similarities to that articulated by Rawls in his recent *The Law of Peoples* (Harvard University Press, 1999). It may well be true, as some argue, that his argument there is inconsistent with his earlier arguments for the original position in *A Theory of Justice*. This, however, would only

indicate that liberalism can reasonably retreat from the cosmopolitanism that may have been implicit in his early theory, and perhaps even that it should.

9. Inevitably, though, aspects of this view will receive at least a partial defense in the course of the larger argument to follow. In this respect I direct the reader's attention especially to the discussion of legitimacy and my two-tiered approach to problems of political morality in chapter three.

Chapter 1

1. Notwithstanding Hobbes, for whom all migration would have been voluntary, since actions "that have their beginning from Aversion, or Feare of those consequences that follow the omission, are *voluntary actions."* Thomas Hobbes, *Leviathan,* ed. Richard Tuck (Cambridge: Cambridge University Press, 1994), p. 45 (emphasis in original).
2. Thomas Sowell, *Race and Culture: A World View* (New York: Basic Books, 1994), p. 69.
3. Aderanti Adepoju, "The Politics of International Migration in Post-Colonial Africa," in Robin Cohen (ed.), *The Cambridge Survey of World Migration* (Cambridge: Cambridge University Press, 1995), p. 170. Henceforth I shall refer to this book simply as *Survey.*
4. *Ibid.,* pp. 170–1.
5. Celestine Bohlen, "Albanian Refugees in Italy Are in a Crowded Limbo," in *The New York Times* on the World Wide Web (www.nytimes.com), March 18, 1997.
6. Carl-Ulrik Schierup, "Former Yugoslavia: Long Waves of International Migration," in *Survey,* p. 288.
7. "Whereabouts of Kosovo Refugees," in *The New York Times* on the World Wide Web (www.nytimes.com), May 28, 1999.
8. Robert Scally, "The Irish and the 'Famine Exodus' of 1847," in *Survey,* p. 81. I consider the Great Famine again briefly in chapter 6.
9. Klas-Göran Karlsson, "Migration and Soviet Disintegration," in *Survey,* p. 488.
10. Sowell, *Race and Culture,* p. 188.
11. *Ibid.,* p. 186.
12. See *ibid.,* pp. 186–7.
13. Thomas Sowell, *Migrations and Cultures: A World View* (New York: BasicBooks, 1996), p. 248.
14. Adepoju, "The Politics of International Migration in Post-Colonial Africa," pp. 167–9.
15. The citations and figures about Germany and eastern Europe in this paragraph are all from the opening pages of Heinz Fassmann and Rainer Münz, "European East-West Migration, 1945– 1992," in *Survey,* pp. 470–72. See also their Table 14.1 on p. 471.
16. To give just one example, taken more or less at random: Philip Martin, under the heading "Why Migration?", writes, "Migration occurs because of demand-pull factors that draw migrants into industrial countries, supply-push factors

that push them out of their own countries, and networks of friends and relatives already in industrial societies who serve as anchor communities for newcomers." From "The Migration Issue," in Russell King (ed.), *The New Geography of European Migrations* (London and New York: Belhaven Press, 1993), p. 4.

17. Cf., for example, the quote from Martin in the previous note.

18. Bernard Bailyn, in his "Introduction" to Nicholas Canny (ed.), *Europeans on the Move: Studies on European Migration, 1500–1800* (Oxford: Clarendon Press, 1994), similarly refers to the need to "relate large-scale phenomena to micronarratives[, bypassing] loose, abstract categories like 'push' and 'pull', 'poverty', 'mobility', and 'discontent' in favour of specific events and detailed circumstances, precise triggers of dislocation and propulsion, and precisely delineated decisions and choices" (p. 5). I had thought the text made it sufficiently clear, but since several readers have questioned it, let me repeat here that my use of the push-pull model, which recent scholarship has (correctly) criticized as inadequate, does not constitute an endorsement of it. If, being an underpaid assistant professor, I buy a cheap but adequate closet organizer at K-Mart, my purchase in no way implies the view that my new possession is the best way of organizing one's closet. If it suffices to bring some temporary order into my belongings, I am content to leave the task of discovering the best such method to those whose job it is to design closet organizers. In the same fashion, the push-pull model is "out there" and is convenient for my present limited purposes; since this book is not intended to provide a social-scientific explanation of migration flows, I cheerfully leave the task of finding the best model for such flows to others, better suited to it than I. Push-pull here is simply my closet organizer for human motives, and nothing further should be read into it.

19. Jon Gjerde, "The Scandinavian Migrants," in *Survey*, pp. 85–6.

20. Georg Fertig, "Transatlantic Migration from the German-Speaking Parts of Central Europe, 1600–1800: Proportions, Structures, Explanations," in Canny, *Europeans on the Move*, p. 208.

21. The final citation and the numbers for Jews leaving Russia are from Sowell, *Migrations and Cultures*, p. 264.

22. For a brief history of the Jews' dispersal throughout the world, and of the difficulties they have faced nearly everywhere they went, including the examples cited in the text, see Ch. 6, "Jews of the Diaspora," in Sowell, *Migrations and Cultures*. For a treatment of Jews in Nazi Germany and earlier in tsarist Russia, see Colin Holmes, "Jewish Economic and Refugee Migrations, 1880–1950," in *Survey*, pp. 148–53.

23. See Tanya Basok and Alexander Benifand, "Soviet Jewish Emigration," in *Survey*, pp. 502–506, esp. p. 503. Total Soviet Jewish emigration for the years mentioned in the text can be found in their Table 14.8 on p. 502.

24. See Karlsson, "Migration and Soviet Disintegration," p. 488.

25. *Ibid.*, p. 486.

26. Fassmann and Münz, "European East-West Migration," p. 477.

27. Karlsson, "Migration and Soviet Disintegration," p. 488.

28. Fassmann and Münz, "European East-West Migration," in Table 14.2, p. 473; see also pp. 475–6.
29. Rudolph J. Vecoli, "The Italian Diaspora, 1876–1976," in *Survey,* pp. 116–18.
30. Gjerde, "The Scandinavian Migrants," p. 89.
31. Scally, "The Irish and the 'Famine Exodus,'" p. 81.
32. Jan Lucassen, "Emigration to the Dutch Colonies and the USA," in *Survey,* pp. 24–5.
33. See Sowell, *Migrations and Cultures,* p. 344.
34. Christopher Caldwell, "Germany Goes Amerikanisch," from the December 1998 issue of *The American Spectator,* at www.spectator.org/archives/98–12_caldwell.html.
35. Ida Altman, "Spanish Migration to the Americas," in *Survey,* pp. 29, 30.
36. Vecoli, "The Italian Diaspora," p. 116.
37. Walter Nugent, *Crossings: The Great Transatlantic Migrations, 1870–1914* (Bloomington: Indiana University Press, 1992), p. 35. Nugent emphasizes the effect of advances in transportation, particularly steam-powered sea voyages: "Its [migration's] magnitude in the late nineteenth century . . . was unprecedented, thanks to steamship and steam railway networks after 1870, and most dramatically in the 1880s" (p. 11; see also pp. 31–2). He also notes "the creation of a railroad network and more regular passenger sailings" in Germany, as well as that of "a network of railroads and canals" in America, as a condition making possible the great transatlantic migrations of the nineteenth century in "Migration from the German and Austro- Hungarian Empires to North America," in *Survey,* p. 104.
38. Nugent, *Crossings,* p. 34.
39. See Nugent, *Crossings,* p. 48 for the British; p. 53 for Irish women; and p. 67 for German farm families.
40. Ewa Morawska, "East Europeans on the Move, "in *Survey,* p. 98.
41. Gérard Noiriel, "Russians and Armenians in France," in *Survey,* p. 145.
42. *Idem.*
43. Altman, "Spanish Migration to the Americas," pp. 29–30 (references omitted).
44. Sowell, *Migrations and Cultures,* pp. 5, 6. Sowell lists a number of other illustrations of this phenomenon as well; on this topic in general, see pp. 4–9.
45. *Crossings,* p. 59. The internal quote is from Kristin Hvidt, *Flight to America: The Social Background of 300,000 Danish Emigrants* (New York: Academic Press, 1975), p. 192.
46. All quotations in this paragraph are from Herbert S. Klein, "European and Asian Migration to Brazil," in *Survey,* pp. 208–9.
47. For France's low birth rate, see Nugent, *Crossings,* ch. 3 ("Fertility and Mortality"), esp. p. 19 and Table 6 on p. 20. The quote from Cohen is from his editorial introduction to "Part Five: Migration in Europe, 1800–1950," in *Survey,* p. 124.
48. Gérard Noiriel, "Italians and Poles in France, 1880–1945," in *Survey,* p. 143.
49. Gérard Noiriel, "Russians and Armenians in France," in *Survey,* p. 145.
50. Sowell, *Race and Culture,* p. 69.
51. Seymour Phillips, "The Medieval Background," in Canny, p. 15, fn. 16.

52. *Idem.*
53. Ulrich Im Hof, *The Enlightenment* (Oxford and Cambridge, Mass.: Blackwell, 1994), p. 223.
54. *Ibid.,* p. 228.
55. *Ibid,* p. 231–2 (travel literature); 232–3 (cartography, botany, zoology, and ethnology).
56. Ong Jin Hui, "Chinese Indentured Labour: Coolies and Colonies," in *Survey,* pp. 51–2.
57. Nugent discusses Canada's policies for populating its own western frontier in *Crossings,* pp. 142–8.
58. *Ibid.,* p. 152.
59. *Ibid.,* p. 120. See also p. 119 for this "second stage of its [Argentina's] immigration history."
60. As quoted in *ibid.,* p. 159.
61. Julian L. Simon, *The Economic Consequences of Immigration* (Cambridge, Mass.: Basil Blackwell, 1989).
62. Roy Beck, *The Case Against Immigration: The moral, economic, social, and environmental reasons for reducing U.S. immigration back to traditional levels* (New York: W.W. Norton & Company, 1996), p. 136.
63. Noiriel, "Russians and Armenians in France," p. 145.
64. Alan Dowty makes the same point from the opposite perspective, explaining the Soviet controls on emigration: "A large-scale exodus would have constituted an unacceptable blow to Soviet self-esteem. Soviet leaders saw themselves as engaged in an ongoing struggle with hostile forces throughout the world. That some Soviet citizens might prefer to live elsewhere, especially in the capitalist West, was highly threatening." *Closed Borders: The Contemporary Assault on Freedom of Movement* (New Haven: Yale University Press, 1987), p. 73.
65. Fassmann and Münz, "European East-West Migration," p. 475.
66. *Spheres of Justice: A Defense of Pluralism and Equality* (New York: Basic Books, Inc., Publishers, 1983), p. 49. Walzer writes, "Perhaps every victim of authoritarianism and bigotry is the moral comrade of a liberal citizen: that is an argument I would like to make. But that would press affinity too hard . . ." (49).
67. These arguments are made at great length for the contemporary American case in Peter Brimelow, *Alien Nation: Common Sense About America's Immigration Disaster* (New York: HarperPerennial, 1996), chs. 7 and 8; and in Beck, *The Case Against Immigration*, chs. 5–7 and 10.
68. Of course, racist motivations were mixed with genuine economic fears about cheap Chinese labor taking American jobs. Such mixed motives can in practice often be hard to untangle.
69. Quoted in Joseph H. Carens, "Nationalism and the Exclusion of Immigrants: Lessons from Australian Immigration Policy," in Mark Gibney (ed.), *Open Borders? Closed Societies? The Ethical and Political Issues* (Westport, Conn.: Greenwood Press, 1988), p. 45. Carens himself quotes the passage from H.I. London, *Non-White Immigration and the "White Australia" Policy* (New York: New York

University Press, 1970), p. 98. Carens's essay provides a good brief overview and a critical discussion of the policy.

70. *Ibid.,* p. 49.

71. Joseph H. Carens, "Immigration, Political Community, and the Transformation of Identity: Quebec's Immigration Policies in Critical Perspective," in Joseph H. Carens (ed.), *Is Quebec Nationalism Just? Perspectives from Anglophone Canada* (Montreal & Kingston: McGill-Queen's University Press, 1995), p. 29.

72. Beck, *The Case Against Immigration,* p. 230.

73. *Ibid.,* p. 231.

74. *Ibid.,* p. 233.

Chapter 2

1. Two important anthologies are Warren F. Schwartz (ed.), *Justice in immigration* (Cambridge: Cambridge University Press, 1995) and Brian Barry and Robert E. Goodin (eds.), *Free Movement: Ethical issues in the transnational migration of people and of money* (University Park, PA: The Pennsylvania State University Press, 1992), though, as the subtitle indicates, not all the essays in the latter deal with the migration of people. Another collection is Mark Gibney (ed.), *Open Borders? Closed Societies? The Ethical and Political Issues* (New York, London, and Westport, CT: Greenwood Press, 1988), though the second half of this collection is specifically about the problem of refugees. For Carens, see note 30. In addition to works already cited in the introduction and its accompanying notes, see also Herman R. van Gunsteren, "Admission to Citizenship," *Ethics* 98.4 (1988): 731–41; and Timothy King, "Immigration from Developing Countries: Some Philosophical Issues," *Ethics* 93.3 (1983): 25–36.

2. See, for example, the literature cited in the introduction, note 2. In addition to those references, Matthew Gibney has also recently made the same observation, noting that "those few who have considered these issues ['entrance policy'] almost invariably argue for radical changes in the policies of liberal democracies." Gibney is referring to "writers in the major impartialist strands of political theory, liberalism and utilitarianism;" but since the only example of a "partialist" thinker to whom he devotes attention and who writes specifically about immigration is Walzer (see below), his description essentially corroborates my characterization of the literature as a whole. (See Gibney, "Liberal Democratic States and Responsibilities to Refugees," *American Political Science Review* 93.1 [March 1999], p. 171.) The one significant exception to the claim made here about the general trend of the literature is Michael Walzer, *Spheres of Justice* (New York: Basic Books, Inc., 1983), ch. 2 ("Membership"). Because his argument is such a superb illustration of the claims I make concerning the connection between views on immigration and different conceptions of political community, I consider Walzer's argument separately in the second half of chapter five. Also worth noting for their attempt to defend (on the whole) current state practice with regard to immigration are Jules L. Coleman and Sarah K.

Harding, "Citizenship, the demands of justice, and the moral relevance of political borders," in Schwartz, *Justice in immigration,* pp. 18–62. Insofar as their argument rests upon a Kymlickian claim that borders help protect individuals' access to the good of membership in a political community (see esp. pp. 40–46), the doubts I raise in chapter five about the adequacy of Kymlicka's defense of community apply equally to their particular defense of state control over immigration.

3. Peter Brimelow, *Alien Nation: Common Sense About America's Immigration Disaster* (New York: HarperPerennial, 1996); Roy Beck, *The Case Against Immigration: The moral, economic, social, and environmental reasons for reducing U.S. immigration back to traditional levels* (New York: W.W. Norton & Company, 1996); Chilton Williamson, Jr., *The Immigration Mystique: America's False Conscience* (New York: BasicBooks, 1996). Page references for citations from these works will be given in the text, together with the author's last name when the source of the quote is not clear from the context.

4. Recall Brian Barry's observation, cited in the introduction, note 2, of a "consensus among the contributors [to the volume in question] that morality ideally mandates open borders."

5. Cf. the following statement by Carens: "Americans' concern for the economic well-being of those who are already citizens and their descendants is clearly a central motivation of those who want to restrict immigration in order to maintain the welfare state. But the priority of liberty in the Rawlsian version of social contract theory makes such a concern irrelevant" ("Immigration and the Welfare State," in Amy Gutmann [ed.], *Democracy and the Welfare State* [Princeton: Princeton University Press, 1988], pp. 215–16). Similarly, Carens writes elsewhere of the application of an international difference principle: "[O]ne could not justify restrictions [on immigration] on the grounds that immigration would reduce the economic well-being of current citizens . . . . So, the economic concerns of current citizens are essentially rendered irrelevant" ("Aliens and Citizens: The Case for Open Borders," *The Review of Politics* 49.2 [Spring 1987], p. 262).

6. Cf. Williamson, p. xii (paragraph division omitted): "Therefore, at the level of what passes for serious public debate, immigrationists and anti-immigrationists, liberals, conservatives, and moderates, have—until lately, anyway—confined themselves largely to the economic argument: Immigration increases, immigration does not increase but rather decreases, American prosperity, as measured by the gross domestic product and econometric standards of efficiency. The rather offensive superficiality of the discussion that necessarily results is an evasion, rather than a denial, of the essentially moral nature of the problems posed by immigration."

7. See, for example, pages 5–9, and also p. 259, which lists as one of the principles that ought to guide American immigration policy, "Immigration must be treated as a luxury for the United States, not as a necessity" (original in italics). His elaboration of this and his other three principles over the following pages

make it clear that, in his view, America is entitled to choose the policy that is best for America.

8. Cf. Walzer, *Spheres of Justice,* p. 31: "The primary good that we distribute to one another is membership in some human community." Note that neither this nor Brimelow's formulation entails that a community is *required* to maintain itself in existence, only that democracy implies its right to do so.

9. To be somewhat more precise: Brimelow does not regard high immigration itself as undemocratic; rather, it is the way in which this has come about—through the unintended consequences of the 1965 Immigration Act, consequences which it was denied would occur—that has deprived Americans of their democratic self-government. Americans could, of course, democratically choose mass immigration, and thus voluntarily allow their nation to be transformed (see previous note), but in the present circumstances they have been denied that opportunity. See, for example, Brimelow, pp. 20–22, "Americans Ought to be Asked."

10. In the same place, Brimelow also defines a "nation-state" as "*the political expression of a nation*" (203; emphasis in original).

11. Cf. note 6.

12. The quote continues with this rhetorical question, to which Williamson's implied answer is clear: "Is *any* nation justified in committing its citizens to anything beyond the welfare of their families and their country, their chosen or appointed work, and their God?" (29; emphasis in original)

13. Interestingly, Brimelow uses the same image, though in a slightly different way: "[I]mmigration enthusiasts have been able to get away with treating American immigration history as a sort of Rorschach blot, into which they can read their personal preoccupations" (14).

14. See Beck, ch. 2; Williamson, ch. 2; and Brimelow, chs. 2–5. The summary in the preceding paragraph is drawn from their accounts.

15. Frederick G. Whelan, "Citizenship and the Right to Leave," *American Political Science Review* 75.3 (Sept. 1981), p. 651.

16. *Idem.*

17. Frederick G. Whelan, "Citizenship and Freedom of Movement: An Open Admission Policy?", in Mark Gibney (ed.), *Open Borders? Closed Societies? The Ethical and Political Issues* (Westport, CT: Greenwood Press, 1988), p. 22.

18. *Idem.* The reference to a "liberal base" is from *ibid.,* p. 23.

19. *Ibid.,* p. 23. This argument seems quite similar to Joseph Carens's recognition of a "public order restriction" (see n. 32), according to which "liberty may be restricted for the sake of liberty," as a qualification of his argument for open borders. But Carens too emphasizes that the restrictions which could be justified under such a proviso are in reality quite limited: even though "some restrictions on immigration would be justified under the public order principle . . . it is important to recall all the qualifications that apply to this. In particular, the need for some restriction would not justify any level of restriction whatsoever or restrictions for other reasons, but only that level of restriction essential to maintain

public order. This would surely imply a much less restrictive policy than the one currently in force which is shaped by so many other considerations besides the need to maintain public order." See Carens, "Aliens and Citizens," pp. 258–60.

20. *Ibid.*, p. 34. The characterization of these perspectives as "hybrid" is Whelan's own; see p. 23.

21. Lest I leave the impression that Whelan's articles themselves are such a hodge-podge, let me quickly add that, to the contrary, they are models of analytical clarity and are extremely helpful, especially in their use of the canon to shed light on immigration puzzles. My point here is simply that they do not really present a particularly strong a defense of the state's right to regulate immigration.

22. Mark Gibney, *Strangers or Friends: Principles for a New Alien Admission Policy* (Westport, CT: Greenwood Press, 1986), p. ix. Further references will be identified by page number in parentheses within the text.

23. In fairness, some readers will no doubt level precisely the opposite charge at me (though I do not make the same claim to be striking a balance between current practice and a properly moral policy, since I regard current practice as already striking a by-and-large defensible balance); and it may be that Gibney's emphasis derives in part from a sort of strategic consideration. Viewing prevailing intellectual trends within liberal political theory, I am inclined to think that political community and self-government need defense more than do international moral obligations; but perhaps Gibney, looking upon prevailing international law and policy, thought the opposite. If that were the case, then our differences in approach would conceal a significant shared middle ground. I do think it is fair to say, though, that the goals which Gibney seeks to balance— individual rights vs. communal autonomy—seem somewhat *ad hoc*, less defended than assumed.

24. Though my own approach, as will become clear later, differs significantly from Gibney's, I do think that his HP is a promising starting-point for reflection and possesses the significant virtue of seeking to correct specific wrongs in which the party responsible for the injustice, the party suffering it, and the precise nature of the harm itself can all be concretely identified. In my view, however, the virtue of this is less what Gibney seems to think, namely, that it allows us to specify precisely what our moral duties (and their limits) are—since, after all, we can presumably specify our duties in any number of ways, some of them more, others less reasonable—than that it eschews attempts to achieve an imagined state of ideal justice in favor of addressing particular and identifiable historical wrongs. Obviously, the same reason leads me to be more skeptical of his BRP.

25. Gibney does point out, correctly, that a country's HP obligations are presumably largely within its own control. Yet one of his own favorite examples of how HP obligations originate raises doubts about this. Gibney argues that under the HP, countries engaged in a war, because of the special duty not to harm noncombatants, may acquire an obligation to admit as immigrants (though not necessarily permanent ones) noncombatants whose security is

threatened by their military actions. Unless we assume that there are no just wars, however, this seems perverse; it would mean that a country engaged in a just war would have to take special precautions—positive actions, that is, exceeding the normal limitations imposed by just war theory, such as not targeting civilians—to protect the citizens of its hostile opponent. Since such requirements might significantly discourage or hamper the fighting of even a justified war, it is hard to know why we would want to impose them; and, indeed, I think that only an extremely rule-governed approach to morality, like Gibney's, would produce such a conclusion. Gibney's casual attitude toward foreign policy considerations in the context of the Cold War presents a similar example; see, e.g., pp. 124, 143–4.

26. This emphasis on autonomy leads him at times to say peculiar things, such as when he writes, in discussing policy towards Haiti, that "alien admissions might well be the only effective means of protecting the autonomy of individuals singled out for death or persecution" (123). I should not have thought that protecting autonomy was our chief concern in a case like this. Indeed, the same could be said of Gibney's presentation of the Harm Principle in these terms (79–80); since he emphasizes that it is only intended to address serious harms, it is not clear why we need to defend it on the basis of autonomy, the implications of which appear much more far-reaching.

27. Bruce A. Ackerman, *Social Justice in the Liberal State* (New Haven and London: Yale University Press, 1980), p. 95; emphasis, in both citations, in the original.

28. Veit Bader, "Citizenship and Exclusion: Radical Democracy, Community, and Justice. Or, What Is Wrong with Communitarianism?", *Political Theory* 23.2 (May 1995), p. 213; see also his argument for this view on pp. 213–16.

29. Onora O'Neill, "Justice and Boundaries." In Christine Chwaszcza and Wolfgang Kersting, *Politische Philosophie der internationalen Beziehungen* (Frankfurt: Suhrkamp, 1998). The first citation is on p. 518, the second and third are on p. 520. As the third makes clear (and as the second obscures), O'Neill's argument is intended to refute considerably more than merely the case for "absolute" sovereignty, something which I do not defend here and which is hardly a part of most people's ordinary assumptions about the state's powers.

30. See Joseph H. Carens, "Compromises in Politics," in *Nomos*, vol. XXI, *Compromise in Ethics, Law, and Politics* (New York: New York University Press, 1979), pp. 123–41 (hereafter CiP); "Aliens and Citizens: The Case for Open Borders," *The Review of Politics* 49.2 (Spring 1987), pp. 251–73 (hereafter AaC); "Who belongs? Theoretical and legal questions about birthright citizenship in the United States," *University of Toronto Law Journal* XXXVII.4 (Fall 1987), pp. 413–43 (hereafter WB); "Nationalism and the Exclusion of Immigrants: Lessons from Australian Immigration Policy," in Mark Gibney (ed.), *Open Borders? Closed Societies? The Ethical and Political Issues* (New York and Westport, Conn.: Greenwood Press, 1988), pp. 41– 60 (hereafter Austr); "Immigration and the Welfare State," in Amy Gutmann (ed.), *Democracy and the Welfare State* (Princeton: Princeton University Press, 1988), pp. 207–30 (hereafter IWS);

"Membership and Morality: Admission to Citizenship in Liberal Democratic States," in William Rogers Brubaker, *Immigration and the Politics of Citizenship in Europe and North America* (Lanham, MD: University Press of America, 1989), pp. 31–49 (hereafter MemaM); "Migration and Morality: A liberal egalitarian perspective," in Brian Barry and Robert E. Goodin (eds.), *Free Movement: Ethical issues in the transnational migration of people and money* (University Park, PA: The Pennsylvania State University Press, 1992), pp. 25–47 (hereafter MigaM); "Democracy and Respect for Difference: The Case of Fiji," *University of Michigan Journal of Law Reform* 25.3–4 (Spring and Summer 1992), pp. 547–631 (hereafter Fiji); "The Rights of Immigrants," in Judith Baker (ed.), *Group Rights* (Toronto: University of Toronto Press, 1994), pp. 142–63 (hereafter RoI); "Immigration, Political Community, and the Transformation of Identity: Quebec's Immigration Policies in Critical Perspective," in Carens (ed.), *Is Quebec Nationalism Just? Perspectives from Anglophone Canada* (Montreal and Kingston: McGill-Queen's University Press, 1995), pp. 20–81 (hereafter Quebec); "Realistic and Idealistic Approaches to the Ethics of Migration," *International Migration Review* XXX.1 (Spring 1996), pp. 156–70 (hereafter RealIdea); "Reconsidering Open Borders," *International Migration Review* XXXIII.4 (Winter 1999), pp. 1082–97 (hereafter ROB); and *Culture, Citizenship, and Community: A Contextual Exploration of Justice as Evenhandedness* (Oxford: Oxford University Press, 2000; hereafter CCC). References to these works will be given in the text, using the abbreviated identifications indicated here whenever the source is not immediately clear from the context.

31. See Robert Nozick, *Anarchy, State, and Utopia* (New York: Basic Books, 1974) and John Rawls, *A Theory of Justice* (Cambridge, MA: The Belknap Press, 1971). In dealing with utilitarianism, Carens relies on no single book (indeed, he mentions the significant disagreements within utilitarianism), but in a note he refers to works by Richard Brandt, Peter Singer, R.M. Hare, and Amartya Sen and Bernard Williams.

32. Carens does recognize that Rawlsian theory would permit "public order" restrictions on immigration; that is, "liberty may be restricted for the sake of liberty" (AaC, 259). So if immigration would lead to a complete breakdown of order, it could be limited. But, Carens notes, in ideal theory this would hardly apply; and even in the non-ideal real world, he argues, the restrictions that it would justify are very few in number.

33. For the "public order restriction," see the previous note.

34. Though even this, of course, can be very important; consider the effect of American Supreme Court decisions, for example, in which a single suit brought by a single individual can have very far-reaching social consequences. The Court's First Amendment jurisprudence seems to offer especially good evidence of this.

35. Also interesting are some examples Carens offers of reasons why people might want to migrate: "Economic opportunities for particular individuals might vary greatly from one state to another [even under an international difference prin-

ciple]. One might fall in love with a citizen from another land, one might belong to a religion which has few followers in one's native land and many in another, one might seek cultural opportunities that are only available in another society" (AaC, 258). These examples, with which we may well sympathize, are revealing. For they all describe only individual motives, whereas the problem which public policy generally seeks to address is large migrations of many people, in numbers sufficient to affect society in important ways. Furthermore, policy inevitably operates in general categories and normally cannot examine the details of each particular situation. One could grant the force of all of Carens's examples and still think the state should have a power to regulate immigration.

36. It is, of course, possible to make a liberal case for the preservation of culture. The most prominent such argument is that of Will Kymlicka; see *Liberalism, Community, and Culture* (Oxford: Clarendon Press, 1989) and *Multicultural Citizenship: A Liberal Theory of Minority Rights* (Oxford: Clarendon Press, 1996). Arguably, though, Kymlicka's argument itself is intended to preserve only liberal cultures. He is quite explicit, for instance, that his argument rests upon the fundamental value of individual autonomy (*Multicultural Citizenship*, 152–63) and that he views culture as of only instrumental value: "Cultures are valuable, not in and of themselves, but because it is only through having access to a societal culture that people have access to a range of meaningful options" (*Multicultural Citizenship*, 83). Worth considering in this regard are, for example, his distinction between "external protections" and "internal restrictions" and the claim that minority cultures are entitled to exercise only the former (*Multicultural Citizenship*, 35–44); or his distinction between culture as a "context of choice" and the particular "character" of that culture at any given time, of which only the first is entitled to protection (*Liberalism, Community, and Culture*, 166–7). Thus his argument may actually parallel Carens's here in interesting ways; on Carens, see the following discussion in the text of a possible modified perfectionist principle. I discuss Kymlicka's argument in greater detail in the first half of chapter five. Incidentally, I think it also worth mentioning that Carens's characterization of what an individual would or would not be willing to do is not, in my view, obviously correct.

37. Interestingly, James Woodward takes precisely the opposite position from Carens's: "restrictions on entry, in my argument, have the status of non-ideal, second-best solutions to problems of preserving institutions and policies we care about in an imperfect world. In a better world, in which even extensive immigration would not threaten these policies and institutions, my view is that the case for restrictions on entry would be far weaker, even if the result were radically to undermine distinctive national and cultural identities" ("Commentary: Liberalism and migration," in Barry and Goodin, *Free Movement*, p. 80).

38. But see also the later article in which Carens returns to the question of whether movement can be restricted for the sake of the welfare state, using again the example of Canada and the United States, but denies that immigration may be

restricted in such a situation: "[I]n the end I cannot see that sovereignty makes that much difference from a liberal egalitarian perspective. Despite my attachment to Canada's social welfare policies, I do not think they justify restrictions on movement" (Migam, 42). In a recent clarification, Carens has emphasized that this is indeed his view: "I intended to argue only that it would be permissible, under some circumstances to require people to be residents for a modest period before gaining access to (some) welfare state programs" (ROB, 1083, fn. 2). Thus the argument about the welfare state does not provide any significant exception to the general argument for open borders.

39. Carens also considers this possibility, though I believe less deeply than in the Fiji article, in "Immigration, Political Community, and the Transformation of Identity: Quebec's Immigration Policies in Critical Perspective," where he defends Quebec's right to place certain limits on immigration. I simply offer two observations about this essay: (1) as is his wont, Carens makes a point of referring to the "Aliens and Citizens" article, saying that he has already made the principled argument for open borders there and in the current article wishes to focus on a slightly different question (Quebec, 28, and also fn. 6); and (2) the restrictions which Carens is prepared to accept are only those intended to preserve French as the common language of Quebec—hardly a very robust vision of a shared way of life. A fuller consideration of this essay would not, I think, alter the conclusions I reach after considering the Fiji piece. An abridged version of the Fiji article also appears as chapter nine of CCC (pp. 200–59).

40. Here Carens footnotes his own argument to this effect elsewhere (MemaM).

41. Here Carens does concede the possibility of some restrictions for the sake of culture; but this is the example of an already liberal Japan.

42. Carens himself does not take up the issue of immigration in his discussion of Fiji.

43. This does still leave the possibility that Carens might entertain restrictions on immigration from rich countries to poor ones; on this possibility, see note 54.

44. I deliberately set aside as a topic for another time the question of whether Carens has exhausted the possibilities within liberalism—though, as my very brief comments in the introduction suggest, I do not think he has. Also, since Carens's reliance in the "Aliens and Citizens" article on the anti-perfectionist argument has loomed large in my explication, it is only fair to note that, in a recent essay discussing his current assessment of the case for open borders (an essay written in response to an earlier published version of my argument here), he has explicitly distanced himself from that early, severely anti-perfectionist position: "If I were restating the argument today, I would detach it more sharply from an anti-perfectionist account, and I would acknowledge more clearly that there can be justifiable reasons for restricting free movement that would be compatible with a commitment to equal moral worth" (ROP, 1088). Nevertheless, his modest reformulation there is, as he himself puts it, "methodological rather than . . . substantive" (ROB, 1084), it is quite similar to the other recent writings that I discuss later, and, by reaffirming the fundamental validity of his earlier argument (see esp. ROB, 1096– 7), it substantially validates my conclu-

sion here, that his essential argument for open borders has remained consistent through the course of his numerous publications on the topic. Carens's recent book on justice (*Culture, Citizenship, and Community: A Contextual Exploration of Justice as Evenhandedness,* Oxford University Press, 2000), a conscious effort to make room within liberal theory and practice for considerations of culture, also gives evidence of his desire to move away from an arid and illusory "neutrality." Just how far from it he has succeeded in moving is an interesting question; see my review of the book, "A Different Kind of Liberalism?" (forthcoming in *Review of Politics* 63.2 [Spring 2001]).

45. The characterization, with which I agree, is Carens's (AaC, 271, at fn. 1).

46. I discuss the American case in the first half of chapter four.

47. Carens is careful to point out, however, that "I'm not sure whether the contextualist approach is ultimately satisfactory" (Austr, 43). The argument in "Aliens and Citizens," in other words, remains necessary. He also ends the article by coyly stating, "Perhaps we should challenge the right of every state to keep people out. But that is the turtle [i.e., premise] I promised not to turn over" (Austr, 59). ("Turtle" here refers to a metaphor which Carens borrows from Clifford Geertz. Its meaning is as I have indicated.) Carens also avoids this issue in a similar (though perhaps, given the context, justifiable) fashion elsewhere: "The conventional view is that states normally have no moral (or legal) obligation to admit aliens (apart from refugees). In this essay, I will not directly challenge that view because I am focusing on people who are already present, living in the country, not those knocking at the door. Still, the conventional view is not as securely founded as people sometimes assume. I have criticized it in ['Aliens and Citizens']" (MemaM, 164–5, at fn. 3).

48. Responding to an earlier published version of this argument, Carens criticized a quite similar description I had given of the realism/idealism distinction as a kind of "strategic" move. He wrote, "I regard this approach as much more than a tactical concession to the power of the forces opposing open borders. Adopting as presuppositions moral views that one knows to be widely shared by others is one way of participating in the process of democratic deliberation, even if one wishes to challenge those presuppositions at another moment of the process" (ROB, 1088). I am not entirely sure what to make of this. I should have regarded the temporary adoption of views that one rejects and intends to challenge, for the purpose of reaching agreement about other matters, as precisely a "tactical" concession. Certainly it is not a substantive one. Nor does the existence of a simultaneous commitment to democratic deliberation seem to make any difference in this regard. It shows only that one prefers to debate and vote (perhaps a number of times over the years) rather than fight for what one would regard as the perfectly just outcome; that one prefers, in other words, tactical concessions (perhaps a succession of them) to war. That is no doubt a good thing, much to be desired, but I do not see how it represents a more-than-tactical concession with regard to one's actual views on the particular matter, such as immigration, under debate.

49. The contrast between realism and idealism is, I think, merely Carens's most recent and fullest articulation of a distinction he has hinted at in various ways in his earlier work. This is evident not only from the piece on "Compromises in Politics," but also from suggestions in some of his earlier writing specifically on immigration. Thus in "Immigration and the Welfare State," for example, Carens closes with a section entitled "Political Theory and Political Realities" (228–30). Here he addresses the question of the extent to which the ideals discovered by political theory should give way to the practical possibilities imposed by particular circumstances, arguing that although the latter will inevitably constrain what we can actually achieve, political theory must nevertheless pursue the task of discovering "what the citizens' deepest convictions are or ought to be, even if they cannot act upon them" (229). Similarly, in "Migration and morality: A liberal egalitarian perspective," he refers at one point to a distinction between the "morally required" and the "morally permissible" (41; the same distinction is discussed in his article on Fiji), and in concluding that article he notes, "Liberal egalitarians are committed to an idea of free movement, with only modest qualifications. That idea is not politically feasible today and so it mainly serves to provide a critical standard by which to assess existing restrictive practices and policies" (45). Thus it is fair to say that the question of how theoretical ideals ought to guide political action has concerned Carens for a while. But, as I have argued in the text, the distinction (whether in its earlier or current, more clearly stated form) between realism and idealism does not, I think, affect either Carens's steadfast commitment to open borders as the ideal toward which we should strive and by which actual practices are to be measured or his argument's fundamental basis in a certain set of liberal principles.

50. See also ROB, p. 1095: "[T]he primary audience I had in mind in developing the open borders argument was one that shared my liberal commitments, broadly speaking."

51. This paragraph is drawn from my forthcoming review (see n. 44) of *Culture, Citizenship, and Community,* as are a number of my other comments here on that book.

52. Such changes in article can at times be significant: consider the difference between Sabine's *A History of Political Theory* and Strauss and Cropsey's *History of Political Philosophy.*

53. Carens consistently adds the qualifying reference to modern political conditions when making this claim, though without elaboration. I might add that this combination of a deep skepticism about whether any universal morality actually exists with a willingness to apply the standards of a particular morality universally is, I think, symptomatic not only of Carens's thought but of much contemporary liberalism: the reluctance to recognize and affirm genuine moral truths as such is not matched by a reluctance to hold others to one's own particular standards. It is this combination that directly leads to what I describe in the text as the making of demands upon others that they inevitably regard

as unjustified. In a funny way, Carens's argument (again, like those of many others) is both too relativist and too universalist for my taste. My own approach here is, I think, almost the opposite: I am less abashed about recognizing the claims of a universal morality, but much more cautious in my views about how those claims can and should be applied within different, particular contexts.

54. Perhaps this is all that Carens intends to claim. There are passages in his work that might support such a reading, particularly when we recognize that the countries of the world that share liberal principles are also, by and large, its wealthiest countries. I have already pointed to several of these passages in discussing the circumstances under which Carens might be prepared to admit some limited application of the perfectionist principle. Remember, too, that Carens countenanced certain perfectionist policies on the island of Fiji only because they were not "dependent upon the subordination of any other group," which he clearly does not think can be said of contemporary restrictions on immigration by the wealthy nations of the liberal West. Such passages might lend credence to a reading of Carens's argument as addressed only to liberal countries, since they emphasize his deep belief that when *those* countries, which are on the whole fairly prosperous, seek to limit immigration, they are really acting to perpetuate their own position of unjust privilege in the world. But emphasizing this aspect of his argument would only exacerbate the misleadingness of calling it a case for open borders. For then (a) it would be *not* a case for open borders, but rather for a world in which some countries opened their borders while others did not; and (b) it would in an important sense no longer be an argument fundamentally about immigration at all, but rather one about economic redistribution, towards which immigration would be one means. Such a reading would also raise a problem noted by Woodward, that the two parts of Carens's Rawlsian argument for free movement—that it is a fundamental liberty, and that it is an important way of helping satisfy an international difference principle—do not complement, but are rather in tension with, one another ("Commentary," pp. 60–62). Woodward himself suggests that the motive of economic redistribution ultimately motivates Carens's argument and is responsible for its appeal (62).

55. As the claims about liberal democracy as a universal moral norm cited in the previous paragraph suggest, this is certainly a plausible interpretation, particularly, one might think, for non-liberals. In chapter three I argue that the same general problem I pose here to Carens, of reconciling broad claims about immigration policy with a due regard for the range of legitimate political differences, is faced by any claim that all countries are obliged to follow the same immigration policy, whatever it might be.

56. Carens response to me in ROB (1095–97) suggests that he takes this to be my criticism of his argument. I hope that the present restatement clarifies my view.

57. I want to emphasize that this argument would apply with equal force, in only slightly altered form, to an (apparently?) internal disagreement, such as would

occur if, for example, a critic were to say to Carens, "I too make a liberal argument, but I believe that you have misstated liberal premises, and therefore I reach a different conclusion." Though I raise it briefly at the close of my discussion of Carens, this is not an argument I wish to press here, because I seek to construct an argument based upon premises that can command wider agreement. It is, however, an argument no less important than the one pressed in the text.

58. This kind of gridlocked failure to confront one another's premises characterizes much of the debate about immigration. A nice illustration of this situation is the collection of essays entitled *Free Movement,* edited by Brian Barry and Robert Goodin. This book is divided into sections, each of which represents a different philosophical approach. Thus there are contributions from the perspectives of liberal egalitarianism, libertarianism, Marxism, natural law, and political realism. Within each section are three essays, one on the transnational movement of people, one on the movement of money, and finally a response. The result is a series of essays exploring the implications of these different perspectives for immigration. The essays themselves are very interesting and stimulating, and they are quite useful for showing the resources available within various traditions for considering immigration. But the very organization of the book virtually guarantees that no confrontation *among* these various approaches can take place. So one gets arguments about just what, for example, natural law has to say about immigration, but no reasons why we should follow one of these approaches rather than another and thus no reasons why we should pursue any of the particular policy recommendations—except that we already happen to be Marxists, libertarians, or whatever the case may be. Thus the volume, interesting though it is, inadvertently provides a kind of microcosm of the immigration debate as a whole.

59. For my part, I am doubtful that Carens (or anybody) can make good on this claim. To be more precise: the claim that all peoples should embrace liberal democracy could mean two different things. It could mean that any regime other than liberal democracy (subject to the ordinary range of variability dictated by historical differences among communities) is unjustifiable and illegitimate. Or it could mean simply that, as a general rule, peoples are likely to be better governed (leaving open the precise meaning of that phrase) under liberal democracy than under other alternatives. As the next chapter will make clear, I disagree with the first, stronger claim. I would, however, endorse some version of the weaker one.

60. John Rawls, "The Law of Peoples," *Critical Inquiry* 20.1 (Autumn 1993): 48, n. 17. For another, and even more clearly opposed, dissenting voice, see the very interesting article by Jeremy Rabkin, "Liberalism and Nationality: Grotius, Vattel and Locke," *Review of Politics* 59.2 (Spring 1997): 293–322.

61. "It [the sovereign state] is the site of the most fundamental division between inside and outside, us and them, domestic and foreign, the sphere of citizen entitlements and that of strategic responses. It is the center surrounded by a periphery and the community surrounded by danger." William Connolly, *Identity*

Difference: Democratic Negotiations of Political Paradox (Ithaca: Cornell University Press, 1991), p. 201. Further references to this work will be given by page number in parentheses within the text and identified when necessary as ID.

62. See Julia Kristeva, *Strangers to Ourselves* (New York: Columbia University Press, 1991); and *Nations without Nationalism* (New York: Columbia University Press, 1993).

63. London and New York: Routledge, 1994.

64. *Ibid.,* p. 123. For the metaphorical use of "migrancy," see esp. pp. 22–9; for it as a causal factor in our contemporary situation, consider pp. 107–10.

65. Bonnie Honig's new book, *Democracy and the Foreigner* (Princeton: Princeton University Press, 2001), evidently fills the gap I note by providing a significant postmodern treatment of immigration. It has appeared too recently to be included here.

66. Without identity, "I would not be, do, or achieve anything. Neither would we. Nor would there be an I or we to criticize for failure in this regard. Identity, in some modality or other, is an indispensable feature of human life" (ID, 158).

67. "An identity is established in relation to a series of differences that have become socially recognized" (ID, 64).

68. See also p. 67: "Now, the paradoxical element in the relation of identity to difference is that we cannot dispense with personal and collective identities, but the multiple drives to stamp truth upon those identities function to convert differences into otherness and otherness into scapegoats created and maintained to secure the appearance of a true identity."

69. See, e.g., p. 15: "In this study explorations of identity and difference at the level of individual and group relationships outstrip those at the level of interstate relations. The academic division of labor between political theory and international relations theory is one that I have not escaped, even as I now recognize the imperative to scramble it . . . . I begin to think about this issue in the present study, but the words break off before the pertinent questions have been pushed far enough." Connolly begins to address such questions in ch. 7, "The Politics of Territorial Democracy."

70. The phrase is from Benedict Anderson, *Imagined Communities: Reflections on the Origin and Spread of Nationalism,* 2nd ed. (London and New York: Verso, 1991).

71. In this connection one is obliged to cite the by now hackneyed but nonetheless tragic example of the former Yugoslavia.

72. I say "some form" because, when he does begin to speak about democracy in international relations, Connolly makes it clear that the traditional model of territorial government, reserving authority and control over a particular area solely to the state in question, is in his view no longer tenable. "Perhaps today the state, as the legitimate center of sovereignty, citizen loyalty, and political dissent, must give more ground to other modes of political identification . . . . Perhaps today the state must be thought and lived as one site of membership, allegiance, obligation, and political mobilization on a globe that presents other viable possibilities of identification, inside and outside state boundaries" (ID, 215).

73. "A collective identity recapitulates the contingent, conflicted character of personal identity; it also *inflates* tendencies in the latter to dogmatize its configuration when confronted by disruptive contingencies" (ID, 204; emphasis in original).

74. "Central to the project of retheorizing democracy to fit the circumstances of late-modern life is the task of rethinking the contemporary relation between sovereignty and democracy" (215). See also the criticism of "the territorial base of contemporary democratic ideals," pp. 217–18.

75. Connolly calls this situation "the globalization of contingency" and says that it is "the defining mark of late modernity" (ID, 25).

76. But see ID, xi: "Finally, agonistic democracy challenges the confinement of democracy to the governmental institutions of the territorial state. The politics of identity\difference flows beneath, through, and over the boundaries of the state. It overflows state boundaries when the state constitutes a set of differences to protect the certainty of its collective identity and whenever the established identity of a sovereign state itself becomes an object of politicization." If agonistic democracy requires thus challenging sovereignty and collective national identities, and if it calls for the kind of "strife" in the polity to which I earlier alluded, then some version of open borders might be a more necessary implication than I am suggesting here.

77. Minneapolis: University of Minnesota Press, 1995. References will be given by page number in parentheses within the text and identified when necessary as EP.

78. See note 75.

79. See also EP, 22, where Connolly writes of the globalization of contingency, "The politics of enclosed territories, while certainly pertinent to these issues, is no longer sufficient to them. What is needed politically, today and tomorrow, is a series of cross-national, nonstatist movements organized across state lines, mobilized around specific issues of global significance, pressing states from inside and outside simultaneously to reconfigure established convictions, priorities, and policies . . . . For today it is necessary to disturb and challenge . . . a variety of presumptions, understandings, and loyalties inscribed in the nation-state." It is also worth pointing out in this connection that Connolly now includes in the list of factors creating the globalization of contingency the presence of "refugees" and "legal and illegal immigrants" within the state (xxiii).

80. In noting how these issues have by this time become explicit in Connolly's language, I would also direct attention to the presence of two relevant metaphors that play a role in "Tocqueville, Religiosity, and Pluralization" (EP, ch. 6): that of "nomadism" (see pp. 178ff.) and that of "migration" (see pp. 184ff.). Cf. the passage by Chambers cited earlier about the proper stance of the cultural critic.

81. EP, pp. 135–61.

82. Connolly lists "the rights of refugees" and "state immigration policies" (EP, 156–7), among other things, as examples of such issues.

83. It is interesting to compare this account with the distinction often made between "ethnic" and "civic" nationalism.

84. See n. 2.

85. Immigration and citizenship are closely linked for Walzer because of his argument that a state must extend the opportunity for citizenship to all people residing in its territory for any significant length of time. See *Spheres of Justice,* pp. 52–61.

86. Princeton: Princeton University Press, 1990. References will be given by page number in parentheses within the text.

87. Her (in)complete list: "among others women, Blacks, Chicanos, Puerto Ricans and other Spanish-speaking Americans, American Indians, Jews, lesbians, gay men, Arabs, Asians, old people, working-class people, and the physically and mentally disabled" (40).

88. See esp. p. 184: "I assert, then, the following principle: a democratic public should provide mechanisms for the effective recognition and representation of the distinct voices and perspectives of those of its constituent groups that are oppressed or disadvantaged."

89. See also p. 172: "Membership in a social group is a function not of satisfying some objective criteria, but of a subjective affirmation of affinity with that group, the affirmation of that affinity by other members of the group, and the attribution of membership in that group by persons identifying with other groups."

90. Young's proposal for group representation includes a "group veto power regarding specific policies that affect a group directly" (184). Perhaps one might say that national groups would exercise this veto power to reject policies that would limit their control over immigration.

91. For a lengthier critique of community as a political ideal (though not explicitly with reference to national identity), see pp. 227–36. "The most serious consequence of the desire for community, or for copresence and mutual identification with others, is that it often operates to exclude or oppress those experienced as different" (234).

92. Young's criticism of decentralization and municipal autonomy is also provocative in this regard. She writes, "Where there are diverse and unequal neighborhoods, towns, and cities, whose residents move in and out of one another's locales and interact in complex webs of exchange, only a sovereign authority whose jurisdiction includes them all can mediate their relations justly" (250). More generally: "The principle is simple: wherever actions affect a plurality of agents in the ways I have specified, all those agents should participate in deciding the actions and their conditions" (251). Since these descriptions arguably apply today to the world as a whole, one could plausibly claim that this line of argument points toward a loose cosmopolitan federation permitting free mobility among various member regional (and themselves federal) governments.

93. I should concede that I am somewhat less confident of this conclusion than I am in the case of Connolly, the clear implication of whose argument seems to me open borders. Young, after all, is sympathetic to groups, as I have discussed in the text; still, as I have also shown there, her remarks about national groups

display a considerable amount of skepticism and even hostility. Thus I think that the argument in the text pursues the implications of her views in a persuasive fashion. It is possible, though, that she might endorse some kind of middle position: just as she supports special rights for various domestic social groups as a way of countering privilege and oppression, so too might one argue that disadvantaged nationalities are also entitled to special protections—among them, perhaps, greater control over immigration—against the predations of more prosperous and powerful nations, which would not be entitled to exercise the same control over their borders as a way of buttressing and maintaining their own privileged position. Against this, however, remains the "normative ideal of city life" with all its implications for mobility; it suggests, I think, that even if disadvantaged nationalities were entitled to special forms of protection, rigidly defined borders might not be among them. It also seems to me that the dangers of permitting a state to reify and enforce, through immigration controls, a particular, official version of the "national" identity—with all the potential consequences this implies for the various sub-groups within the state who depart from this identity in various ways and who are Young's central focus—would probably outweigh, from the point of view of Young's theory, any possible benefits of such an approach. On this point cf. also n. 91. But there is no doubt room for further argument about this.

94. Though her new book has appeared too recently to be included here (cf. n. 65), a pair of articles—which the book presumably incorporates in some form—by Bonnie Honig buttresses this suggestion that postmodernism is another of the several academic forces operating to erode the state's conventional approach towards immigration. Honig argues that America has historically sought to use immigrant infusions of energy and pluralism to shore up various myths about American democracy and national identity and to symbolize a metaphorical refounding of the regime, thus reassuring us of our continuing vitality and goodness. Because this very project of ongoing national restoration, however, depends necessarily upon the immigrants' *foreignness*— they can reinvigorate us only by being in important respects different from us— it simultaneously generates feelings of anxiety and xenophobic resentment. To break out of this cycle of injustice and transform our nervous manipulation of foreigners into a more genuine openness toward and engagement with their otherness, Honig proposes a "democratic cosmopolitanism," which seeks to empower the exploited and excluded by increasing opportunities for participation and mobilization at both sub- and transnational levels. This democratic cosmopolitanism does not aim directly at abolishing the state, since the state remains an important locus for fighting certain injustices. Clearly, though, it does (and is intended to) weaken the claims of the state—particularly with regard to distinctions such as alien/citizen, immigrant/native, them/us—in the name of a demos that "is dispersed" and "exceeds the states it seems to presuppose." Bonnie Honig, "Ruth, the Model Emigrée: Mourning and the Symbolic Politics of Immigration," *Political Theory* 25.1 (February 1997), p. 113. See also Honig,

"Immigrant America? How Foreignness 'Solves' Democracy's Problems," ABF Working Paper #9707 (Chicago: American Bar Foundation, 1997).

95. Quoted in Brimelow, *Alien Nation,* p. 233.

96. For the tension between pluralism and pluralization, see the introduction ("Introduction: The Pluralist Imagination") to EP, esp. pp. xiii-xv. Nevertheless, consider the following passage from ID: "You could not be what you are unless some possibilities of life had been forgone ('to do is to forgo'). And you now depend upon the difference of the other for your identity. Recognition of these conditions of strife and interdependence, especially when such recognition contains an element of mutuality, can flow into an ethic in which adversaries are respected and maintained in a mode of agonistic mutuality, an ethic in which alter-identities foster agonistic respect for the differences that constitute them, an ethic of care for life" (166). Though Connolly is not using it in that context, this could be a description of the pluralistic system of states.

97. *Irish Impressions* (London: W. Collins Sons & Co. Ltd., 1920), pp. 20–21. Further references will be given by page number in parentheses within the text.

98. Chesterton offers another humorous example of this phenomenon: "Suppose a man has to write on a particular subject, let us say America; if he has a day to do it in, it is possible that, in the last afterglow of sunset, he may have discovered at least one thing which he himself really thinks about America. It is conceivable that somewhere under the evening star he may have a new idea, even about the new world. If he has only half an hour in which to write, he will just have time to consult an encyclopaedia and vaguely remember the latest leading articles. The encyclopaedia will be only about a decade out of date; the leading articles will be aeons out of date—having been written under similar conditions of modern rush. If he has only a quarter of an hour in which to write about America, he may be driven in mere delirium and madness to call her his Gigantic Daughter in the West, to talk of the feasibility of Hands Across the Sea, or even to call himself an Anglo-Saxon, when he might as well call himself a Jute" (19–20).

99. Thomas Hobbes, *Leviathan,* ed. Richard Tuck (Cambridge: Cambridge University Press, 1994), p. 91. Further references will be given by page number in parentheses within the text.

100. Cf. also John Locke, *Second Treatise of Government,* ed. Peter Laslett (Cambridge: Cambridge University Press, 1988): "Could [people] be happier without it, the *Law,* as a useless thing would of it self vanish; and that ill deserves the Name of Confinement which hedges us in only from Bogs and Precipices. So that, however it may be mistaken, *the end of Law* is not to abolish or restrain, but *to preserve and enlarge Freedom:* for in all the states of created beings capable of Laws, *where there is no Law, there is no Freedom.* For *Liberty* is to be free from restraint and violence from others, which cannot be, where there is no Law . . ." (pp. 305–6).

101. Beck, *The Case Against Immigration,* p. 49.

102. In this context, one might think of black Americans' repeated (and quite plau-

sible) complaints that they have been shouldered aside by wave after wave of immigrants, always being shoved back to the bottom of the heap, and of Booker T. Washington's famous appeal to white industrialists, seeking to recruit labor, to "cast down your bucket where you are." Quoted by Beck, *The Case Against Immigration,* p. 169; on the impact of immigration on black Americans generally, see Beck, chs. 8 and 9.

Chapter 3

1. Consider, for example, my discussion in chapter four of the view that America is a "universal nation" in the sense of being committed to certain liberal political principles that are universal in scope; see in particular the passages quoted there from Carens and Schuck.

2. This seems to be how Julian Simon understands America (he also thinks that immigrants as a general rule do contribute to the nation's economic prosperity); see, for instance, his brief article, "The case for greatly increased immigration," *The Public Interest,* no. 102 (Winter 1991), pp. 89–103, which seems intelligible only if based upon such a view.

3. To some extent, of course, these restrictions are self-enforcing—how many Muslims dream of migrating to Israel, after all (to the *Jewish* Israel, that is, not simply to the territory, repopulated and transformed)?—and thus may not always need to be enacted into law. That seems to me, however, a practical consideration to be determined according to particular circumstances and not to affect the theoretical point.

4. Thomas Jefferson, *Notes on the State of Virginia* (Chapel Hill: University of North Carolina Press, 1982), pp. 84–5.

5. Consider, for example, James M. Buchanan, "A two-country parable," in Warren F. Schwartz (ed.), *Justice in immigration* (Cambridge: Cambridge University Press, 1995): "[T]he effects of adding new members extend well beyond those that might be measured in economic terms and . . . become especially important in modern democratic states. The institutional parameters that have made some of these states relatively 'rich' are often not understood, and the fragility of those parameters in the face of noninformed politicization must be incorporated in any calculus of evaluation. Action toward potential immigrants that may seem motivated by considerations of justice or compassion may generate results that are directionally reversed from those initially anticipated" (p. 65).

6. Michael Walzer, *Spheres of Justice* (New York: Basic Books, Inc., 1983), p. 31.

7. Such identities are in this sense "imagined" ones; see Benedict Anderson, *Imagined Communities: Reflections on the Origin and Spread of Nationalism,* 2nd ed. (London and New York: Verso, 1991). Edmund Burke also emphasized the artificial nature of political communities, though in a positive sense: "In a state of *rude* nature there is no such thing as a people. A number of men in themselves have no collective capacity. The idea of a people is the idea of a corporation. It is wholly artificial; and made like all other legal fictions by common

agreement" (*An Appeal from the New to the Old Whigs,* in Burke, *Further Reflections on the Revolution in France,* ed. Daniel E. Ritchie [Indianapolis: Liberty Fund, 1992], pp. 163–4).

8. Oxford: Clarendon Press, 1995. Page references will be given in parentheses within the text.

9. Joseph H. Carens, "Democracy and Respect for Difference: The Case of Fiji," *University of Michigan Journal of Law Reform* 25.3–4 (Spring and Summer 1992), p. 605.

10. In chapter four, for example, I argue that, as a result of changes wrought by immigration over the past decades, the traditional ethnocultural conception of German national identity could no longer be maintained; the recent changes in German citizenship laws are in a sense an attempt to bring the conception of national identity implicit in those laws into closer correspondence with the actual composition of the people living there.

11. This leaves open the question of exactly how national identities are formed. I assume that this process occurs differently in different places, though we may be able to detect certain commonalities that are repeated in more than one place. One implication of this line of argument, of course, is that the manner of a nation's founding may not affect the reality or legitimacy of its identity at a later date; cf. Burke's reference to "the time of prescription which, through long usage, mellows into legality governments that were violent in their commencement" (*Reflections on the Revolution in France,* ed. J.G.A. Pocock [Indianapolis: Hackett Publishing Company, 1987], p. 145). There is a sizeable body of literature on nationalism and nationality, most of it historical and sociological. Some important works are Anderson, *Imagined Communities;* Ernest Gellner, *Nations and Nationalism* (Oxford: Basil Blackwell, 1983); Liah Greenfield, *Nationalism: Five Roads to Modernity* (Cambridge: Harvard University Press, 1992); Eric Hobsbawm, *Nations and Nationalism Since 1780* (Cambridge: Cambridge University Press, 1990); Anthony D. Smith, *The Ethnic Origins of Nations* (Oxford: Basil Blackwell, 1986); Charles Tilly, *The Formation of National States in Western Europe* (Princeton: Princeton University Press, 1975); and Eugen Weber, *Peasants into Frenchmen* (London: Chatto & Windus, 1979). Recently, nationalism has also begun to attract the attention of political theorists; see in particular two valuable collections of essays, Ronald Beiner (ed.), *Theorizing Nationalism* (Albany: SUNY Press, 1999) and Robert McKim and Jeff McMahan (eds.), *The Morality of Nationalism* (Oxford and New York: Oxford University Press, 1997).

It leaves open too the question of what exactly constitutes this broad popular support over time or how one might recognize it. Obviously, I am not referring to the existence of democratic political institutions. A phrase like "popular sovereignty," broadly understood, might come closer to capturing my meaning. Though I cannot address this problem at length here, I would suggest that Locke's notion of tacit consent might provide a good place to begin thinking about it. My discussion of Walzer in chapter five, and in particular of the distinction between stronger and weaker senses of self-determination that one can detect in his work, deals with some of these matters; what I am describing here is more like the weaker, "passive" meaning of self-determination that I identify there.

12. David Hume once made a similar point: "The vulgar are apt to carry all *national characters* to extremes; and having once established it as a principle, that any people are knavish, or cowardly, or ignorant, they will admit of no exception, but comprehend every individual under the same censure. Men of sense condemn these undistinguishing judgments: Though at the same time, they allow, that each nation has a peculiar set of manners, and that some particular qualities are more frequently to be met with among one people than among their neighbours" ("Of National Characters," in *Essays Moral, Political, and Literary,* ed. Eugene F. Miller [Indianapolis: Liberty Fund, 1985], p. 197, emphasis in original).

13. In my view, this is not even true of liberalism, even if, for example, Carens's arguments about its Rawlsian, Nozickian, and utilitarian varieties are correct, as they may be. My brief discussion a bit later in the chapter of some of the ways in which even we Americans—who might well be expected to distinguish relatively clearly between culture in general and political culture in particular— blur the line between culture and politics may be suggestive in this regard.

14. Cf. Habermas's idea of "constitutional patriotism," which I briefly discuss in the consideration of Germany in chapter four.

One might also use this argument in an entirely different way: to concede that open borders push all countries in the direction of liberalism, but to claim that this is justifiable because liberalism is superior to other forms of government, and that, despite the convergence in political cultures, considerable divergence will nevertheless continue to exist among cultures at large (national identities). This argument is, I think, considerably stronger than the one in the text with regard to its use of the distinction between political culture and culture in general. My objection to it is the one already mentioned in the text: it assumes that non-liberal polities are illegitimate.

15. See Alexis de Tocqueville, *Democracy in America,* ed. J.P. Mayer, tr. George Lawrence (New York: Perennial Library, 1988), p. 287.

16. Though I have freely adapted his argument here for my own purposes, I have been helped in thinking about these matters by James W. Ceaser, *Liberal Democracy and Political Science* (Baltimore and London: Johns Hopkins University Press, 1990).

17. I assume here for the purposes of argument that we are dealing with legitimate political systems. I say more about this aspect of the argument later in the chapter.

18. One might consider an alternative situation in which a non-democratic polity desired to keep out those with democratic inclinations. This might be a matter of excluding people with a clearly expressed hostility toward the non-democratic system in question or a stated desire to transform it; or one of excluding those whose more democratic socialization has simply made them people who are likely to be problematic subjects in a non-democratic polity. (This latter situation, though, appears to fit more neatly the next category discussed in the text, of attempts to restrict immigration in order to protect the political culture, rather than the specific insitutions of the political system itself.) Either of these

cases seems to me potentially justifiable: since I do not assume (as I have suggested; cf. note 11) that all polities are required to govern themselves by means of democratic institutions in order to be legitimate, then a legitimate non-democratic regime would presumably have the same right to protect itself that a legitimate democratic regime would. The argument, in other words, is not intended to work in only one direction.

19. For a statement of the view that liberal countries may be entitled, even upon liberal principles, to restrict immigration as a form of "self-preservation" in a non-ideal world, see Frederick G. Whelan, "Citizenship and Freedom of Movement: An Open Admission Policy?" in Mark Gibney (ed.), *Open Borders? Closed Societies? The Ethical and Political Issues* (Westport, CT: Greenwood Press, 1988), pp. 16–23, esp. the summary on p. 22.

20. Tocqueville, *Democracy in America,* pp. 287–94, 442–9, and esp. 542–6. Tocqueville famously declared religion "the first of their [American] political institutions" (292).

21. Recall, for example, Carens's use, at least in his earlier articles, of the Rawlsian anti-perfectionist argument to rule out immigration policies designed to preserve a certain cultural way of life.

22. I have found Bernard Yack, "The Myth of the Civic Nation," *Critical Review* 10.2 (Spring 1996), pp. 193–211 quite helpful in thinking about these matters.

23. I offer this example purely for the sake of argument, not necessarily because it is true in any uncomplicated sense.

24. These examples also suggest the more complicated case of a population which is divided into two (or more) reasonably distinct and identifiable sub-"peoples," one of which is a clear majority. In such a case, policies might really reflect the majority's identity, but they could do so consistently, and perhaps oppressively, at the expense of the other group(s). I confess that I am not sure exactly how to respond to such a difficult case, in which it is not clear that there is *a* people or national identity at all. It seems to point somewhat beyond the scope of my present focus, raising questions of, for instance, secession. My earlier suggestion that a national identity must really have some empirical foundation (American identity is not based upon the shared use of the Chinese language) may have some helpful implications in this regard, since it would raise doubts about a postulated national identity that simply ignored the existence of a substantial segment of the population. My discussion of German immigration and naturalization law in the next chapter is relevant here; see also the thoughts on self-determination in my discussion of Walzer in chapter five.

25. Compare the somewhat similar though not identical approach of Jules L. Coleman and Sarah K. Harding: "Our approach to the normative question is to see whether important aspects of the immigration policies of the nations we consider can be defended as reflecting or consistent with alternative plausible conceptions of justice. So we look first for common elements in these practices and then ask ourselves whether these can be plausibly construed as implementing an appropriate ideal or demand of justice. In other words, before suggesting

reform of existing policies, we take the view that the theorist's responsibility is to try first to make the best case for existing practices. The criticisms that stick are those that emerge after a practice has received the most sympathetic understanding and found to fall short." ("Citizenship, the demands of justice, and the moral relevance of political borders," in Schwartz, *Justice in immigration,* p. 18). Coleman and Harding reach many of the same conclusions I do, but they follow a somewhat different path, basing their argument upon Kymlicka's good of membership in a cultural community, which should, they argue, be fairly distributed according to a theory of distributive justice.

26. It is not accidental that this discussion of legitimacy and illegitimacy avoids the language of rights, which would surely be the most common way in our contemporary world of attempting to draw the distinction between just and unjust regimes. Though I confess to some skepticism that such a thing as "rights" exists in a more than legal and artificial sense, I do actually think that the language of rights can be quite useful for certain limited purposes, roughly as a way of expressing our sense that the most serious forms of injustice, such as those discussed in the text, violate something important in human nature and should be avoided. My reluctance to speak in terms of rights is therefore primarily strategic, because the actual history of what Mary Ann Glendon has called "rights talk" shows pretty clearly that rights, over time, become a way of dealing with a vastly greater portion of moral and political life than my much narrower view considers appropriate. In contemporary America, indeed, the language of rights is about the only common language we possess any longer for discussing such matters. I regard this as, if not a necessary, at least a highly likely consequence of the internal logic of the concept of rights. One of Palgrave's reviewers, critical of my reluctance to employ the language of rights, suggested that I might be avoiding it out of a presupposition "that rights claims are absolute, a view too much shaped by some features of American jurisprudence." It seems to me that, whether they need be or not, rights claims often are taken as absolute (Dworkinian "trumps"), and that the slightest acquaintance with the European Court of Human Rights—which is supposed to employ a non-absolute conception of rights—shows pretty clearly that the explosive and kudzu-like potential of rights is much more than an American phenomenon. Indeed, though I am no expert on international law, it seems obvious to even a casual observer that the domestic history of rights within Western liberal democracies is now being re-enacted on the international scene via the idea of human rights. For these reasons, and because the whole thrust of my argument is to move in the opposite direction from that in which rights have been and are taking us, I prefer to avoid the language of rights whenever possible.

27. Examples such as these show how problematic it is to draw the clear distinction that Stephen R. Perry blithely takes for granted in his consideration of immigration: "At least three arguments might be advanced to defend the claim that outsiders can be excluded from a state because they do not share the cultural heritage of some or all of its inhabitants . . . . The first argument begins with

the premise that one of the purposes of the state is simply to serve and protect the shared culture, which would be regarded as a valuable way of life in itself . . . . This kind of communitarian (or perhaps perfectionist) entrenchment of a particular culture within the political framework of a state is contrary to liberal thought . . . . In this essay I say nothing about either the moral legitimacy of such states or the extent to which they are justified in limiting immigration on this basis. This is due in part to my uncertainty concerning what ought to be said about these matters, but also in part to the fact that our primary concern must be with the formulation of a just immigration policy for liberal societies like our own. Accordingly, I will not consider the first argument further . . ." ("Immigration, justice, and culture," in Schwartz, *Justice in immigration,* p. 111). I do not deny that Perry's assumption reflects one important aspect of liberalism; but, as the discussion in the text shows, this kind of sweeping claim can only be regarded as an oversimplification.

28. Jean Hampton implicitly, I think, points to the centrality of this question of legitimate preferences, when she notes that the "legitimacy of the nation-state" and the "moral importance of nations" are at the heart of debates over immigration ("Immigration, identity, and justice," in Schwartz, *Justice in immigration,* p. 78). Stephen R. Perry makes the same point explicitly: "The question of whether and under what circumstances it is permissible to exclude outsiders from joining a political community is just one aspect of the larger issue of whether and to what extent the differential treatment of compatriots [from other persons in the world] is justified" ("Immigration, justice, and culture," p. 96).

29. Miller's *On Nationality,* already referred to, is one recent attempt to provide such a book; Yael Tamir, *Liberal Nationalism* (Princeton: Princeton University Press, 1995) is another, though it takes liberalism for granted "as the starting point" (p. 4). The same question lies at the heart of much of Michael Walzer's work.

30. As I sit here putting the finishing touches to this manuscript, a news story raising this very question has catapulted onto the international scene: the Taliban's attempt to destroy a number of religious images throughout Afghanistan, including in particular a pair of ancient stone Buddhas widely regarded as artistic masterpieces. The *New York Times* quotes an Iranian official who described the monuments as "part of the 'country's cultural and national heritage [belonging] to the history of the region's civilization in which all humanity has a share.'" Similarly, the Islamic Educational, Scientific and Cultural Organization referred to the statues as "a universal human heritage." See "Taliban Fire Mortars at Afghan Buddha Statues," *The New York Times* on the web (www.nytimes.com), March 2, 2001.

31. Recently this claim has been most extensively discussed by Will Kymlicka, whose argument I consider in chapter five.

32. There could, of course, be a culture so stifling, brutal, or oppressive that it could in no way be defended as promoting individual or human flourishing. This, however, merely suggests a positive answer to the previous question raised: some cultures really are broadly superior to others.

33. This way of thinking about the matter is different from the one considered previously. The possibility considered there was whether a more-or-less stable culture turns out to be instrumentally important for individual flourishing; it thus provides (as do the first two possibilities considered, in different ways) what one might call a second-order justification for the communities that people form. The possibility being considered here is rather that social life is an inherent part of human life, that to deny it is to deny a part of our nature; it would thus provide a defense of community as such, valuable and worth protection in its own right. The difference between these approaches becomes apparent, I hope, in my discussion of Kymlicka in chapter five.

34. Aristotle, *The Politics of Aristotle,* tr. Ernest Barker (London, Oxford, and New York: Oxford University Press, 1958), pp. 3–7 (the quoted passage is on p. 5).

35. St. Augustine, *Concerning the City of God Against the Pagans,* tr. Henry Bettenson (London and New York: Penguin Books, 1984), p. 868. Augustine expressed the two-sidedness of human nature when he wrote, "For the human race is, more than any other species, at once social by nature and quarrelsome by perversion" (508).

36. Hume, *Essays Moral, Political, and Literary.* The first phrase is from "Of the First Principles of Government" (p. 33); the second from "Of National Characters" (p. 202).

37. "Community has been a central concept of political and legal philosophy since its beginning" (Carl J. Friedrich, "The Concept of Community in the History of Political and Legal Philosophy," in Friedrich [ed.], *Community, Nomos* II [New York: The Liberal Arts Press, 1959], p. 3).

38. The following two chapters will, in their different ways, be devoted to illustrating this particular claim.

39. Or, perhaps more precisely, it is to insist that they adopt one of the views of political community that might justify the policy, since it seems unlikely that each possible way of life uniquely determines one and only one immigration policy (though equally unlikely that a given way of life excludes no potential policies).

40. I should perhaps forestall potential concerns by noting simply that I do not intend to endorse complete state discretion; chapter six takes up this question

Chapter 4

1. Kenneth K. Lee, *Huddled Masses, Muddled Laws: Why Contemporary Immigration Policy Fails to Reflect Public Opinion* (Westport, Connecticut: Praeger, 1998), p. 14.

2. The rough shape of this history can be found in many sources. Some that I have found useful are William S. Bernard's contribution ("Immigration: History of U.S. Policy," pp. 486–95) to Stephan Thernstrom (ed.), *Harvard Encyclopedia of American Ethnic Groups* (Cambridge, MA: The Belknap Press of Harvard University Press, 1980), also collected as "A History of U.S. Immigration Policy" in Easterlin, Ward, Bernard, and Ueda, *Immigration* (Cambridge,

Massachusetts: The Belknap Press of Harvard University Press, 1982), pp. 75–105, which extends through the critical Immigration Act of 1965; and Keith Fitzgerald, *The Face of the Nation: Immigration, the State, and the National Identity* (Stanford, California: Stanford University Press, 1996), a very detailed account which also ends with the 1965 legislation. Detailed accounts of post-1965 legislation can be found in several articles by Peter Schuck that have been collected in his recent *Citizens, Strangers, and In-Betweens: Essays on Immigration and Citizenship* (Boulder, Colorado: Westview Press, 1998) (see especially chs. 2–5); and in Reed Ueda, *Postwar Immigrant America: A Social History* (Boston and New York: Bedford Books of St. Martin's Press, 1994).

3. The overall limit of 150,000 is also from the 1924 Act, which was more restrictive than the initial 1921 Act had been. Note, incidentally, that by using the census of 1890 as the baseline for calculating national limits, Congress managed to exclude a significant portion of the late-eighteenth-century, southern and eastern European immigrants from the population that would determine the composition of future immigration.

4. Rita J. Simon and Susan H. Alexander, *The Ambivalent Welcome: Print Media, Public Opinion and Immigration* (Westport, Connecticut: Praeger, 1993), pp. 40–41.

5. *Ibid.,* p. 45. Simon and Alexander do, however, go on to note the ambivalence of this public opinion, as I discuss later in the text.

6. *Ibid.,* p. 244.

7. See, for example, Peter Skerry, "Individualist America and Today's Immigrants," *The Public Interest* no. 102 (Winter 1991), p. 111, where he suggests that our current policy of family reunification "is informed by the belief that stable, intact families promote the economic and social well-being of immigrants."

8. See, for example, Ueda, *Postwar Immigrant America,* who argues that the Quota Acts of the 1920s were not only restrictionist but also "selective:" they "constituted a selective control system over immigration that would make it serve more efficiently the nation's economic needs . . ." (p. 25).

9. Lee, *Huddled Masses, Muddled Laws,* p. 9.

10. This account relies heavily on that in Lee, *Huddled Masses, Muddled Laws,* the central concern of which is to explain the gap between American public opinion and immigration policy and which describes the relevant congressional debates in great detail, using internal memos from the lobbying office that carefully nurtured the left-right, pro-immigration coalition as part of a deliberate strategy. The description I have given here of the legislative process behind our immigration laws will be readily recognizable as an essentially pluralist one. The most noted proponent of pluralism is Robert A. Dahl; see, for example, *A Preface to Democratic Theory* (Chicago: The University of Chicago Press, 1956); *Who Governs? Democracy and Power in an American City* (New Haven: Yale University Press, 1961); *Dilemmas of Pluralist Democracy: Autonomy vs. Control* (New Haven: Yale University Press, 1982); and *Democracy and its Critics* (New Haven: Yale University Press, 1989). By offering the description in the text, I do not intend to endorse pluralism as a comprehensive account of the American political sys-

tem, only to suggest that it seems to explain the formation of immigration policy nicely (see esp. Lee, ch. 6, "The Left-Right Alliance," pp. 89–126). As Lee puts it, "A modified pluralist theory most comprehensively explains the divergence between public opinion and public policy on immigration . . ." (91; by calling it "modified," Lee refers to the role of ideas as discussed in the text). For another excellent account of recent immigration politics, one that also discusses the formation of a pluralist coalition as it was shaped by certain ideas influential at the time, see Peter H. Schuck, "The Politics of Rapid Legal Change: Immigration Policy, 1980–1990," in *Citizens, Strangers, and In-Betweens*, pp. 91–138 (esp. 110–37). For criticisms of pluralism and the excesses of interest-group politics, see Theodore J. Lowi, *The End of Liberalism: The Second Republic of the United States* (New York: W. W. Norton, 1979).

11. Though he was obviously not referring specifically to contemporary interest-group politics, James Madison gave the classic account of "faction" in American politics—describing how our system attempts both to control and to manipulate factions—in Federalist 10; see Jacob E. Cooke (ed.), *The Federalist* (Middletown, CT: Wesleyan University Press, 1961), pp. 56–65. (Madison's treatment of faction is also important for the development of pluralist theory.) In general, the *Federalist*'s account of our government's structure offers a brilliant discussion of both how that structure rests upon popular will (see, for example, Federalist 37: "The genius of Republican liberty, seems to demand on one side, not only that all power should be derived from the people; but, that those entrusted with it should be kept in dependence on the people, by a short duration of their appointments; and, that, even during this short period, the trust should be placed not in a few, but in a number of hands" [Cooke, p. 234]), and also of how it attempts to moderate and channel that popular will. The best example of the latter is no doubt Madison's famous discussion of the separation of powers and checks and balances; see esp. papers 48 and 51 (Cooke, pp. 332–38 and 347–53, respectively).

12. Ben J. Wattenberg, *The First Universal Nation: Leading Indicators and Ideas about the Surge of America in the 1990s* (New York: The Free Press, 1991).

13. *Ibid.*, p. 24. Wattenberg explicitly links this fact to contemporary trends in immigration: "[I]n the quarter-century since 1965 about 14 million immigrants have come to the U.S. . . . And about 85 percent of these are *not* of white European ancestry. Americans, for the first time, can be accurately said to come from 'everywhere'" (10, emphasis in original). And later, discussing the demographic composition of the American population, he writes, "A threshold was passed, probably with the passage of the 1965 immigration law. America is becoming the world's first universal nation" (75).

14. For an account of this particular transformation, see Lee, *Huddled Masses, Muddled Laws*, pp. 101–6.

15. Peter Brimelow, *Alien Nation: Common Sense About America's Immigration Disaster* (New York: HarperPerennial, 1996), pp. 204–5 (emphasis in original).

16. *Ibid.*, p. 212 (and in general pp. 211–16). The point about America's significant ethnic and cultural homogeneity can be found on 206. Brimelow's second

through fifth chapters, which make the point that current high levels of immigration, far from being an inevitable part of a continuous American tradition, are rather the direct (and therefore reversible) consequence of the Immigration Act of 1965, in their own way underscore the "intermittent" nature of American immigration; see, *inter alia,* pp. 28–33.

17. Chilton Williamson, Jr., *The Immigration Mystique: America's False Conscience* (New York: BasicBooks, 1996), p. 21; the discussion makes up Williamson's second chapter, pp. 21–79.

18. Roy Beck, *The Case Against Immigration: The moral, economic, social, and environmental reasons for reducing U.S. immigration to traditional levels* (New York: W.W. Norton & Company, 1996), p. 38.

19. *Ibid.;* the first quote is from p. 36, the second from p. 49. On public opposition to the Great Wave of immigration, see pp. 42–7; on the Great Wave's atypical place in the overall history of American immigration prior to 1965, see pp. 37–42. In general on these issues, see Beck's second chapter, "Learning from the Great Wave," pp. 35–50.

20. See note 4 above.

21. Ueda, *Postwar Immigrant America,* p. 1.

22. Simon and Alexander, pp. 45–6. "Ambivalent" is also the word used by these authors in the title of their own volume, *The Ambivalent Welcome.*

23. *Ibid.,* p. 46.

24. For a discussion of Proposition 187, see Schuck, *Citizens, Strangers, and In-Betweens,* ch. 6 ("The Message of Proposition 187: Facing Up to Illegal Immigration").

25. Schuck, *Citizens, Strangers, and In-Betweens,* p. 144. Schuck's essay "Reform Continues: 1990–1998," in *ibid.,* pp. 139–48, contains a nice account of the ambivalence (a word he also uses) of contemporary American attitudes towards immigration. He also links the harsh treatment of illegal immigrants to the relatively favorable treatment of legal ones: "But even the IIRIRA's recklessness and unfairness [toward illegal immigrants] should not obscure a fundamental fact about immigration politics: Challenges to the high levels of *legal* immigration set in the 1990 law, such as the Jordan Commission's proposal to reduce legal admissions by more than one-third, have all failed" (145, emphasis in original).

26. Kenneth Lee argues that the rise in illegal immigration in the 1970's (and since) has provided cover to politicians who could appear tough on immigration by passing harsh legislation with regard to illegal immigrants while continuing to support legislation allowing very high levels of legal immigration; in this sense, he says, "illegal immigration helped 'save' legal immigration" (Lee, *Huddled Masses, Muddled Laws,* p. 146; see in general the argument on pp. 139–46).

27. Williamson notes (critically) the way in which "universalism" in the first sense (a large and diverse immigrant stream) feeds into and reinforces "universalism" in the second sense (the central unifying role of certain political ideals applicable to all people): "Given the degree to which a common commitment to a demo-

cratic ideal has helped to bind an ethnically heterogeneous nation together, this unifying ideal will become even more critical in the future as America becomes still more heterogeneous" (*The Immigration Mystique,* p. 137).

28. Michael Walzer, *On Toleration* (New Haven: Yale University Press, 1997), p. 94. Note, incidentally, how Walzer's defense of a state's right to fashion immigration policy in light of its particular traditions and identity leads in the American case (in Walzer's view) towards a position potentially open to considerable immigration.

29. Schuck, *Citizens, Strangers, and In-Betweens,* pp. 76–7 (endnote omitted); see also Ueda, *Postwar Immigrant America,* for a similar statement in a discussion of early American naturalization policy: "Most important, the origins of naturalized citizenship were presumed to lie in the idea of 'volitional allegiance' that characterized citizenship generally. The adoption of American citizenship by aliens, the transference of allegiance to the United States, emanated from individual choice and self-interest. Naturalization was based on the autonomy and liberty of the individual. This theoretical character of naturalization meant practically that an alien had to initiate and control the pursuit of citizenship and nationality. Government would only set basic rules of procedure. The applicant would decide how and when naturalization would fit into his or her life. Naturalization would be a reflection of the republican values of personal liberty and consent. For most of the nineteenth century, naturalization policy reflected fully these inclusive and voluntary principles" (27; paragraph division and endnote omitted).

30. Joseph H. Carens, "Aliens and Citizens: The Case for Open Borders," *Review of Politics* 49.2 (Spring 1987), p. 269 (emphasis in original; paragraph division omitted). Note that, in light of the passage quoted earlier (see note 28), Walzer and Carens may be in closer agreement on the nature of American political identity than on the general question of the state's authority to determine its membership.

31. Williamson, *The Immigration Mystique,* pp. 134–5 (emphasis in original). Also worth pondering in this connection is the following passage from Williamson, written partly in response to Wattenberg's labeling the United States the first universal nation: "The propositionists [those who consider the essence of American identity its being 'dedicated to a proposition'] assert their claim for America's uniqueness in the history of the world by denying the American nation a coherent personality, the attribute most wholly unique to any human individual or group . . . . Ben Wattenberg's 'first universal nation' manifestly would be no nation at all, which is why the concept is so attractive, and also useful, to those who have an interest in denying that the United States is a nation in the traditional cultural, ethnic, and geopolitical sense of the term" (113–14).

32. For Carens's argument that the original position ought to be applied globally, see "Aliens and Citizens," pp. 255–57; for Rawls's view, see "The Law of Peoples," *Critical Inquiry* 20.1 (Autumn 1993), pp. 54–5.

33. See, for example, Charles R. Beitz, *Political Theory and International Relations* (Princeton: Princeton University Press, 1979); and Jürgen Habermas, "Citizenship and National Identity: Some Reflections on the Future of Europe," in Ronald Beiner (ed.), *Theorizing Citizenship* (Albany: State University of New York Press, 1995), pp. 255–81.

34. Jeremy Rabkin, "Grotius, Vattel, and Locke: An Older View of Liberalism and Nationality," *Review of Politics* 59.2 (Spring 1997), p. 295 and pp. 317–18 (paragraph division omitted).

35. Thomas G. West, *Vindicating the Founders: Race, Sex, Class, and Justice in the Origins of America* (Lanham, MD: Rowman & Littlefield, 1997), p. 156.

36. Brimelow, *Alien Nation*, p. xviii.

37. I suspect that the number of different and not always harmonious principles is even greater than this. "Among the most salutary lessons that jurisprudence can learn from study of our republican regime are lessons about its complexity . . . . From the *Federalist* we learn that the constitutional design is meant to accommodate diverse elements of the public good—'combining the requisite stability and energy in government with the inviolable attention due to liberty, and to the republican form' and 'mingling them together in their due proportions.' . . . And the study of our history confirms what Tocqueville so powerfully teaches—that conflicts between claims for equality and claims for liberty are endemic to our kind of society. The same is true of other disparate desiderata of our complex liberal polity—majority rule and property rights, personal liberty and domestic tranquility, popular government and the rule of law." See Harry M. Clor, "Constitutional Interpretation and Regime Principles," in Robert A. Goldwin and William A. Schambra (eds.), *The Constitution, the Courts, and the Quest for Justice* (Washington, D.C.: American Enterprise Institute, 1989), p. 131. I am indebted to Clor's article for helping me think about the complexity of the American polity.

38. Though I cannot pretend to do justice here to Rogers Smith's massive *Civic Ideals: Conflicting Visions of Citizenship in U.S. History* (New Haven: Yale University Press, 1997), a brief comment on both its similarity to and difference from my approach here is in order. Just as I identify here universalist or particularist interpretations of American identity, so too does Smith describe different strands within American citizenship. He identifies three such strands, which he calls the democratic, republican, and ascriptive visions of citizenship. In this sense, there is a certain similarity between our general descriptions of American identity as containing diverse elements. But in contrast to my fairly neutral presentation of the two competing interpretations of America, Smith is quite explicit in his judgement that the liberal strand represents what is best in American citizenship, the ascriptive strand what is worst, and that Americans should strive to perfect their liberal ideals and to overcome the ascriptive elements from their past (a fairly easy argument once ascriptivism has been more or less equated with racism). It would require many more pages than I have here to sort out exactly how far Smith and I can travel down the same road together;

but I am suspicious of the theoretical typology upon which Smith builds his argument, because I am not sure that the distinctions in question are as neat as that typology suggests. At the risk of exaggerating slightly, there are, I think, no such thing as "liberal principles" in the abstract, to which we can compare the practice of an ostensibly liberal country. Rather, as I suggested in my introduction, liberalism seeks to balance a variety of different goals, and therefore, because different countries balance them differently, there are a variety of liberalisms, each of them combining elements from Smith's various strands (including ones related to his ascriptivism, which is a broader category than mere racism or sexism) in its own ways. (To paraphrase Justice Stewart on pornography: I'm not sure I can define liberal democracy, but I know it when I see it.) This, if true, means that American liberal democracy, for example, is not just a stew of poorly matched ingredients, heavy on the potatoes, light on the carrots, but is rather at some level a coherent whole, a complex attempt to serve a number of purposes (which Americans may have done more or less well at different times). This, of course, does not preclude arguments about how good the stew tastes, or whether it might be improved by a bit more (or less) salt and pepper. And insofar as this is what Smith is doing, offering his particular argument about the best way to understand American identity and the loftiest aspirations to draw from it, he may well be doing precisely the sort of thing I suggest citizens should do: argue about who they are, and who they hope to become.

39. Cf. West, *Vindicating the Founders,* pp. 147–9.
40. Arthur M. Schlesinger, Jr., *The Disuniting of America* (New York: W.W. Norton & Company, 1992), though not specifically about immigration, is a brief account of several aspects of these "culture wars." The work of a historian with impeccable left-wing credentials, one who is undeniably sympathetic to the claims of America's diverse ethnic and racial groups, the book is nevertheless motivated by the author's concern that increasing ethnic diversity—or, more specifically, increasing ethnic assertiveness and separatism—is threatening the American union. At the same time, Schlesinger clearly believes that this union is based around common allegiance to a certain set of political principles. The book thus provides a nice illustration of how debates over the "universality" of America both underlie a whole range of contemporary issues and also how they can at times confuse typical right-left political divisions.
41. Note that there is presumably at least some common ground between these two, since even defenders of universal liberal principles may allow measures taken to protect those principles themselves. Thus, for example, Carens, in his argument for open borders, concedes that immigration could be restricted if "unrestricted immigration would lead to chaos and the breakdown of order;" this would be "a case of restricting liberty for the sake of liberty" ("Aliens and Citizens," p. 259). For an interesting contemporary example of compromising liberal principles for the sake of liberalism itself, consider the clause in Article 21 of the German constitution, which states, "Parties which, by reason of their aims or the behaviour of their adherents, seek to impair or abolish the free

democratic basic order or to endanger the existence of the Federal Republic of Germany shall be unconstitutional." This provision has been used to ban neo-Nazi parties, for example.

42. One should remember that other classic countries of immigration, such as Canada or Australia, must wrestle with similar problems. And immigration has also played a significant role in shaping the societies of several South American nations, such as Brazil, Argentina, and Chile.

43. The most obvious example of changed circumstances is certainly the problem of illegal immigration, which for most of our history was essentially nonexistent but has assumed enormous proportions in recent decades, becoming the focus of considerable public attention and even outrage. For a consideration of some theoretical problems raised by illegal immigration, see the discussion in Peter H. Schuck and Rogers M. Smith, *Citizenship Without Consent: Illegal Aliens in the American Polity* (New Haven:Yale University Press, 1985).

44. Summaries of these changes can be found in numerous places. See, for example, Rainer Münz and Ralf Ulrich, "Immigration and Citizenship in Germany," *German Politics and Society,* Issue 53, vol. 17, no. 4 (Winter 1999), pp. 12–15; and Davood Rahman-Niaghi, *Ausländerrecht: aber leicht* (Berlin: Rosen Verlag, 2000), ch. 14 ("Die Einbürgerung," pp. 278–94) and ch. 15 ("Anspruchseinbürgerung für Ausländer mit längerem Aufenthalt in Deutschland," pp. 295–308). The German government has also provided a helpful account of the changes at the website www.einbuergerung.de.

45. Rogers Brubaker, *Citizenship and Nationhood in France and Germany* (Cambridge, Mass.: Harvard University Press, 1992), p. 1. Further citations from Brubaker will be identified by page number in parentheses within the text.

46. Friedrich Meinecke, *Weltbürgertum und Nationalstaat* (Munich: R. Oldenbourg Verlag, 1962), p. 10. All translations from the German, unless otherwise noted, are my own.

47. The recent reform changed the law's heading to simply *Staatsangehörigkeitsgesetz,* eliminating the reference to the *Reich.* I have relied upon the texts of German laws (prior to the recent reforms) given in Reinhard Marx, *Kommentar zum Staatsangehörigkeitsrecht* (Neuwied, Kriftel, and Berlin: Luchterhand, 1997). My translations are based upon these texts as well.

48. Marx, *Kommentar,* p. 152. Marx goes on to modify this very stark characterization slightly, claiming that *some* balancing does—and, according to the opinions of the *Bundesverfassungsgericht,* must—take place. But the consideration of the applicant's constitutionally protected interests seems primarily to consist in assuring him a fair hearing; and "as always, in the framework of the [official] discretion with regard to naturalization, the public interests are entitled to paramount significance" (Marx, p. 155). Further references to Marx's commentary will be given by page number in parentheses within the text.

49. Brubaker was writing in 1992; since then, efforts have been made at slowing immigration of ethnic Germans from the East as well as easing naturalization procedures for foreigners raised in Germany. Still, the point remains well-taken.

See also his similar description on p. 176 (subject also to the same qualification): "While politicians of all parties have invoked the limited 'absorptive capacity' [*Aufnahmefähigkeit*] of Germany, especially with respect to Turks, it remains politically unacceptable to make the same argument about ethnic Germans. And while the government has maintained its restrictive citizenship policies toward non-German immigrants, German immigrants continue to enjoy a privileged citizenship status. The availability of a supply of ethnic German immigrants, legally privileged and socially preferred to non-Germans, has revealed the marked ethnocultural inflection in the contemporary German politics of immigration and citizenship."

50. "[E]in Einwanderungsland neuen Typs." Klaus J. Bade (ed.), *Das Manifest der 60: Deutschland und die Einwanderung* (Munich: C. H. Beck, 1994), p. 67 (see generally pp. 66–7).

51. The summary here, including all quotations, is from Bade, *Das Manifest der 60*, pp. 74–78. Nearly identical accounts can be found in several of Bade's other works, for example: "Politik in der Einwanderungssituation: Migration—Integration—Minderheiten," in Bade (ed.), *Deutsche im Ausland—Fremde in Deutschland: Migration in Geschichte und Gegenwart* (Munich: C. H. Beck, 1993), pp. 442–55, see esp. 443–46; *Homo Migrans. Wanderungen aus und nach Deutschland: Erfahrungen und Fragen* (Essen: Klartext, 1994), pp. 53–65; and "Einwanderung und Gesellschaft in Deutschland—quo vadis Bundesrepulik?" in Bade (ed.), *Die multikulterelle Herausforderung: Menschen über Grenzen—Grenzen über Menschen* (Munich: C. H. Beck, 1996), pp. 230–53, see esp. 240–42.

52. It might be suggested that I should give more attention here to asylum, for at least two reasons: it has often been the large numbers of asylum-seekers that have in recent years occasioned strong public opposition to immigration (though this problem has diminished somewhat as the legal changes mentioned in the text, making it more difficult to claim asylum in Germany, have begun to take effect); and, of course, asylum-seekers can only very rarely be expected to share a "German" identity. My reason for not doing so is simply that, if I am right to claim that German citizenship law reflects an ethnocultural national identity, then asylum-seeking immigrants do not pose anything like the direct challenge to that identity that the stark contrast between *Gastarbeiter* and *Aussiedler* does. This is because asylum is necessarily a response to an exceptional situation; and it would be almost perverse to insist that a state be defined by and consistently held to a standard determined by its willingness to offer humanitarian assistance to people in extraordinary circumstances. To this, of course, it might be replied that Germany is a special case, and that its liberal asylum laws have been a defining part of Germany's post-war identity, reflecting, presumably, a new but central element of that identity, namely, Germany's firm commitment to liberal political ideals. This may be true, but I question whether it can really do the work being asked of it here. After all, Germany's newfound liberalism, as reflected by its asylum policy, has coexisted with the ethnocultural identity embodied in its citizenship law for some time; thus the upshot of the criticism seems to be that

these were *always* in contradiction with each other, even if that contradiction has only gradually become obvious. This is a rather large claim, however, and in my view a questionable one; it involves significant assumptions about the nature of liberalism and what kinds of polities are or are not compatible with it. These assumptions are too complex to explore here, but they do suggest the difficulty of drawing clear conclusions about German identity on the basis of asylum policy. For some further (though also brief and fragmentary) comments on these issues, see my later discussion in this section of "constitutional patriotism" as a possible new basis for German identity; and my discussion in the first half of this chapter on liberalism as a part of American identity.

53. The information in this brief history of the *Gastarbeiter* can be found in numerous sources; one concise essay that I have found helpful is Bade, "Einheimische Ausländer: ,Gastarbeiter'—Dauergäste—Einwanderer," in Bade, *Deutsche im Ausland—Fremde in Deutschland,* pp. 393–401.

54. Cornelia Schmalz-Jacobsen and Georg Hansen (eds.), in their *Kleines Lexikon der ethnischen Minderheiten in Deutschland* (Munich: C. H. Beck, 1997), give a figure of 2,014,311 (p. 164), a number which has presumably continued to grow since then.

55. Bade, "Einheimische Ausländer: ,Gastarbeiter'—Dauergäste—Einwanderer," p. 398.

56. It may seem that I am trying to have it two ways here with respect to the descendants of former *Gastarbeiter.* On the one hand, I describe them as being already "German;" on the other, I concede that, even when the possibility has been made available to them, very few have sought to acquire German citizenship, partly from a reluctance to initiate a process that is thought to require "becoming" completely German. So: are these foreigners assimilated—are they really German—or not? This apparent contradiction is exaggerated, however. First, it seems reasonable to think that full assimilation can only occur in an atmosphere of openness or willing acceptance on the part of the majority, mainstream population; current German legal practice suggests that, no doubt for complicated reasons, such acceptance does not yet exist. And second, there are presumably degrees of assimilation, which is not an all-or-nothing affair. Thus we can say that the former *Gastarbeiter* and their descendants are assimilated in the sense of being settled in Germany and having made their permanent home there (and having no other real home), of having to operate in the German culture and inevitably absorbing important parts of it, even if their complete assimilation takes longer and is hampered by a reluctance to view them as truly "German."

57. The number is from Heinz Fassmann and Rainer Münz, "European East-West Migration, 1945–92," in Robin Cohen (ed.), *The Cambridge Survey of World Migration* (Cambridge: Cambridge University Press, 1995), p. 470.

58. The number is from Bade, "Fremde Deutsche: ,Republikflüchtige'—Übersiedler—Aussiedler," in Bade (ed.), *Deutsche im Ausland—Fremde in Deutschland,* p. 405. This brief essay (pp. 401–410) is a very nice treatment of the problems of the *Aussiedler.*

59. Bade, *ibid.,* often refers to their desire to live as "Deutsche unter Deutschen."
60. *Ibid.,* pp. 408–9.
61. *Ibid.,* p. 409.
62. *Ibid.,* p. 407.
63. *Ibid.,* p. 410.
64. Bade, "Einheimische Ausländer: ,Gastarbeiter'—Dauergäste—Einwanderer," p. 400.
65. Jürgen Habermas, "Struggles for Recognition in the Democratic Constitutional State," in Amy Gutmann (ed.), *Multiculturalism: Examining the Politics of Recognition* (Princeton: Princeton University Press, 1994), p. 135. See also Habermas, "Citizenship and National Identity" (full citation in n. 33). Habermas himself explicitly proposes this "constitutional patriotism" as a response to the ethnocultural understanding of German identity discussed in the text: "If the notion that 'we are not a land of immigration' continues to be put forth in the political public sphere in the face of this evidence [to the contrary], this indicates that it is a manifestation of a deep-seated mentality—and that a painful change is necessary in the way we conceive ourselves as a nation. It is no accident that our naturalization decisions are based on the principle of ancestry and not, as in other Western nations, on the principle of territoriality. The shortcomings described above in the way Germany is dealing with the problem of immigration must be understood against the historical background of the Germans' understanding of themselves as a nation of *Volksgenossen* or ethnic comrades centered around language and culture" ("Struggles for Recognition," p. 145). For some interesting criticisms of Habermas's position as an example of "civic nationalism," see Bernard Yack, "The Myth of the Civic Nation," *Critical Review* 10.2 (Spring 1996), pp. 198–200.
66. Habermas, "Struggles for Recognition," p. 139.
67. Habermas, as one would expect, criticizes these restrictions, *ibid.,* pp. 143–48.
68. The difficulty of answering such questions—though not simply with regard to liberalism—was suggested in chapter three. See also note 52 in this chapter, as well as the discussion in my earlier treatment of America referred to there. See chapter three also for a discussion of the relationship between political culture and culture more generally, one which, though it was not written with him in mind, seems relevant to a consideration of Habermas's argument.
69. *Der Spiegel,* January 11, 1999 (no. 2), pp. 22–32.
70. "The Week in Germany," February 12, 1999, published online by the German Embassy at www.germany-info.org.
71. *Der Spiegel,* April 5, 1999 (no. 14), p. 41. As noted later in the text, the new reforms also shorten the time of residence in Germany necessary for a foreigner to apply for citizenship from 15 to 8 years.
72. See Kay Hailbronner, "Die Reform des deutschen Staatsangehörigkeitsrechts," *Neue Zeitschrift für Verwaltungsrecht,* Heft 12 (1999), p. 1274.
73. Before the eight years have expired, naturalization is still possible only at the discretion of the relevant authorities.

74. This implies that a concern for national identity is better able to justify restrictive policies for immigration than for naturalization. I am inclined to agree with that view, which has been defended by writers whose opinions on immigration restrictions themselves are quite opposed; cf. Carens, "Membership and Morality: Admission to Citizenship in Liberal Democratic States," in William Rogers Brubaker (ed.), *Immigration and the Politics of Citizenship in Europe and North America* (Lanham, MD: University Press of America, 1989), pp. 31–49, and Michael Walzer, *Spheres of Justice* (New York: Basic Books, 1983), pp. 52–63. See also Ruth Rubio-Marin, *Immigration as a Democratic Challenge: Citizenship and Inclusion in Germany and the United States* (Cambridge: Cambridge University Press, 2000).

75. For a discussion of this and other questions related to the new laws, see Hailbronner, "Die Reform des deutschen Staatsangehörigkeitsrechts."

76. Evidence of this is the heated discussion that has arisen in the past several months over the suggestion that German culture represents a *Leitkultur,* a leading or dominant culture, that should guide the integration and assimilation of foreigners. A useful summary of the debate over the idea of a *Leitkultur* is presented in the "Chronik" given under the "Dossier" on that subject at the website of the *Frankfurter Allgemeine Zeitung* (www.faz.de; links to the various dossiers, which contain a variety of helpful information, are located on the "Politik" page).

77. Contrast this with the approach of Rubio-Marin, *Immigration as a Democratic Challenge,* who also examines the cases of the United States and Germany, though her specific focus is naturalization rather than immigration. She begins with principles derived from abstract liberal or democratic theory, which she then uses to explain the obligations of contemporary liberal democracies. By contrast, if the case for liberal democracy is, as I believe, to a large extent a practical one—we know liberal democracy is desirable because of its impressive success in providing good governance—then a more cautious approach may be justified. If actual liberal democracies, seeking to do justice to a complex array of moral claims, have regarded certain practices as not incompatible with liberal democratic principles, that is at least a strong prima facie reason for thinking that they are not. My brief comments on Rogers Smith's *Civic Ideals* (note 38) are relevant here as well.

Chapter 5

1. Though he has, in discussing the possibility of open borders, refrained from endorsing that position; see, for example, Will Kymlicka, *Multicultural Citizenship: A Liberal Theory of Minority Rights* (Oxford: Clarendon Press, 1996), pp. 124–6. Further references to this work will be given by page number in parentheses within the text, which I shall identify when necessary with the abbreviation MC.

2. Kymlicka, *Liberalism, Community, and Culture* (Oxford: Clarendon Press, 1989); citations from this book will also be noted by page number within the text, iden-

tified when necessary as LCC. My own discussion focuses mainly on the more recent *Multicultural Citizenship*. The argument remains the same, but the treatment in the later book is more concise. Furthermore, the emphasis in the first book is on the liberal response to communitarianism, that is, on showing that liberalism does not preclude (indeed, requires) a concern for culture; whereas the question of minority rights (also treated in the first book) is the clear focus of the second book. Thus the topics that I am concerned with are more thoroughly dealt with in *Multicultural Citizenship*.

3. Kymlicka specifically characterizes his liberalism as based on individual autonomy, and contrasts it with an account based upon toleration, in MC, chapter 8, introduction and sections 1 and 2.

4. Kymlicka also describes the difference between the two groups in this way: "[I]t is important to distinguish this sort of cultural diversity"—that is, the kind found among immigrant groups—"from that of national minorities. Immigrant groups are not 'nations', and do not occupy homelands. Their distinctiveness is manifested primarily in their family lives and in voluntary associations, and is not inconsistent with their institutional integration. They still participate within the public institutions of the dominant culture(s) and speak the dominant language(s)" (MC, 14).

5. Will Kymlicka, *States, Nations and Cultures* (Assen, the Netherlands: Van Gorcum & Comp., 1997), Lecture 2: "Multicultural Citizenship," p. 54.

6. Kymlicka notes a handful of people who *have* endorsed open borders, Carens among them, at MC, 215, n. 17.

7. Carens, however, discussing this aspect of Kymlicka's argument, suggests that it is actually more sympathetic to open borders than it appears. He points out a footnote in which Kymlicka conditions states' right to exclude outsiders upon the fulfillment of their "redistributive obligations under international justice." But, continues Carens, "Since no rich states come close to meeting what Kymlicka clearly regards as their obligations, this seems to commit him in practice to something close to an open borders argument himself, at least with respect to affluent states." See Carens, *Culture, Citizenship, and Community* (Oxford: Oxford University Press, 2000, p. 68, n. 13.

8. I suspect that another reason for Kymlicka's reluctance to endorse the outright imposition of liberalism, though he does not discuss this factor in his treatment of the problem of illiberal groups, is his argument that people are normally entitled not simply to *any* cultural context of choice, but rather to that provided by their *own* culture (see MC, 84–93). Being deprived of one's own culture is extremely difficult for most people and can even cause them serious harm (consider the sad fate of numerous indigenous peoples). Thus, Kymlicka suggests, "in developing a theory of justice, we should treat access to one's culture as something that people can be expected to want, whatever their more particular conception of the good [that is, we should treat it as a Rawlsian primary good; see LCC, 166]. Leaving one's culture, while possible, is best seen as renouncing something to which one is reasonably entitled" (MC, 86). Obvi-

ously, if this is the case, then forcibly imposing liberalism on a people raises problems that seeking to encourage its liberalization from within does not. Kymlicka offers a briefer but essentially identical treatment of the problem of nonliberal cultures (often repeating practically verbatim passages from the argument in *Multicultural Citizenship*) in *States, Nations and Cultures*, pp. 41–2.

9. Exactly the same sentence is repeated at *States, Nations and Cultures*, p. 34.

10. Consider, for example, the following passage and its implications for immigration policy: "If certain liberties really would undermine the very existence of the community, then we should allow what would otherwise be illiberal measures. But these measures would only be justified as temporary measures, easing the shock which can result from too rapid change in the character of the culture (be it endogenously or exogenously caused), helping the culture to move carefully towards a fully liberal society. The ideal would still be a society where every individual is free to choose the life she thinks best for her from a rich array of possibilities offered by the cultural structure" (MC, 170–1).

11. Recall, in this regard, the passage I cited earlier, in which Kymlicka explains how a culture functions as a context of choice and thus why liberals ought to value culture as the necessary background condition for individual autonomy: "The decision about how to lead our lives must ultimately be ours alone, but this decision is always a matter of selecting what we believe to be most valuable from the various options available, selecting from a context of choice which provides us with different ways of life. This is important because the range of options is determined by our cultural heritage" (LCC, 164–5). This certainly sounds as though the cultural context of choice consists of the particular set of options the culture in question offers its members.

12. For discussions of this example see LCC, 167; MC, 87–8; and *States, Nations and Cultures*, pp. 37–9.

13. *States, Nations and Cultures*, p. 37; see also MC, 87.

14. *Idem.*

15. MC, 87–88; *States, Nations and Cultures*, pp. 37–8.

16. Edmund Burke, *Reflections on the Revolution in France*, ed. J.G.A. Pocock, (Indianapolis: Hackett Publishing Company, 1987), pp. 36–7.

17. This is how Stephen R. Perry, for instance, interprets Kymlicka's idea of cultural structure (as opposed to character). See Perry, "Immigration, justice, and culture," in Warren F. Schwartz (ed.), *Justice in immigration* (Cambridge: Cambridge University Press, 1995), pp. 116–17 (where he suggests that even language belongs to the character, rather than the structure, of a community) and 114.

18. Michael Walzer, *Spheres of Justice* (New York: Basic Books, Inc., 1983), p. 6; original in italics. Further references to this work will be given by page number in parentheses within the text, identified when necessary as SOJ.

19. Obviously, this assumes that membership comes along with, or should come along with, birth into a given community. I do not examine that assumption here, though parts of Walzer's discussion—his prohibition on expelling mem-

bers, or his argument that full membership (citizenship) must be offered to all residents of a given territory—would be relevant to its defense.

20. The italics are Walzer's, but he has borrowed the phrase "communities of character" from the Austrian socialist Otto Bauer; see SOJ, 325, n. 31.

21. Joseph H. Carens, "Aliens and Citizens: The Case for Open Borders," *The Review of Politics* 49.2 (Spring 1987), p. 267; emphasis in original.

22. Walzer, "The Moral Standing of States: A Response to Four Critics," *Philosophy & Public Affairs* 9.3 (Spring 1980), p. 210. The book on just war is, of course, *Just and Unjust Wars: A Moral Argument with Historical Illustrations* (New York: Basic Books, Inc., 1977).

23. This presumption plays an important role in Walzer's argument. Consider "The Moral Standing of States," p. 212, where Walzer speaks of "a morally necessary presumption: that there exists a certain 'fit' between the community and its government and that the state is 'legitimate.' . . . This presumption is simply the respect that foreigners owe to a historic community and to its internal life." He also writes, "Foreigners are in no position to deny the reality of that union [between community and government], or rather, they are in no position to attempt anything more than speculative denials" (212). He does concede that in some cases the presumption of "fit" between a people and its government "can be rebutted and disregarded" (212), and suggests several circumstances that might justify this: "[s]truggles for secession or liberation," "civil war," or a government's "massacre or enslavement of its own citizens or subjects" (217; see in general 216–18).

24. Walzer, *Thick and Thin: Moral Argument at Home and Abroad* (Notre Dame: University of Notre Dame Press, 1994), p. 78.

25. Walzer, "Nation and Universe," *The Tanner Lectures on Human Values XI* (Salt Lake City: University of Utah Press, 1990), p. 536.

26. See note 23.

27. See the passage quoted in part earlier: "Only if the state makes a selection among would-be members and guarantees the loyalty, security, and welfare of the individuals it selects, can local communities take shape as 'indifferent' associations [as neighborhoods, that is], determined solely by personal preference and market capacity. Since individual choice is most dependent upon local mobility, this would seem to be the preferred arrangement in a society like our own. The politics and the culture of a modern democracy probably require the kind of largeness, and also the kind of boundedness, that states provide" (SOJ, 38–39).

28. One could plausibly argue, I think, that the broadest community of shared meanings will vary with the object of debate—for some purposes it might be a very local community indeed (Americans sometimes think of education in this way, for example, though that view is of course disputed), for others it might conceivably be the world as a whole. Such an argument would not, though, disprove Walzer's suggestion that most of the time and for most purposes the most relevant community is the state.

29. For an attempt by Walzer to think about some of these problems, see *Thick and*

Thin, ch. 4, "Justice and Tribalism: Minimal Morality in International Politics" (pp. 63–83).

30. Which is not to say, of course, that different social worlds never have anything in common or that they are unrecognizable to each other as shared worlds of meaning; only that in most of our social interactions, the meanings at stake will be relatively particular, "thick," rather than the vaguer and "thinner" meanings that might conceivably be shared across communities; see the distinction between "minimal" and "maximal" morality in *Thick and Thin*, ch. 1, "Moral Minimalism" (pp. 1–19).

31. This does not mean, of course, that distinct communities will always disappear if they lack this control. Carens misses this point, I think, when he criticizes Walzer's claim that "[t]he distinctiveness of cultures and groups depends upon closure and, without it, cannot be conceived as a stable feature of human life" (SOJ, 39). Carens responds by quite reasonably pointing out, using the example of culturally distinct cities and regions in the United States, that more forces are at work here: "What makes for distinctiveness and what erodes it is [*sic*] much more complex than political control of admissions" ("Aliens and Citizens," p. 267). But the point, of course, is really that without control over admissions, groups can do very little to protect their own conceptions of membership and community; they are required to leave themselves vulnerable to extinction, subject to the winds of fortune. This distinction is clearer in a slightly different formulation of Walzer's: "Neighborhoods can be open only if countries are at least *potentially* closed" (SOJ, 38; my emphasis).

32. *Thick and Thin*, p. 67.

33. *Ibid.*, p. 68; emphasis in original.

34. *Ibid.*, pp. 81–2.

35. *Ibid.*, p. 83.

36. This may be a good place to insert a brief comment on the difference between our arguments. Although I think that some such argument as Walzer raises on the edifice of self-determination is quite probably correct, I have not actually made that argument myself. My own argument in chapter three was a weaker, negative one: that our lack of widely persuasive answers to certain fundamental questions about whether groups are entitled to prefer their own members, the plausibility of answering those questions in a way that would support such preference, and the broad coercion that would be required to prohibit countries from acting preferentially combine to create a presumption in favor of allowing actually existing communities to attempt to preserve their own identities. Such an argument can potentially be endorsed even by those who do not themselves share Walzer's deeper commitment to communal self-determination.

37. Patrick Thornberry, "The Democratic or Internal Aspect of Self-Determination with Some Remarks on Federalism," in Christian Tomuschat (ed.), *Modern Law of Self-Determination* (Dordrecht, Boston, and London: Martinus Nijhoff Publishers, 1993), p. 101.

38. *Idem.*

39. *Idem.*
40. *Ibid.*, p. 102.
41. "Nation and Universe," p. 554.
42. "The Moral Standing of States," p. 228.
43. Some sense of Walzer's broader political views can be found (among other places) in *Radical Principles: reflections of an unreconstructed democrat* (New York: Basic Books, Inc., 1980), as well as in his frequent contributions to the journal *Dissent,* of which he has for years been co-editor.
44. *Just and Unjust Wars,* p. 87.
45. *Ibid.*, p. 88.
46. *Ibid.*, p. 89.
47. In fairness, I should perhaps quote a passage from the very same work which describes self-determination in a different way. The following seems to me an excellent description of the "passive" view of self-determination: "The rights of states rest on the consent of their members. But this is consent of a special sort. State rights are not constituted through a series of transfers from individual men and women to the sovereign or through a series of exchanges among individuals. What actually happens is harder to describe. Over a long period of time, shared experiences and cooperative activity of many different kinds shape a common life. 'Contract' is a metaphor for a process of association and mutuality, the ongoing character of which the state claims to protect against external encroachment. The protection extends not only to the lives and liberties of individuals but also to their shared life and liberty, the independent community they have made, for which individuals are sometimes sacrificed. The moral standing of any particular state depends upon the reality of the common life it protects and the extent to which the sacrifices required by that protection are willingly accepted and thought worthwhile" (*Just and Unjust Wars,* 54).
48. *Thick and Thin,* p. 37.
49. It is this blurring between the ideas of self-determination and something like participatory democracy that accounts, I think, for the occasional uncertainty in *Spheres of Justice* about whether Walzer understands himself to be presenting a theory which applies to all different cultural groups or political communities, illustrated at times by references to (in particular) American democracy; or whether his theory really only applies, at least in its fullest form, to democracies; or whether it even proposes democracy, at some level, as a norm for all communities.
50. The first quotation is from "The Moral Standing of States," p. 217; the second from *Just and Unjust Wars,* p. 101.
51. "The Moral Standing of States," p. 226.
52. *Ibid.*, p. 228.
53. *Ibid.*, p. 229.
54. Perhaps it would be better to avoid the language of self-determination altogether, since it invites ambiguity; I am open to this possibility, though I am not sure that there is a better alternative readily available whose common usage would serve the purpose. The phrase "popular sovereignty," broadly understood, has a certain

value, I think (cf. chapter three, n. 11; the corresponding discussion in the text there, on the sense in which a legitimate national identity need be "democratic," is also relevant here); but it no doubt carries connotations similar to those of self-determination. Perhaps what matters here is a broad notion of "consent:" the idea that a given way of life, whatever it may be, is at some level willingly adopted by the people in question (cf. Walzer's own description of "consent of a special sort" in the passage I have quoted here in n. 46). In this sense, of course, people could "consent" to live under any number of arrangements, not just those of a liberal democracy. Though his meaning is not precisely the same, Hume captures something of this idea when he writes, "Nothing appears more surprizing to those, who consider human affairs with a philosophical eye, than the easiness with which the many are governed by the few; and the implicit submission, with which men resign their own sentiments and passions to those of their rulers. When we inquire by what means this wonder is effected, we shall find, that, as FORCE is always on the side of the governed, the governors have nothing to support them but opinion. It is therefore, on opinion only that government is founded; and this maxim extends to the most despotic and most military governments, as well as to the most free and most popular. The soldan of EGYPT, or the emperor of ROME, might drive his harmless subjects, like brute beasts, against their sentiments and inclination: But he must, at least, have led his *mamalukes,* or *praetorian bands,* like men, by their opinion" ("Of the First Principles of Government," in Hume, *Essays Moral, Political, and Literary,* ed. Eugene F. Miller [Indianapolis: Liberty Fund, 1985], pp. 32–3). Hume's point is that all governments rely at some level upon an acknowledgement of their legitimacy on the part of their subjects. Perhaps we could say that when a people consents to its common life in this broad sense, that suffices to establish its right to self-determination in the sense of freedom from unwanted outside interference. At any rate, if we do continue to use the language of self-determination, we should emphasize its "passive" meaning, remembering that it is intended to protect peoples' ways of life, not to impose new restrictions on the kinds of lives they are permitted to live.

55. *Just and Unjust Wars,* p. 54.
56. We should, I think, be mildly troubled by the way in which a preference for some form of participatory democracy seems to sneak back—in a way that seems as much normative as descriptive—into Walzer's account of self-determination or politics at the deepest level. That account takes as its basis the modern state. Thus Walzer begins the chapter in *Spheres of Justice* on political power by writing, "I shall begin with sovereignty, political command, authoritative decision making— the conceptual foundation of the modern state. Sovereignty by no means exhausts the field of power, but it does focus our attention on the most significant and dangerous form that power can pursue; as *state power,* it is also the means by which all the different pursuits, including that of power itself, are regulated. . . . Political power protects us from tyranny . . . and itself becomes tyrannical" (281; emphasis in original). But this vision of the political world is one in which force, or coercion, is central, a constitutive element (compare the definition of "politi-

cal power" offered by John Locke in the very first chapter of his *Second Treatise:* "Political power, then, I take to be a right of making laws, with penalties of death, and consequently all less penalties for the regulation and preserving of our property, and of employing the force of the community in the execution of such laws, and in the defence of the commonwealth from foreign injury, and all this only for the public good"); whereas force in all its forms is utterly excluded from Walzer's description of an ideal politics. This attempt to revive a participatory politics of activist, democratic citizens within the context of the modern state inevitably sounds somewhat ominous, for exactly the reasons recognized by Walzer in the "Socialist Citizen" essay discussed in my concluding paragraphs: it threatens to compel citizens to engage in a kind of political activity for which many, even most, of them will often have no desire. I see no reason to view this as any less potentially repressive than the denial of opportunities for political participation. In trying to revive a participatory politics within the modern state, Walzer reveals his debt to Rousseau and recalls all the tensions and problems of the latter's project. At the same time, Walzer is, I think, more sensitive than Rousseau to these difficulties (as the following paragraphs, again, suggest), and this is part of what makes his work, in my view, so very interesting.

57. Walzer, *Obligations: Essays on Disobedience, War, and Citizenship* (New York: Simon and Schuster, 1970), p. 228. The essay is in *Obligations,* pp. 229–38.

58. *Ibid.,* p. 230.

59. *Ibid.,* p. 231.

60. *Ibid.,* p. 235.

61. *Ibid.,* p. 235.

62. *Just and Unjust Wars,* p. 54.

Chapter 6

1. Michael Walzer, *Spheres of Justice: A Defense of Pluralism and Equality* (New York: Basic Books, Inc., 1983), p. 51.

2. Guy S. Goodwin-Gill, *The Refugee in International Law* (Oxford: Clarendon Press, 1983), p. 215.

3. *Ibid.,* p. 19.

4. The Convention is reprinted in *ibid.,* pp. 247–69; the definition quoted is on p. 253.

5. *Ibid.,* pp. 15–16. For a concise summary of protections of the refugee's right to asylum found in different domestic constitutions and immigration laws, see Richard Plender, *International Migration Law: Revised Second Edition* (Dordrecht, the Netherlands, Boston, and London: Martinus Nijhoff Publishers, 1988), pp. 404–11.

6. Goodwin-Gill, *The Refugee in International Law,* p. 13.

7. Atle Grahl-Madsen, *The Status of Refugees in International Law,* vol. 1 (The Netherlands: A.W. Sijthoff-Leyden, 1966), p. 79.

8. The benefits that follow designation as a refugee are considerable: "Ironically, for many persons on the brink of disaster, refugee status is a privileged position.

In contrast to other destitute people, the refugee is eligible for many forms of international assistance, including material relief, asylum, and permanent resettlement" (Andrew E. Shacknove, "Who is a Refugee?" *Ethics* 95.2 [January 1985]: 276). See also Goodwin-Gill, *The Refugee in International Law,* p. 224: "In many respects, refugees enjoy a legal standing superior to that of citizens in their own country. The existence of the class of refugees not only imports legal consequences for states in regard to *non-refoulement* and standards of treatment, but also an entitlement to exercise protection on behalf of refugees."

9. Shacknove, "Who is a Refugee?", p. 274.

10. *Ibid.,* p. 276.

11. *Ibid.,* p. 277. For an earlier challenge to restrictive definitions of "refugee," see Austin T. Fragomen, Jr., "The Refugee: A Problem of Definition," *Case Western Reserve Journal of International Law* 3.1 (Winter 1970), pp. 45–69.

12. Walzer, *Spheres of Justice,* p. 48.

13. Shacknove might not entirely agree with this claim. Part of his point is that the severity of, say, a famine is often due less to natural, unpreventable events than to the failure of governments to respond to them adequately. Even granting this, though, I think that we would not blame incompetence or corruption in the same way that we would policies of deliberate persecution.

14. I avoid saying that they have a "right" to immigrate in order to forestall the misinterpretation warned against in the introduction to this chapter, that of mistaking the suggestions urged here for abstract principles admitting no exceptions. They are guides to action—and weighty ones—but the appropriate course of action in any given case will depend upon its particular circumstances.

15. Quoted in Walzer, *Spheres of Justice,* p. 46 (the passage is from *Leviathan,* ch. 30).

16. It may, however, also be worth pointing out the more sobering (and typically Hobbesian) sentence that immediately follows the passage cited by Walzer: "And when all the world is overchargd with Inhabitants, then the last remedy of all is Warre; which provideth for every man, by Victory, or Death" (Thomas Hobbes, *Leviathan,* ed. Richard Tuck [Cambridge: Cambridge University Press, 1991], p. 239).

17. I note here that there is some overlap between the "truly desperate" and the group of "involuntary migrants" that I tried to delineate, in a similarly narrow fashion, in chapter one, though the two groups are presumably not identical.

18. More or less detailed accounts of the Famine can be found in many sources. I have drawn the information in this brief description from the following: S.J. Connolly (ed.), *The Oxford Companion to Irish History* (Oxford: Oxford University Press, 1998); D.J. Hickey and J.E. Doherty (eds.), *A Dictionary of Irish History Since 1800* (Totowa, New Jersey: Barnes & Noble Books, 1981); James Lydon, *The Making of Ireland: From ancient times to the present* (London and New York: Routledge, 1998), pp. 301–5; Colin Thomas and Avril Thomas, *Historical Dictionary of Ireland* (Lanham, Md.: The Scarecrow Press, Inc., 1997); and Peter Gray's concise and readable contribution to the "Discoveries" series, *The Irish Famine* (New York: Harry N. Abrams, Inc., 1995).

19. Quoted in Gray, *The Irish Famine,* p. 139.

20. Quoted in Lydon, *The Making of Ireland,* p. 303.

21. Walzer, who argues that refugees do have a claim to admission, suggests that even among refugees countries may select those whom they will admit on the basis of their own self-understandings: "[W]hen the number increases, and we are forced to choose among the victims, we will look, rightfully, for some more direct connection with our own way of life" (*Spheres of Justice,* p. 49).

22. Matthew Gibney has recently made an argument, quite similar to the one proposed here, that attempts to address at least some of these questions. He suggests that the principle of "humanitarianism" should guide liberal democracies' response to the dilemma of refugees (by which term he refers to a group larger than that included in the conventional definition). His humanitarian principle is an attempt to balance our moral obligations towards refugees, grounded in our common humanity, with both the ethical commitment of the state to protect its own citizens and with the constraints on state impartiality that democracy imposes. His argument is especially powerful because he challenges states to live up to certain moral requirements towards outsiders, in a way that would alter current state practices, without holding them to an account of their moral duties exceeding that which most of them already accept. For example, his argument need not require states either to accept more total immigrants than they currently do, or to abandon immigration preferences for close family members. The chief practical effect of adopting his humanitarian principle would be to alter the composition of current immigration streams, essentially replacing many economic or non-immediate family immigrants with refugees. Because his argument pays such careful attention to states' obligations toward their own members and also to the real-world constraints affecting political responses towards refugees, his conclusions are difficult to reject. See Matthew J. Gibney, "Liberal Democratic States and Responsibilities to Refugees," *American Political Science Review* 93.1 (March 1999), pp. 169–81.

23. E.M. Forster, "What I Believe," in *Two Cheers for Democracy* (New York: Harcourt, Brace and Company, 1951), p. 68.

24. Plender, *International Migration Law,* p. 367.

25. *Ibid.,* p. 365.

26. The passages quoted from the Universal Declaration on Human Rights, as well as references to the other international agreements, can be found at *idem*.

27. *Ibid.,* pp. 365–6.

28. Provisions of selected other countries are described at *ibid.,* pp. 367–9. Plender also quotes the reference of a member of parliament during a parliamentary debate in the U.K. to "the inherent right of a man to have his wife and children with him." We would add, of course, the right of a woman to have her husband and children with her. See *ibid.,* p. 386, n. 17.

29. *Ibid.,* p. 369. Plender discusses provisions regarding migrant workers on pp. 369–72, and ones regarding refugees on pp. 372–4.

30. *Ibid.,* p. 366.

31. Louis B. Sohn and Thomas Buergenthal (eds.), *The Movement of Persons Across Borders* (Washington, D.C.: The American Society of International Law, 1992).

The rule is stated on p. 8 and again on p. 65; a discussion of it, including evidence for its existence, can be found on pp. 65–70.

32. Edmund Burke, *Reflections on the Revolution in France,* ed. J.G.A. Pocock (Indianapolis: Hackett Publishing Company, 1987), p. 173.

33. *Ibid.,* p. 41.

34. John Locke, *The Second Treatise of Government,* in Peter Laslett (ed.), *Two Treatises of Government* (Cambridge: Cambridge University Press, 1988), p. 331. Locke was not the most sentimental of writers about the family, but even he recognized the "Inclinations of Tenderness and Concern" (p. 309) that parents naturally feel for their children.

35. I should just point out in passing that I do not mean to suggest, by using Burke and social contract theory so closely together, that these two theories are just different versions of the same approach to politics. Obviously, Burke's ascent from the ties of the family to those of the country is rhetorically quite different from, for example, Locke's sharp distinction between political and paternal or parental power. (Though the two are not necessarily incompatible; whereas Burke is describing how our affections expand to include ever more people, Locke is distinguishing between two types of power. So they are making different kinds of points.) I am simply borrowing from them here for my own purposes, using them as a pair of examples that, I hope, help to illustrate how or why we might think of family ties as especially important.

36. Plender, *International Migration Law,* discusses this problem and the varying practice of states on pp. 374–9; he also notes two other commonly encountered problems, marriages of convenience (that is, those entered into solely for the purpose of an alien's gaining admission into foreign territory; see pp. 380–2) and polygamous marriages (pp. 382–4).

37. Sohn and Buergenthal, *The Movement of Persons Across Borders,* p. 68.

38. *Ibid.,* p. 69.

39. Joseph H. Carens, "Aliens and Citizens: The Case for Open Borders," *The Review of Politics* 49.2 (Spring 1987), p. 251.

40. Allen Mandelbaum (tr.), *The Aeneid of Virgil* (New York: Bantam Books, 1981). Quotations from the *Aeneid* are drawn from Mandelbaum's translation; I shall identify them in parentheses within the text by giving the book number in Roman numerals followed by line numbers in Arabic numerals. For the political and historical subject of the poem, cf. W.R. Johnson, *Darkness Visible: A Study of Vergil's Aeneid* (Berkeley: University of California Press, 1976), p. 133: ". . . Vergil's subject is, in large measure, how men and nations have behaved in the past, how they tend now to behave, and why. Vergil's main subject may originally have been the actions of Aeneas and the virtues that Aeneas demonstrates in his actions; but the longer Vergil pondered his contents and design, the more his poem came to be about the nature of history." Johnson's study is an especially provocative example of the second interpretation I shall outline below, paying special attention to what Johnson (with considerable justification) views as the malevolent role of the gods in the poem.

41. The word translated here as "goodness" is the Latin *pietas,* Aeneas' defining virtue, described by R.G. Austin as "a very Roman concept, embracing many aspects of man's relationship to the gods and to fellow men: duty, devoted service, responsibility, compassion, the full consciousness of what is due to others . . . a code of high conduct and an integral part of patriotism in the best sense" (P. Vergili Maronis, *Aeneidos: Liber Primus,* ed. R.G. Austin [Oxford: Clarendon Press, 1971], p. 33).

42. For a good, brief survey of literature on the *Aeneid,* paying special attention to these two competing interpretations, see S.J. Harrison, "Some Views of the *Aeneid* in the Twentieth Century," in S.J. Harrison (ed.), *Oxford Readings in Vergil's Aeneid* (Oxford: Oxford University Press, 1990), pp. 1–20.

43. This view has a long pedigree. As R.D. Williams writes, "The ancient critics were not in doubt about the purpose of the *Aeneid:* it was to glorify Rome and Augustus" (Williams, "The Purpose of the *Aeneid,*" in Harrison, *Oxford Readings in Vergil's Aeneid,*" p. 21). And it continues to have prominent adherents. In the words of Brooks Otis, author of one of the most powerful contemporary defenses of this interpretation, "[T]he *Aeneid* is . . . the story of death and rebirth by which unworthy love and destructive *furor* are overcome by the moral activity of a divinized and resurrected hero . . . . Essentially the real 'plot' of the *Aeneid* is that of the formation and victory of the *Augustan* hero" (Otis, "The Odyssean *Aeneid* and the Iliadic *Aeneid,*" in Steele Commager [ed.], *Virgil: A Collection of Critical Essays* [Englewood Cliffs, N.J.: Prentice-Hall, Inc., 1966], pp. 92 [first sentence quoted] and 95 [second sentence quoted; emphasis in original]).

44. For a very strong statement of such a view, see Adam Parry, "The Two Voices of Virgil's *Aeneid,*" in Commager, *Virgil,* pp. 107–23.

45. Wendell Clausen, "An Interpretation of the *Aeneid,*" in Commager, *Virgil,* p. 82. Clausen's essay is a very fine treatment of the poem.

46. This too helps capture the difference in emphasis between my position and Walzer's. As I suggested in the previous chapter, in discussing the ambiguous meaning of "self-determination" in Walzer's work, my worry is that he smuggles into that principle a preference for a particular sort of democratic, political activity that actually threatens to restrict, rather than enlarge, the range of communities that people may build for themselves.

47. For a very engaging account of Stevenson's last years, see Richard A. Bermann, *Home from the Sea: Robert Louis Stevenson in Samoa,* tr. Elizabeth Reynolds Hapgood (Indianapolis: The Bobbs-Merrill Company, 1939).

48. From Robert Louis Stevenson, *Collected Poems,* ed. Janet Adam Smith (Soho Square, London: Rupert Hart-Davis, 1950), p. 130.

49. The plaques are described in Bermann, p. 279.

50. Letter from Stevenson to Sidney Colvin, late November 1893, in Ernest Mehew (ed.), *Selected Letters of Robert Louis Stevenson* (New Haven: Yale University Press, 1997), p. 563.

51. St. Augustine, *Concerning the City of God against the Pagans,* tr. Henry Bettenson (London and New York: Penguin Books, 1984), p. 877.

Bibliography

Ackerman, Bruce A. *Social Justice in the Liberal State*. New Haven and London:Yale University Press, 1980. Ch. 3, "Citizenship," pp. 69–103.

Anderson, Benedict. *Imagined Communities: Reflections on the Origin and Spread of Nationalism*. 2nd ed. London and NewYork:Verso, 1991.

Anzovin, Steven (ed.). *The Problem of Immigration*. NewYork:The H. Wilson Company, 1985.

Aristotle. *The Politics of Aristotle*. Tr. Ernest Barker. London, Oxford, and NewYork: Oxford University Press, 1958.

St. Augustine. *Concerning the City of God Against the Pagans*. Tr. Henry Bettenson. London and NewYork: Penguin Books, 1984.

Bade, Klaus J. (ed.). *Das Manifest der 60: Deutschland und die Einwanderung*. Munich: C.H. Beck, 1994.

———— (ed.). *Deutsche im Ausland—Fremde in Deutschland: Migration in Geschichte und Gegenwart*. Munich: C.H. Beck, 1993.

———— (ed.). *Die multikulturelle Herausforderung: Menschen über Grenzen—Grenzen über Menschen*. Munich: C.H. Beck, 1996.

————. *Homo Migrans: Wanderungen aus und nach Deutschland. Erfahrungen und Fragen*. Essen: KlartextVerlag, 1994.

————. "Immigration and Social Peace in United Germany." *Daedalus*, vol. 123, no. 1 (Winter 1994), pp. 85–106.

Bader, Veit. "Citizenship and Exclusion: Radical Democracy, Community and Justice. Or, What is Wrong with Communitarianism?" *Political Theory*, vol. 23, no. 2 (1995), pp. 211–46.

Barbalet, J.M. *Citizenship: Rights, Struggle and Class Inequality*. Minneapolis: University of Minnesota Press, 1988.

Barbieri, Jr., William A. *Ethics of Citizenship: Immigration and Group Rights in Germany*. Durham, NC: Duke University Press, 1998.

Barry, Brian and Goodin, Robert E. (eds.). *Free Movement: Ethical issues in the transnational migration of people and of money*. University Park, PA: The Pennsylvania State University Press, 1992.

Bauböck, Rainer. *Transnational Citizenship: Membership and Rights in International Migration.* Hants, England: Edward Elgar, 1994.

Beck, Roy. *The Case Against Immigration: The moral, economic, social, and environmental reasons for reducing U.S. immigration back to traditional levels.* New York: W.W. Norton & Company, 1996.

Beiner, Ronald. "Citizenship." In *What's the Matter With Liberalism?* (Ch. 5, pp. 98–141). Berkeley, Los Angeles, and Oxford: University of California Press, 1992.

―――― (ed.). *Theorizing Citizenship.* Albany: State University of New York Press, 1995.

―――― (ed.). *Theorizing Nationalism.* Albany: SUNY Press, 1999.

Beitz, Charles R. *Political Theory and International Relations.* Princeton: Princeton University Press, 1979.

Bell, Ian. *Dreams of Exile: Robert Louis Stevenson: A Biography.* New York: Henry Holt and Company, 1992.

Bermann, Richard A. *Home from the Sea: Robert Louis Stevenson in Samoa.* Tr. Elizabeth Reynolds Hapgood. Indianapolis: The Bobbs-Merrill Company, 1939.

Bernard, William S. "A History of U.S. Immigration Policy." In Easterlin, Ward, Bernard, and Ueda (eds.). *Immigration.* Cambridge, MA: The Belknap Press of Harvard University Press, 1982, pp. 75–105.

Borjas, George J. "The New Economics of Immigration." *The Atlantic Monthly,* vol. 278, no. 5 (November 1996), pp. 72–80.

Bouscaren, Anthony T. *International Migrations Since 1945.* New York: Frederick A. Praeger, Publisher, 1963.

Brimelow, Peter. *Alien Nation: Common Sense about America's Immigration Disaster.* New York: Harper Perennial, 1996.

Brown, Peter G. and Shue, Henry (eds.). *Boundaries: National Autonomy and its Limits.* Totowa, New Jersey: Rowman and Littlefield, 1981.

Brubaker, Rogers. *Citizenship and Nationhood in France and Germany.* Cambridge, MA: Harvard University Press, 1992.

Brubaker, William Rogers (ed.). *Immigration and the Politics of Citizenship in Europe and North America.* Lanham, New York, London: University Press of America (with the German Marshall Fund of the United States), 1989.

Buchanan, James M. "A two-country parable." In Schwartz, *Justice in immigration,* pp. 63–6.

Burke, Edmund. *An Appeal from the New to the Old Whigs.* In Ritchie, Daniel E. (ed.). *Further Reflections on the Revolution in France.* Indianapolis: Liberty Fund, 1992, pp. 73–201.

――――. *Reflections on the Revolution in France.* Ed. J.G.A. Pocock. Indianapolis: Hackett Publishing Company, 1987.

Caldwell, Christopher. "Germany Goes Amerikanisch." *The American Spectator,* online archives (www.spectator.org/archives/98–12_caldwell.html).

Canny, Nicholas (ed.). *Europeans on the Move: Studies on European Migration, 1500–1800.* Oxford: Clarendon Press, 1994.

Carens, Joseph H. "Aliens and Citizens: The Case for Open Borders." *Review of Politics,* vol. 49, no. 2 (Spring 1987), pp. 251–73.

———. "Compromises in Politics." In *Compromise in Ethics, Law, and Politics (Nomos,* vol. XXI). New York: New York University Press, 1979, pp. 123–41.

———. *Culture, Citizenship, and Community: A Contextual Exploration of Justice as Evenhandedness.* Oxford: Oxford University Press, 2000.

———. "Democracy and Respect for Difference: The Case of Fiji." *University of Michigan Journal of Law Reform,* vol. 25, nos. 3 and 4 (Spring and Summer 1992), pp. 547–631.

———. "Immigration and the Welfare State." In Gutmann, Amy (ed.). *Democracy and the Welfare State.* Princeton: Princeton University Press, 1988, pp. 207–30.

———. "Immigration, Political Community, and the Transformation of Identity: Quebec's Immigration Policies in Critical Perspective." In Carens, *Is Quebec Nationalism Just?,* pp. 20–81.

——— (ed.). *Is Quebec Nationalism Just? Perspectives from Anglophone Canada.* Montreal & Kingston: McGill-Queen's University Press, 1995.

———. "Membership and Morality: Admission to Citizenship in Liberal Democratic States." In Brubaker, *Immigration and the Politics of Citizenship,* pp. 31–49.

———. "Migration and Morality: A liberal egalitarian perspective." In Barry and Goodin, *Free Movement,* pp. 25–47.

———. "Nationalism and the Exclusion of Immigrants: Lessons from Australian Immigration Policy." In Gibney, *Open Borders?,* pp. 41–60.

———. "Realistic and Idealistic Approaches to the Ethics of Migration." *International Migration Review,* vol. 30, no. 1 (Spring 1996), pp. 156–70.

———. "Reconsidering Open Borders." *International Migration Review,* vol. 33, no. 4 (Winter 1999), pp. 1082–97.

———. "The Rights of Immigrants." In Baker, Judith (ed.). *Group Rights.* Toronto: University of Toronto Press, 1994, pp. 142–63.

———. "Who Belongs? Theoretical and legal questions about birthright citizenship in the United States." *University of Toronto Law Journal,* vol. XXXVII, no. 4 (Fall 1987), pp. 413–43.

Castles, Stephen and Miller, Mark J. *The Age of Migration: International Population Movements in the Modern World.* 2nd. ed. London: Macmillan Press, 1998.

Ceaser, James W. *Liberal Democracy and Political Science.* Baltimore and London: Johns Hopkins University Press, 1990.

Chambers, Iain. *Migrancy, Culture, Identity.* London and New York: Routledge, 1994.

Chesterton, G.K. *Irish Impressions.* London: W. Collins Sons & Co. Ltd., 1920.

———. "A Note on Emigration." In *The Outline of Sanity.* New York: Dodd, Mead & Company, 1927, pp. 205–38.

Clarke, Paul Barry (ed.). *Citizenship.* London and Boulder, Colorado: Pluto Press, 1994.

Clausen, Wendell. "An Interpretation of the *Aeneid.*" In Commager, *Virgil,* pp. 75–88.

Clor, Harry M. "Constitutional Interpretation and Regime Principles." In Goldwin, Robert A. and Schambra, William A. (eds.). *The Constitution, the Courts, and the Quest for Justice.* Washington, D.C.: American Enterprise Institute, 1989, pp. 115–35.

Cohen, Robin (ed.). *The Cambridge Survey of World Migration.* Cambridge: Cambridge University Press, 1995.

Coleman, Jules and Harding, Sarah K. "Citizenship, the demands of justice, and the moral relevance of political borders." In Schwartz, *Justice in immigration,* pp. 18–62.

Commager, Steele (ed.). *Virgil: A Collection of Critical Essays.* Englewood Cliffs, N.J.: Prentice-Hall, Inc., 1966.

Connolly, S.J. (ed.). *The Oxford Companion to Irish History.* Oxford: Oxford University Press, 1998.

Connolly, William. *The Ethos of Pluralization.* Minneapolis: University of Minnsota Press, 1995.

————. *Identity\Difference: Democratic Negotiations of Political Paradox.* Ithaca: Cornell University Press, 1991.

Cooke, Jacob E. (ed.). *The Federalist.* Middletown, CT: Wesleyan University Press, 1961.

Critical Review, vol. 10, no. 2 (Spring 1996). Special issue on "Nationalism."

Daedalus, vol. 122, no. 3 (Summer 1993). Special issue on "Reconstructing Nations and States."

Daedalus, vol. 123, no. 1 (Winter 1994). Special Issue on "Germany in Transition."

Dauenhauer, Bernard P. *Citizenship in a Fragile World.* Lanham, Maryland: Rowman & Littlefield Publishers, Inc., 1996.

Dowty, Alan. *Closed Borders: The Contemporary Assault on Freedom of Movement.* New Haven and London: Yale University Press, 1987.

Ethics, vol. 98, no. 4 (July 1988). Special issue: "Symposium on Duties Beyond Borders."

Fitzgerald, Keith. *The Face of the Nation: Immigration, the State, and the National Identity.* Stanford, CA: Stanford University Press, 1996.

Forster, E.M. "What I Believe." In *Two Cheers for Democracy* (New York: Harcourt, Brace and Company, 1951), pp. 67–76.

Fowler, Michael Ross and Bunck, Julie Marie (eds.). *Law, Power, and the Sovereign State: The Evolution and Application of the Concept of Sovereignty.* University Park, PA: The Pennsylvania State University Press, 1995.

Fragomen, Jr., Austin T. "The Refugee: A Problem of Definition." *Case Western Reserve Journal of International Law,* vol. 3, no. 1 (Winter 1970), pp. 45–69.

Friedrich, Carl J. "The Concept of Community in the History of Political and Legal Philosophy." In Friedrich, Carl J. (Ed.). *Community* (*Nomos* II). New York: The Liberal Arts Press, 1959.

Gibney, Mark (ed.). *Open Borders? Closed Societies? The Ethical and Political Issues.* New York, London, and Westport, CT: Greenwood Press, 1988.

————. *Strangers or Friends: Principles for a New Alien Admission Policy.* New York, London, and Westport, Connecticut: Greenwood Press, 1986.

Gibney, Matthew. "Liberal Democratic States and Responsibilities to Refugees." *American Political Science Review,* vol. 93, no. 1 (March 1999), pp. 169–81.

Goodin, Robert. "What Is So Special about Our Fellow Countrymen?" *Ethics,* vol. 98, no. 4 (July 1988), pp. 663–86.

Goodwin-Gill, Guy S. *International Law and the Movement of Persons Between States.* Oxford: Clarendon Press, 1978.

———. *The Refugee in International Law.* Oxford: Clarendon Press, 1983.

Grahl-Madsen, Atle. *The Status of Refugees in International Law.* 2 vols. The Netherlands: A.W. Sijthoff-Leyden, 1966.

Gray, Peter. *The Irish Famine.* New York: Harry N. Abrams, Inc., 1995.

Habermas, Jürgen. "Citizenship and National Identity: Some Reflections on the Future of Europe." In Beiner, *Citizenship,* pp. 255–281.

———. "Struggles for Recognition in the Democratic Constitutional State." In Gumann, Amy (ed.). *Multiculturalism: Examining the Politics of Recognition.* Princeton: Princeton University Press, 1994, pp. 107–48.

Hailbronner, Kay. "Die Reform des deutschen Staatsangehörigkeitsrechts." *Neue Zeitschrift für Verwaltungsrecht,* Heft 12 (1999), pp. 1273–80.

Hampton, Jean. "Immigration, identity, and justice." In Schwartz, *Justice in immigration,* pp. 67–93.

Harrison, S.J. (ed.). *Oxford Readings in Vergil's Aeneid.* Oxford: Oxford University Press, 1990.

———. "Some Views of the *Aeneid* in the Twentieth Century." In Harrison (ed.), *Oxford Readings in Vergil's Aeneid,* pp. 1–20.

Henry, James. *Aeneidea, or Critical, Exegetical, and Aesthetical Remarks on the Aeneis,* etc. London: Williams and Norgate, 1873.

Hickey, D.J. and Doherty, J.E. (eds.). *A Dictionary of Irish History Since 1800.* Totowa, New Jersey: Barnes & Noble Books, 1981.

Higgins, Rosalyn. "The Right in International Law of an Individual to Enter, Stay in and Leave a Country." *International Affairs,* vol. 49, no. 3 (July 1973), pp. 341–57.

Hobbes, Thomas. *Leviathan.* Ed. Richard Tuck. Cambridge: Cambridge University Press, 1994.

Honig, Bonnie. "Immigrant America? How Foreignness 'Solves' Democracy's Problems." ABF Working Paper #9707. Chicago: American Bar Foundation, 1997.

———. "Ruth, the Model Emigrée: Mourning and the Symbolic Politics of Immigration." *Political Theory,* vol. 25, no. 1 (Feb. 1997), pp. 112–36.

Hume, David. *Essays Moral, Political, and Literary.* Ed. Eugene F. Miller. Indianapolis: Liberty Fund, 1985.

Ignatieff, Michael. *The Needs of Strangers.* London: Chatto & Windus, The Hogarth Press, 1984.

Im Hof, Ulrich. *The Enlightenment.* Oxford and Cambridge, Mass.: Blackwell, 1994.

International Migration Review, vol. 30, no. 1 (Spring 1996). Special Issue on "Ethics, Migration, and Global Stewardship."

Jacobson, David. *Rights Across Borders: Immigration and the Decline of Citizenship.* Baltimore and London: The Johns Hopkins University Press, 1996.

Jefferson, Thomas. *Notes on the State of Virginia*. Chapel Hill: University of North Carolina Press, 1982.

Johnson, W.R. *Darkness Visible: A Study of Vergil's Aeneid*. Berkeley: University of California Press, 1976.

Kaplan, Robert D. "History Moving North." *The Atlantic Monthly*, vol. 279, no. 2 (February 1997), pp. 21–31.

Kästner, Erich. *Die Konferenz der Tiere*. In Kästner, Erich. *Gesammelte Schriften, Band 7: Romane für Kinder*. Zürich: Atrium Verlag, 1959.

Kennedy, David M. "Can We Still Afford to Be a Nation of Immigrants?" *The Atlantic Monthly*, vol. 278, no. 5 (November 1996), pp. 52–68.

Kennedy, John F. *A Nation of Immigrants*. New York and Evanston: Harper & Row, Publishers, 1964.

King, Russell (ed.). *The New Geography of European Migrations*. London and New York: Belhaven Press, 1993.

King, Timothy. "Immigration from Developing Countries: Some Philosophical Issues." *Ethics*, (April 1983), pp. 525–36.

Klusmeyer, Douglas B. "Aliens, Immigrants, and Citizens: The Politics of Inclusion in the Federal Republic of Germany." *Daedalus*, vol. 122, no. 3 (Summer 1993), pp. 81–114.

Kristeva, Julia. *Nations Without Nationalism*. New York: Columbia University Press, 1993.

———. *Strangers to Ourselves*. New York: Columbia University Press, 1991.

Kymlicka, Will. *Liberalism, Community, and Culture*. Oxford: Clarendon Press, 1989.

———. *Multicultural Citizenship: A Liberal Theory of Minority Rights*. Oxford: Clarendon Press, 1996.

———. *States, Nations and Cultures*. Assen, the Netherlands: Van Gorcum & Comp., 1997.

——— and Norman, Wayne. "Return of the Citizen: A Survey of Recent Work on Citizenship Theory." In Beiner, *Citizenship*, pp. 283–322.

Lee, Kenneth K. *Huddled Masses, Muddled Laws: Why Contemporary Immigration Policy Fails to Reflect Public Opinion*. Westport, CT: Praeger, 1998.

Locke, John. *The Second Treatise of Government*. In Laslett, Peter (ed.). *Two Treatises of Government*. Cambridge: Cambridge University Press, 1988.

Loughlin, Kathleen LaCamera. "Sanctuary Churches." *The Christian Century*, vol. 114, no. 7 (Feb. 26, 1997), pp. 212–13.

Lydon, James. *The Making of Ireland: From ancient times to the present*. London and New York: Routledge, 1998.

Mandelbaum, Allen (tr.). *The Aeneid of Virgil*. New York: Bantam Books, 1981.

Maronis, P. Vergili. *Aeneidos: Liber Primus*. Ed. R.G. Austin. Oxford: Clarendon Press, 1971.

Marshall, T.H. *Citizenship and Social Class and Other Essays*. Cambridge: Cambridge University Press, 1950.

Marx, Reinhard. *Kommentar zum Staatsangehörigkeitsrecht*. Neuwied, Kriftel, and Berlin: Luchterhand, 1997.

McKim, Robert and McMahan, Jeff (eds.). *The Morality of Nationalism*. Oxford and New York: Oxford University Press, 1997.

Mehew, Ernest (ed.). *Selected Letters of Robert Louis Stevenson*. New Haven: Yale University Press, 1997.

Meilaender, Peter C. "A Different Kind of Liberalism?" Review of Carens, *Culture, Citizenship, and Community*. Forthcoming in *Review of Politics*, vol. 63, no. 2 (Spring 2001).

Meinecke, Friedrich. *Weltbürgertum und Nationalstaat*. Munich: R. Oldenbourg Verlag, 1962.

Miller, David. "The Ethical Significance of Nationality." *Ethics*, 98, no. 4 (July 1988), pp. 647– 62.

———. *On Nationality*. Oxford: Clarendon Press, 1995.

Münz, Rainer and Ulrich, Ralf. "Immigration and Citizenship in Germany." *German Politics and Society*, Issue 53, vol. 17, no. 4 (Winter 1999), pp. 1–33.

Murray, Laura M. "*Einwanderungsland Bundesrepublik Deutschland?* Explaining the Evolving Positions of German Political Parties on Citizenship Policy." *German Politics and Society*, Issue 33 (Fall 1994), pp. 23–56.

Nardin, Terry. *Law, Morality, and the Relations of States*. Princeton: Princeton University Press, 1983.

Nett, Roger. "The Civil Right We Are Not Ready For: The Right of Free Movement of People on the Face of the Earth." *Ethics*, 81: 212–27.

Nugent, Walter. *Crossings: The Great Transatlantic Migrations, 1870–1914*. Bloomington: Indiana University Press, 1992.

O'Neill, Onora. "Justice and Boundaries." In Chwaszcza, Christine and Kersting, Wolfgang (eds.). *Politische Philosophie der internationalen Beziehungen*. Frankfurt: Suhrkamp, 1998, pp. 502–20.

Orwell, George. "England Your England." In *A Collection of Essays*. Garden City, NY: Doubleday & Company, Inc., 1954, pp. 257–83.

Otis, Brooks. "The Odyssean *Aeneid* and the Iliadic *Aeneid*." In Commager, *Virgil*, pp. 89–106.

Parry, Adam. "The Two Voices of the *Aeneid*." In Commager, *Virgil*, pp. 107–23.

Perry, Stephen R. "Immigration, justice, and culture." In Schwartz, *Justice in immigration*, pp. 94–135.

Pickus, Noah M.J. (ed.). *Immigration and Citizenship in the Twenty-First Century*. Lanham, MD: Rowman & Littlefield, 1998.

Plender, Richard. *International Migration Law: Revised Second Edition*. Dordrecht, the Netherlands, Boston, and London: Martinus Nijhoff Publishers, 1988.

Putnam, Michael C.J. *The Poetry of the Aeneid: Four Studies in Imaginative Unity and Design*. Cambridge: Harvard University Press, 1965.

Rabio-Marin, Ruth. *Immigration as a Democratic Challenge: Citizenship and Inclusion in Germany and the United States*. Cambridge: Cambridge University Press, 2000.

Rabkin, Jeremy. "Grotius, Vattel and Locke: An Older View of Liberalism and Nationality." *Review of Politics*, vol. 59, no. 2 (Spring 1997), pp. 293–322.

Rahman-Niaghi, Davood. *Ausländerrecht: aber leicht*. Berlin: Rosen Verlag, 2000.

Rawls, John. "The Law of Peoples." *Critical Inquiry,* vol. 20, no. 1 (Autumn 1993), pp. 36–68.

———. *A Theory of Justice.* Cambridge, MA: The Belknap Press, 1971.

Schlesinger, Jr., Arthur M. *The Disuniting of America.* New York: W.W. Norton & Company, 1992.

Schmalz-Jacobsen, Cornelia and Hansen, Georg (eds.). *Kleines Lexikon der ethnischen Minderheiten in Deutschland.* Munich: C.H. Beck, 1997.

Schuck, Peter. *Citizens, Strangers, and In-Betweens: Essays on Immigration and Citizenship.* Boulder, Colorado: Westview Press, 1998.

——— and Smith, Rogers. *Citizenship Without Consent: Illegal Aliens in the American Polity.* New Haven: Yale University Press, 1985.

Schulze, Hagen. "German Unification in the Context of European History." *German Studies Review,* vol. 15, no. 4 (Winter 1992), pp. 7–20.

———. *States, Nations and Nationalism: From the Middle Ages to the Present.* Oxford and Cambridge: Blackwell Publishers, 1996.

Schwartz, Warren F. (ed.). *Justice in immigration.* Cambridge: Cambridge University Press, 1995.

Scott, Franklin D. (ed.). *World Migration in Modern Times.* Englewood Cliffs, N.J.: Prentice-Hall, Inc., 1968.

Serra, Antonio Truyol. *The Principles of Political and International Law in the Work of Francisco de Vitoria.* Madrid: Ediciones Cultural Hispanica, 1946. Ch. 2, "International Order," pp. 51–73.

Shacknove, Andrew E. "Who is a Refugee?" *Ethics,* vol. 95, no. 2 (January 1985), pp. 274–84.

Shapiro, Michael J. and Alker, Hayward R. (Eds.). *Challenging Boundaries: Global Flows, Territorial Identities.* Minneapolis: University of Minnesota Press, 1996.

Sheehan, James J. "National History and National Identity in the New Germany." *German Studies Review,* vol. 15, no. 4 (Winter 1992), pp. 163–74.

Simon, Julian L. "The case for greatly increased immigration." *The Public Interest,* no. 102 Winter 1991), pp. 89–103.

———. *The Economic Consequences of Immigration.* Cambridge, Mass.: Basil Blackwell, 1989.

Simon, Rita J. and Alexander, Susan H. *The Ambivalent Welcome: Print Media, Public Opinion and Immigration.* Westport, CT: Praeger, 1993.

Skerry, Peter. "Individualist America and Today's Immigrants." *The Public Interest,* no. 102 (Winter 1991), pp. 104–18.

Smith, Rogers M. *Civic Ideals: Conflicting Visions of Citizenship in U.S. History.* New Haven: Yale University Press, 1997.

Sohn, Louis B. and Buergenthal, Thomas (eds.). *The Movement of Persons Across Borders.* Washington, D.C.: The American Society of International Law, 1992.

Sowell, Thomas. *Migrations and Cultures: A World View.* New York: BasicBooks, 1996.

———. *Race and Culture: A World View.* New York: BasicBooks, 1994.

Spevack, Edmund. "Ethnic Germans from the East: *Aussiedler* in Germany, 1970–1994." *German Politics and Society,* vol. 13, no. 4 (Issue 37, Winter 1995), pp. 71–91.

Stevenson, Robert Louis. *The Amateur Emigrant.* New York: Charles Scribner's Sons, 1895.

———. *Collected Poems.* Ed. Janet Adam Smith. Soho Square, London: Rupert Hart-Davis, 1950.

———. "The Foreigner at Home." In Gelder, Kenneth (ed.). *Robert Louis Stevenson: The Scottish Stories and Essays.* Edinburgh: Edinburgh University Press, 1989, pp. 233–41.

Tamir, Yael. *Liberal Nationalism.* Princeton: Princeton University Press, 1995.

Thernstrom, Stephan (ed.). *Harvard Encyclopedia of American Ethnic Groups.* (Cambridge, MA: The Belknap Press of Harvard University Press, 1980.

Thomas, Colin and Thomas, Avril. *Historical Dictionary of Ireland.* Lanham, Maryland: The Scarecrow Press, Inc., 1977.

Thornberry, Patrick. "The Democratic or Internal Aspect of Self-Determination with Some Remarks on Federalism." In Tomuschat, Christian (ed.). *Modern Law of Self-Determination.* Dordrecht, Boston, and London: Martinus Nijhoff Publishers, 1993.

de Tocqueville, Alexis. *Democracy in America.* Ed. J.P. Mayer. Tr. George Lawrence. New York: Perennial Library, 1988).

Tuttle, Dale. "The Assimilation of East Germany and the Rise of Identity-Based Violence Against Foreigners in the Unified German State." *German Politics and Society,* Issue 31 (Spring 1994), pp. 63–83.

Ueda, Reed. *Postwar Immigrant America: A Social History.* Boston and New York: Bedford Books of St. Martin's Press, 1994.

van Gunsteren, Herman R. "Admission to Citizenship." *Ethics,* vol. 98, no. 4 (July 1988), pp. 731–41.

Virgil. *Aeneid: Book VIII.* Ed. K.W. Gransden. Cambridge: Cambridge University Press, 1988.

de Vitoria, Francisco. *On the American Indians.* In Pagden, Anthony and Lawrance, Jeremy (eds.). *Francisco de Vitoria: Political Writings.* Cambridge: Cambridge University Press, 1991.

Vogel, Ursula and Moran, Michael (eds.). *The Frontiers of Citizenship.* New York: St. Martin's Press, 1991.

von Dirke, Sabine. "Multikulti: The German Debate on Multiculturalism." *German Studies Review,* vol. 17, no. 3 (Oct. 1994), pp. 513–36.

Wagner, Richard. *Exit: A Romanian Story.* Tr. by Quintin Hoare (original title, *Ausreiseantrag*). London and New York: Verso, 1990.

Walzer, Michael. *Just and Unjust Wars: A Moral Argument with Historical Illustrations.* New York: Basic Books, Inc., 1977.

———. "The Moral Standing of States: A Response to Four Critics." *Philosophy & Public Affairs,* vol. 9, no. 3 (Spring 1980), pp. 209–29.

———. "Nation and Universe." *The Tanner Lectures on Human Values XI.* Salt Lake City: University of Utah Press, 1990, pp. 507–56.

———. *Obligations: Essays on Disobedience, War, and Citizenship.* New York: Simon and Schuster, 1970. Ch. 10: "The Problem of Citizenship," pp. 203–228.

———. *On Toleration.* New Haven: Yale University Press, 1997.

———. *Radical Principles: reflections of an unreconstructed democrat.* New York: Basic Books, Inc., 1980.

———. *Spheres of Justice: A Defense of Pluralism and Equality.* New York: Basic Books, Inc., Publishers, 1983.

———. *Thick and Thin: Moral Argument at Home and Abroad.* Notre Dame: University of Notre Dame Press, 1994.

Wattenberg, Ben J. *The First Universal Nation: Leading Indicators and Ideas about the Surge of America in the 1990s.* New York: The Free Press, 1991.

West, Thomas G. *Vindicating the Founders: Race, Sex, Class, and Justice in the Origins of America.* Lanham, MD: Rowman & Littlefield, 1997.

Whelan, Frederick. "Citizenship and Freedom of Movement: An Open Admission Policy?" In Gibney, *Open Borders?,* pp. 3–39.

———. "Citizenship and the Right to Leave." *American Political Science Review,* vol. 75, no. 3 (September 1981), pp. 636–53.

Williams, R.D. "The Purpose of the *Aeneid.*" In Harrison, *Oxford Readings in Vergil's Aeneid,* pp. 21–36.

Williamson, Jr., Chilton. *The Immigration Mystique: America's False Conscience.* New York: BasicBooks, 1996.

Woodward, James. "Commentary: Liberalism and migration." In Barry and Goodin, *Free Movement,* pp. 59–84.

Yack, Bernard. "The Myth of the Civic Nation." *Critical Review,* vol. 10, no. 2 (Spring 1996), pp. 193–211.

Young, Iris Marion. *Justice and the Politics of Difference.* Princeton: Princeton University Press, 1990.

Index